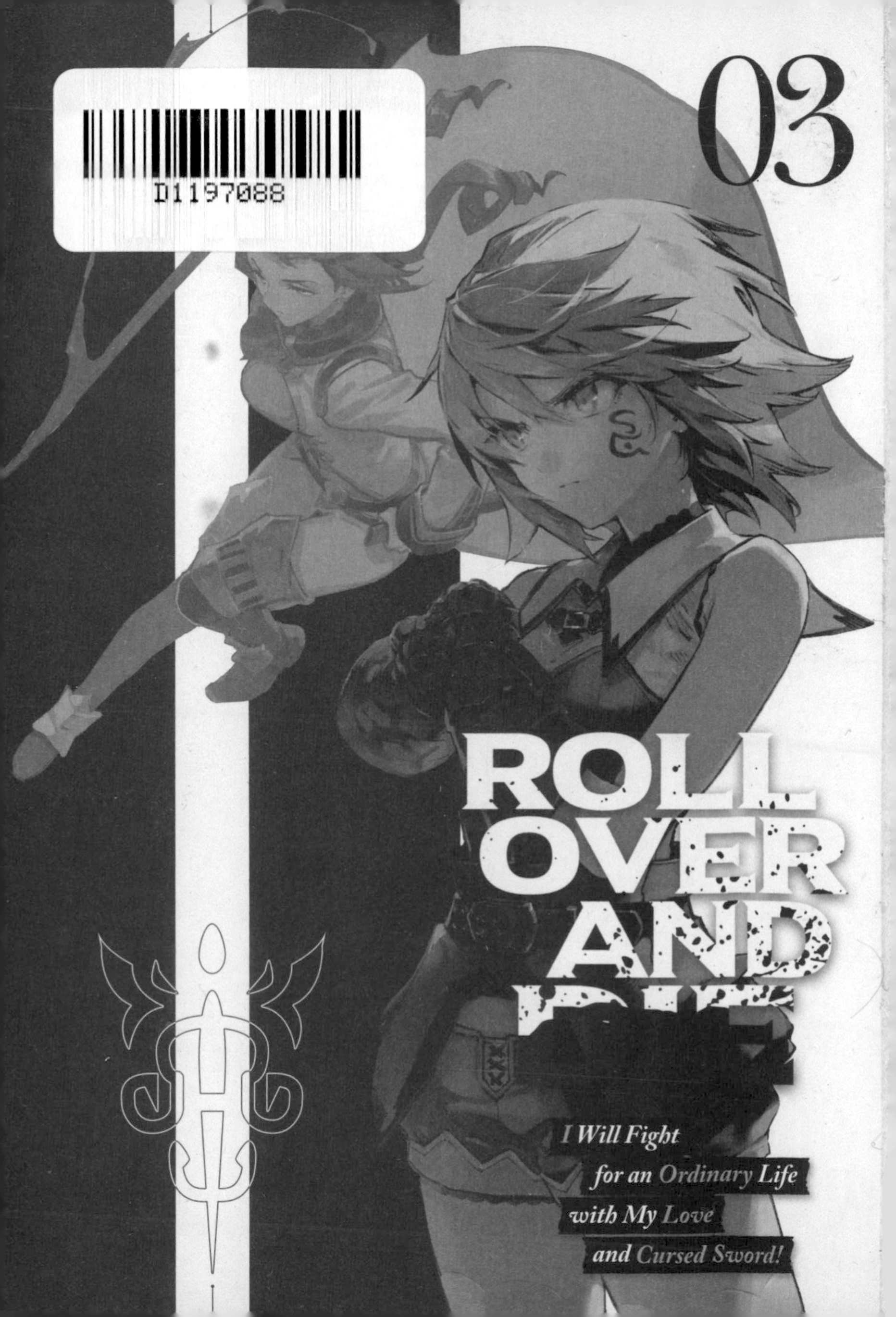
03
ROLL
OVER
AND
I Will Fight
for an Ordinary Life
with My Love
and Cursed Sword!

CONTENTS

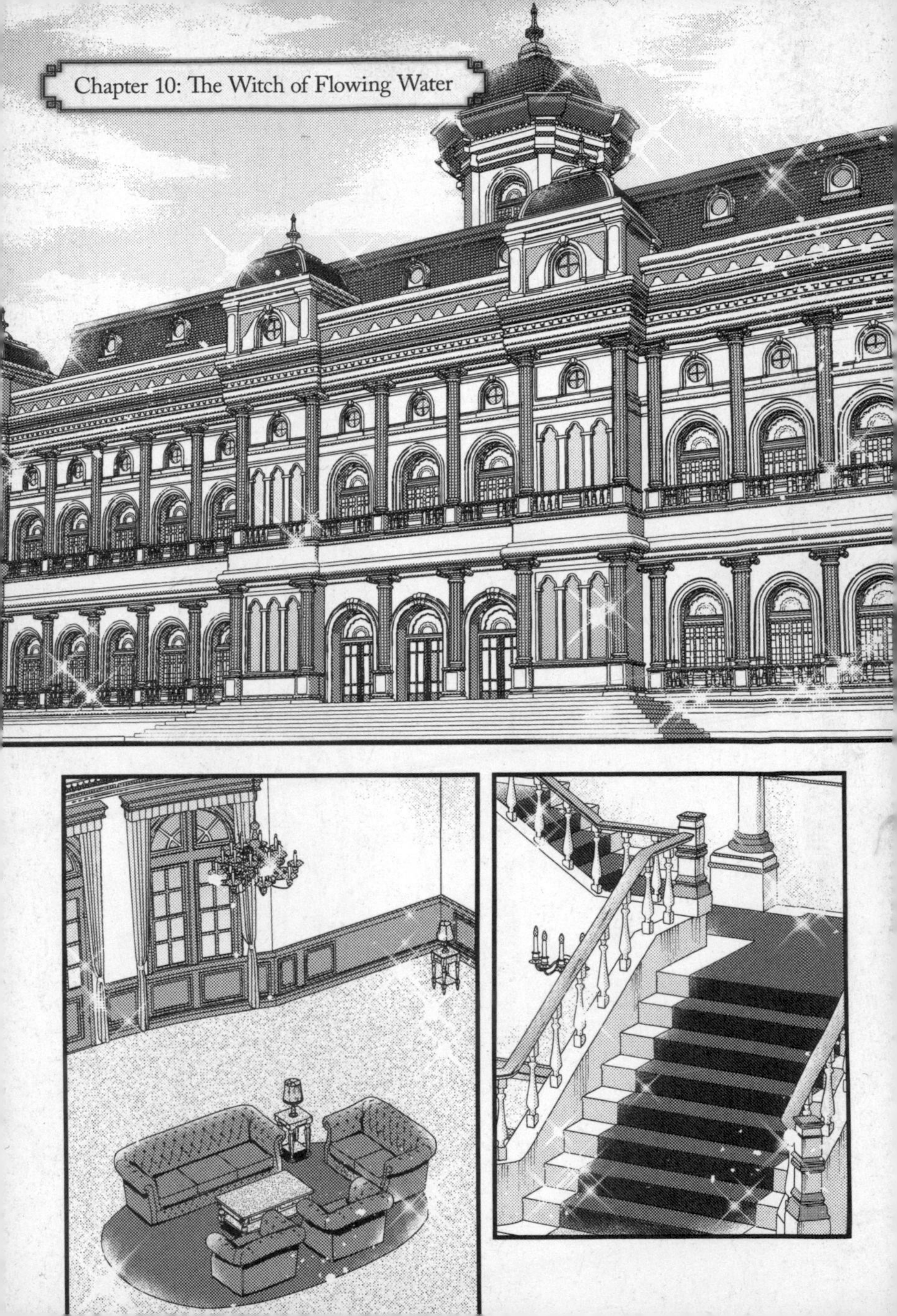
Chapter 10: The Witch of Flowing Water

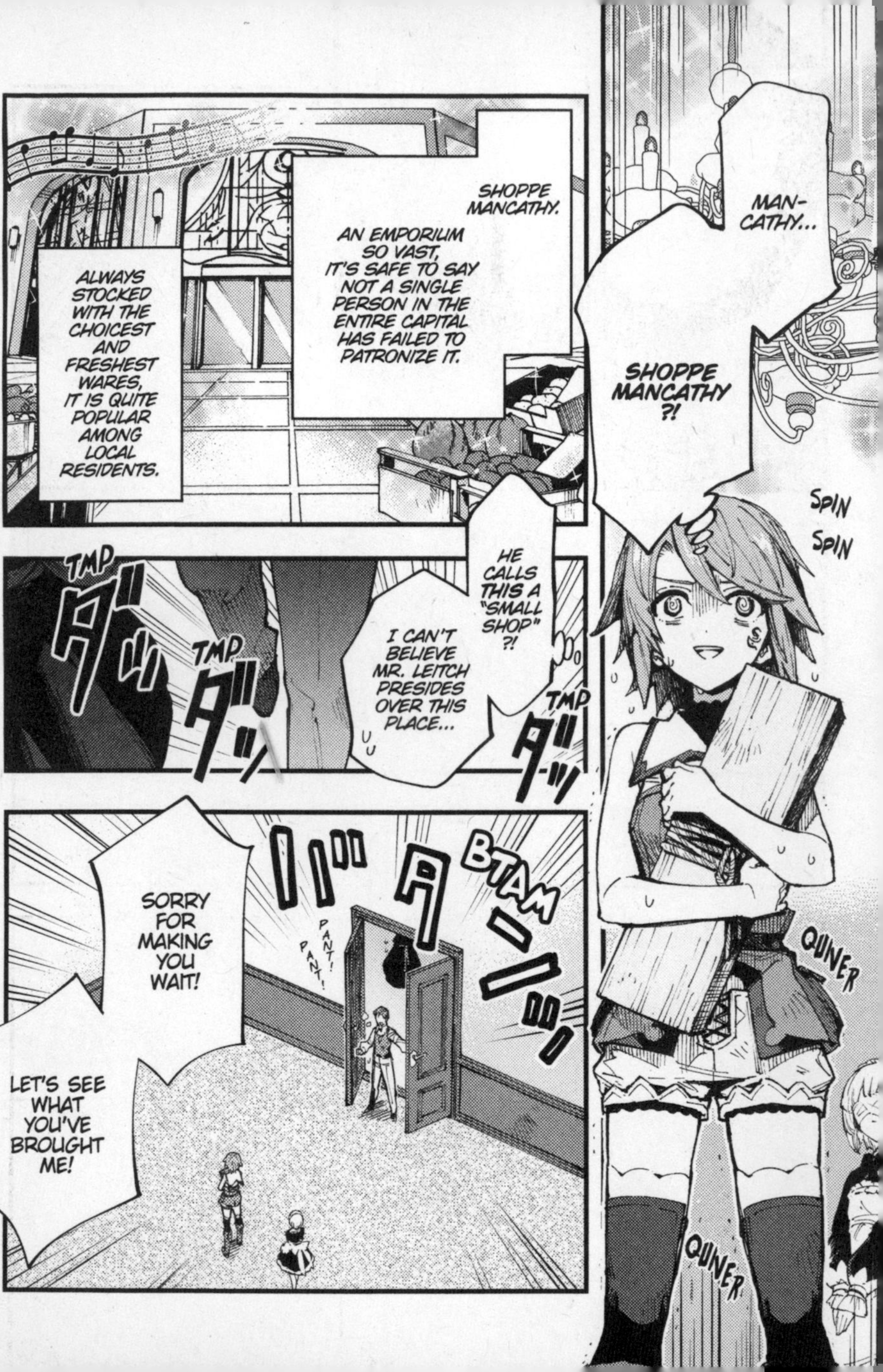
MAN-CATHY...
SHOPPE MANCATHY ?!
SPIN
SPIN
QUNER
QUNER
SHOPPE MANCATHY.
AN EMPORIUM SO VAST, IT'S SAFE TO SAY NOT A SINGLE PERSON IN THE ENTIRE CAPITAL HAS FAILED TO PATRONIZE IT.
ALWAYS STOCKED WITH THE CHOICEST AND FRESHEST WARES, IT IS QUITE POPULAR AMONG LOCAL RESIDENTS.
HE CALLS THIS A "SMALL SHOP" ?!
TMP
I CAN'T BELIEVE MR. LEITCH PRESIDES OVER THIS PLACE...
TMP
TMP
BTAM
PANT! PANT!
SORRY FOR MAKING YOU WAIT!
LET'S SEE WHAT YOU'VE BROUGHT ME!

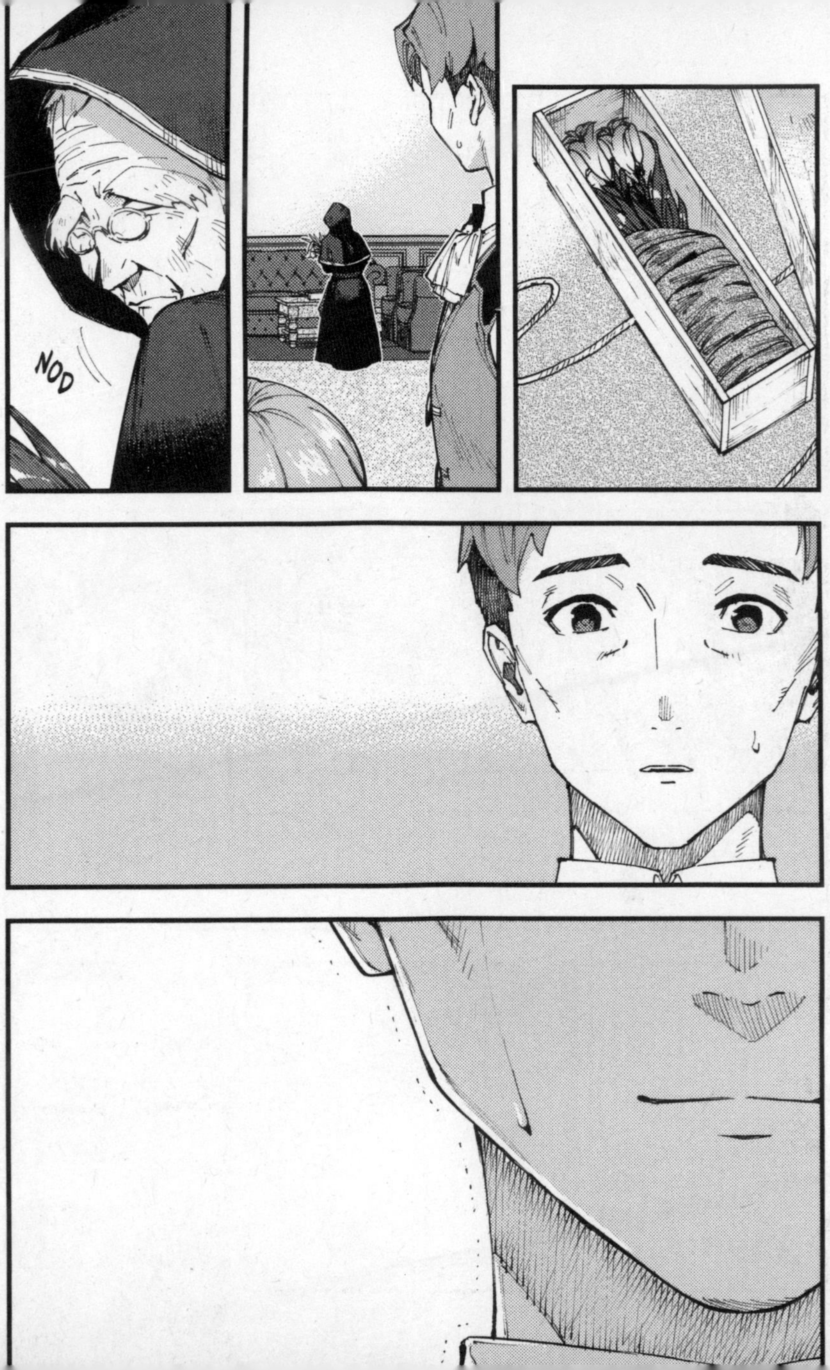
NOD

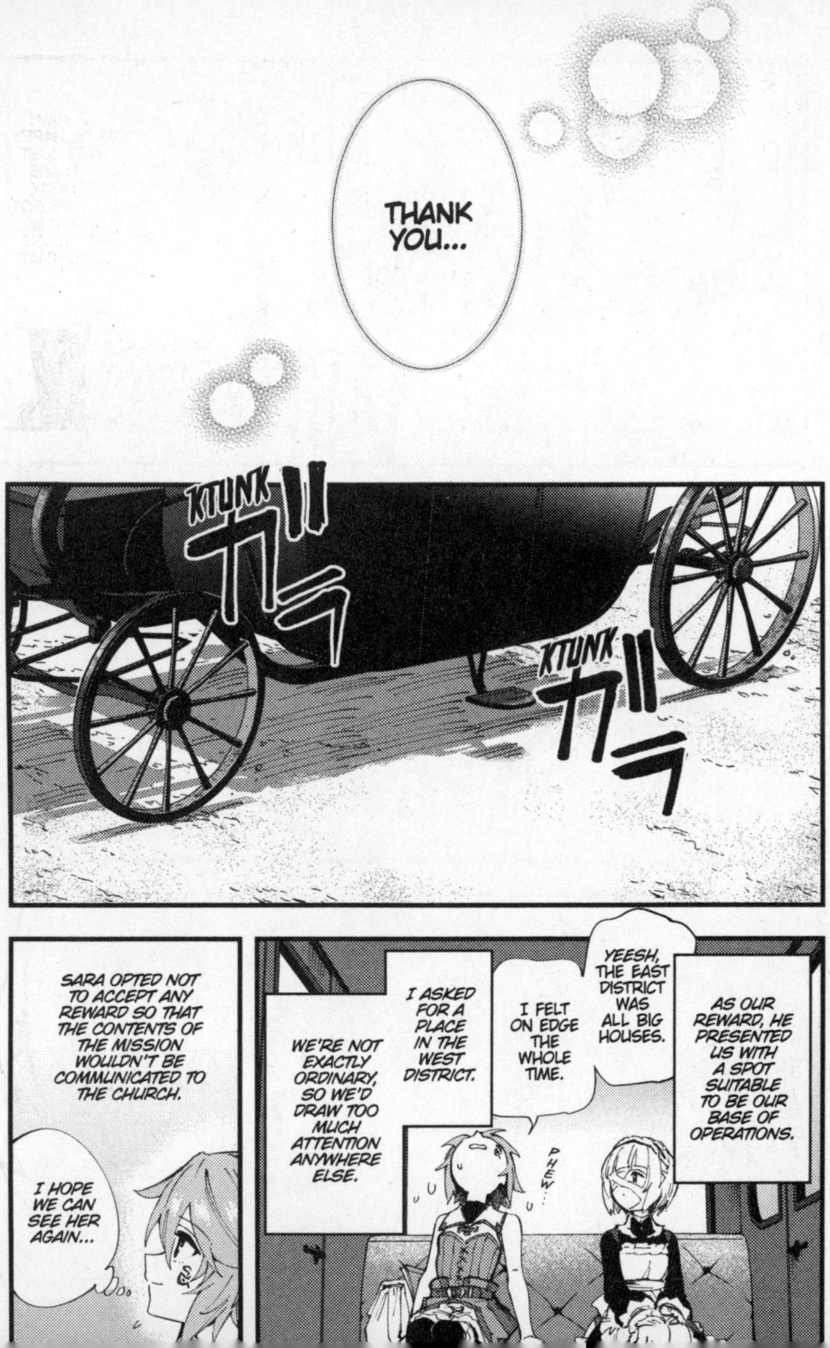
THANK YOU...
KTUNK
KTUNK
AS OUR REWARD, HE PRESENTED US WITH A SPOT SUITABLE TO BE OUR BASE OF OPERATIONS.
YEESH, THE EAST DISTRICT WAS ALL BIG HOUSES.
I FELT ON EDGE THE WHOLE TIME.
I ASKED FOR A PLACE IN THE WEST DISTRICT.
WE'RE NOT EXACTLY ORDINARY, SO WE'D DRAW TOO MUCH ATTENTION ANYWHERE ELSE.
PHEW...
SARA OPTED NOT TO ACCEPT ANY REWARD SO THAT THE CONTENTS OF THE MISSION WOULDN'T BE COMMUNICATED TO THE CHURCH.
I HOPE WE CAN SEE HER AGAIN...

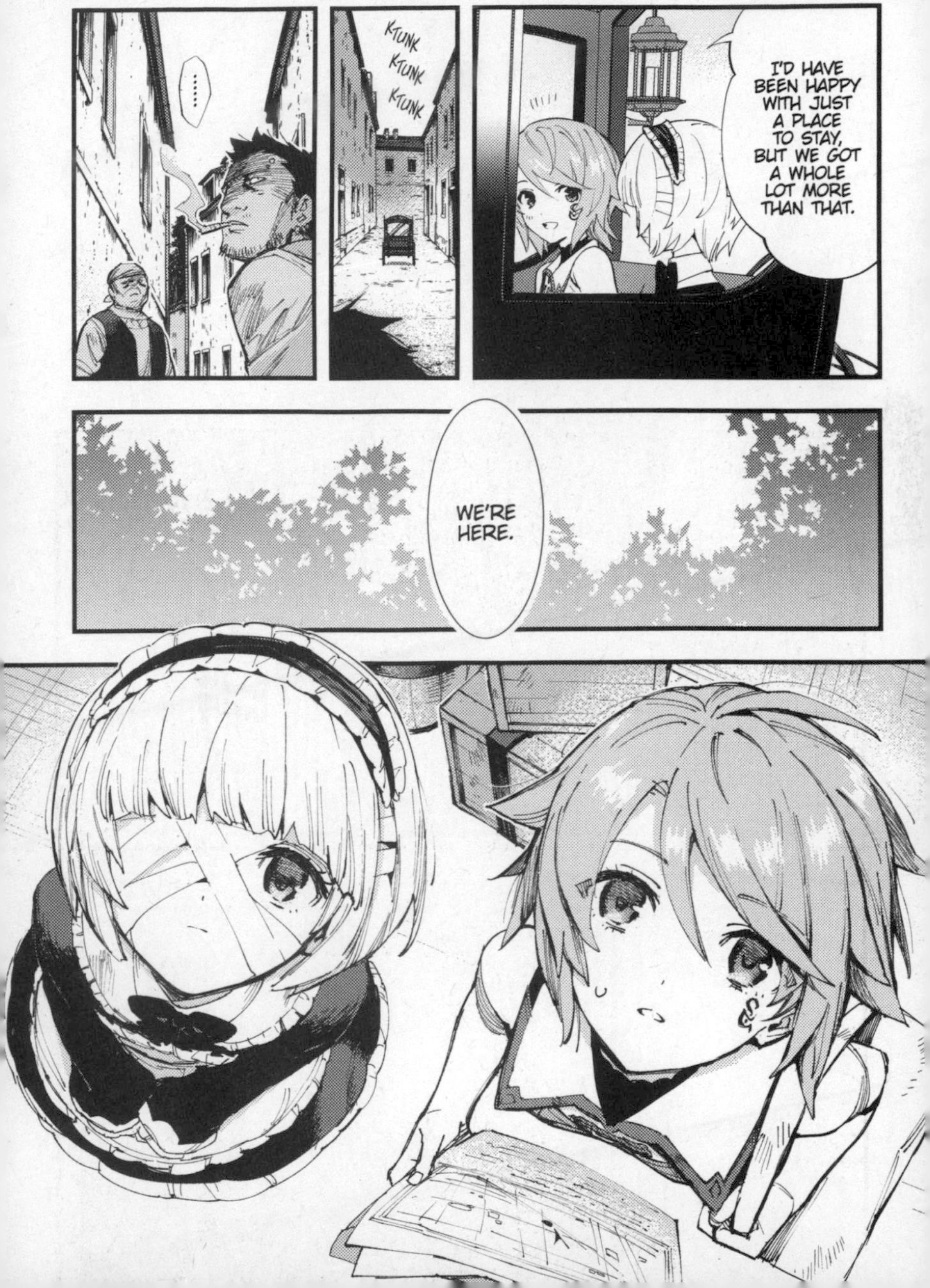
I'D HAVE BEEN HAPPY WITH JUST A PLACE TO STAY, BUT WE GOT A WHOLE LOT MORE THAN THAT.
K-TUNK
K-TUNK
K-TUNK
......
WE'RE HERE.

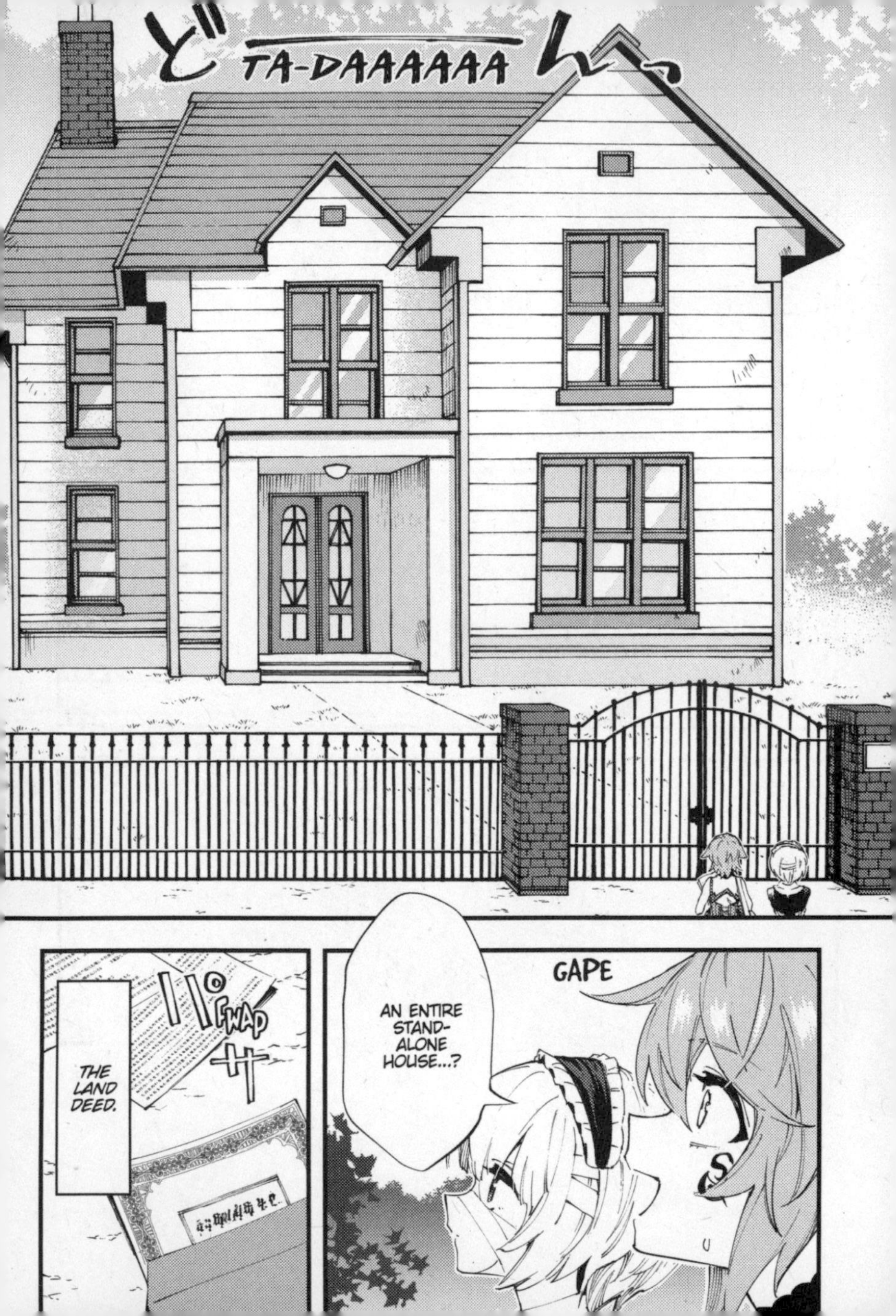
TA-DAAAAAA
GAPE
AN ENTIRE STAND-ALONE HOUSE...?
FWAP
THE LAND DEED.

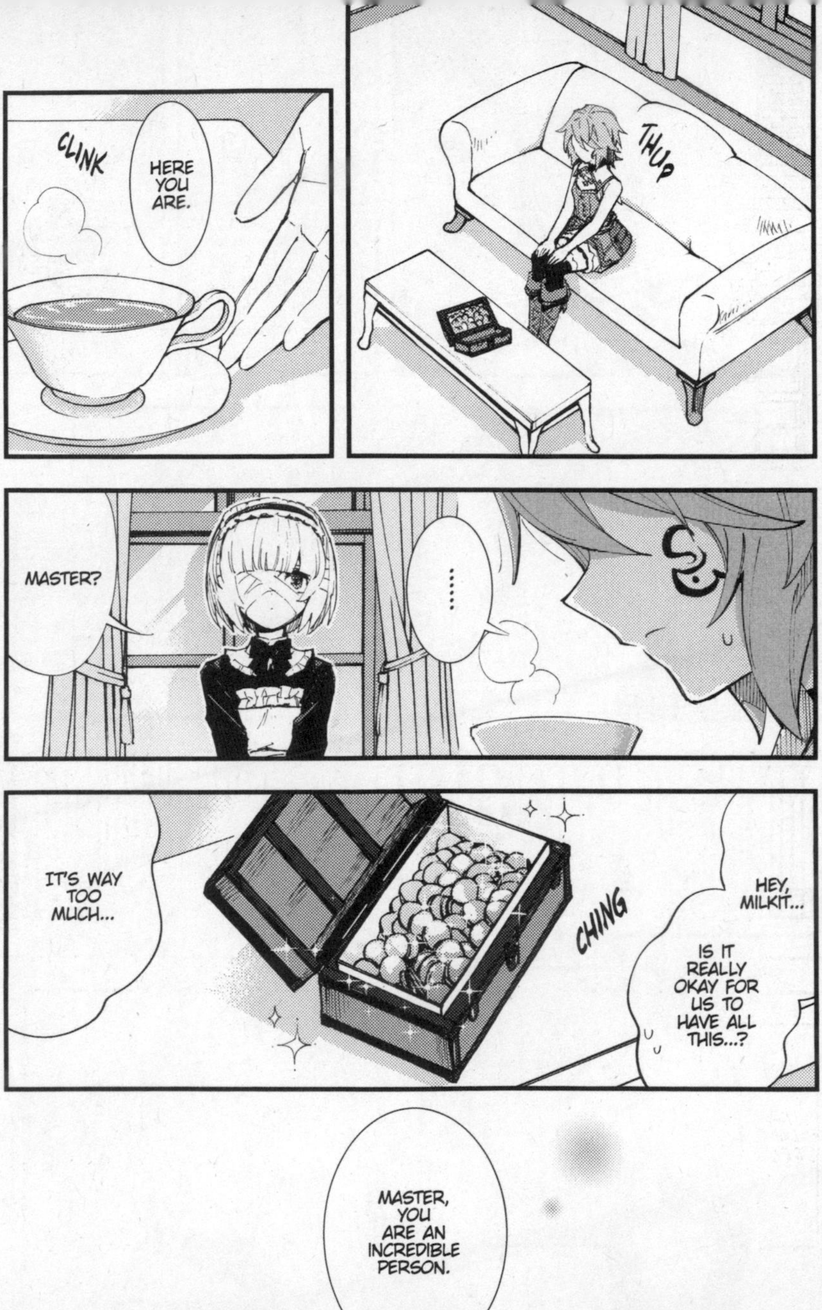
THUD
CLINK
HERE YOU ARE.
......
MASTER?
HEY, MILKIT...
IS IT REALLY OKAY FOR US TO HAVE ALL THIS...?
CHING
IT'S WAY TOO MUCH...
MASTER, YOU ARE AN INCREDIBLE PERSON.

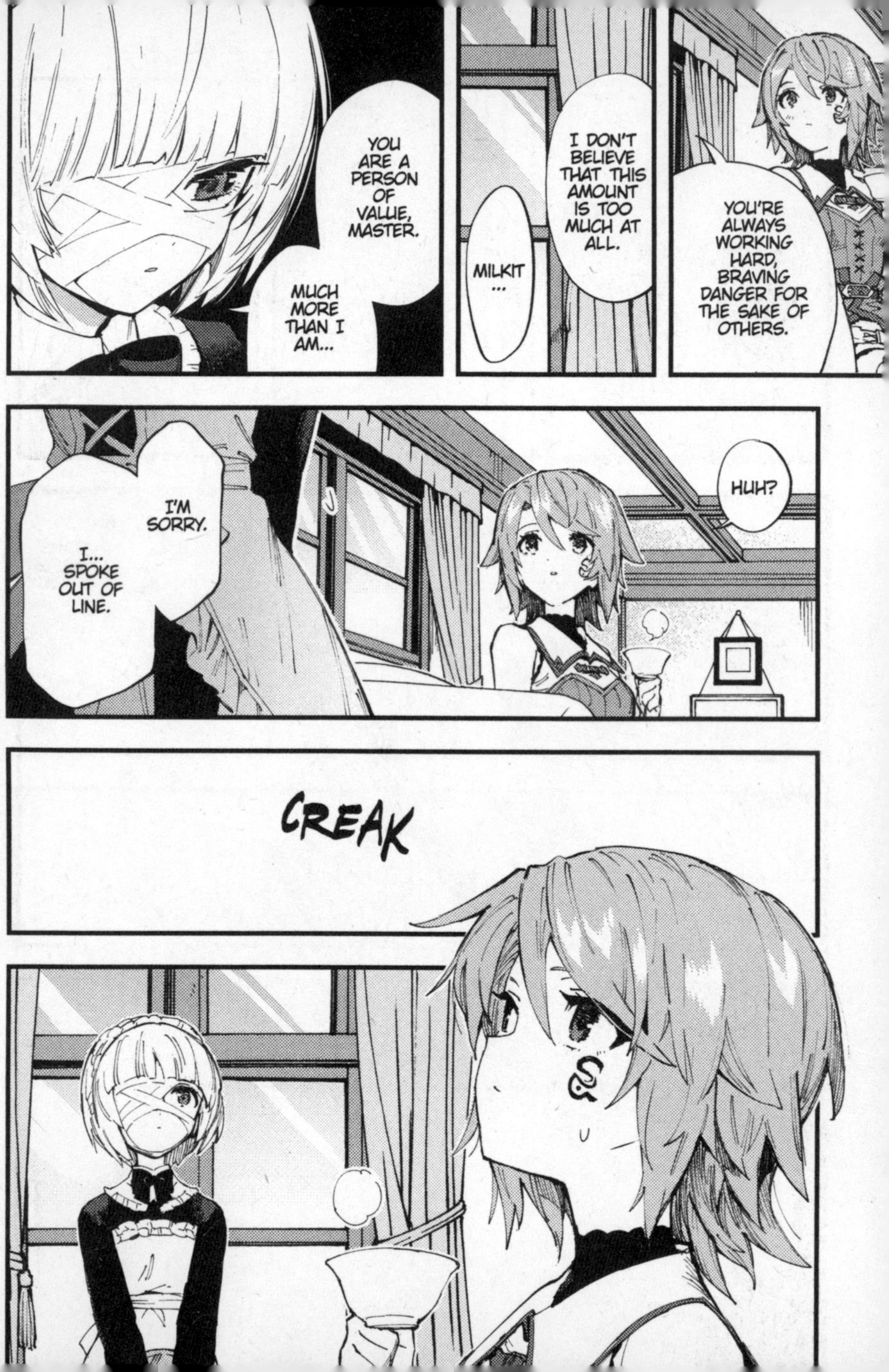
YOU'RE ALWAYS WORKING HARD, BRAVING DANGER FOR THE SAKE OF OTHERS.
I DON'T BELIEVE THAT THIS AMOUNT IS TOO MUCH AT ALL.
MILKIT ...
YOU ARE A PERSON OF VALUE, MASTER.
MUCH MORE THAN I AM...
HUH?
I'M SORRY.
I... SPOKE OUT OF LINE.
CREAK

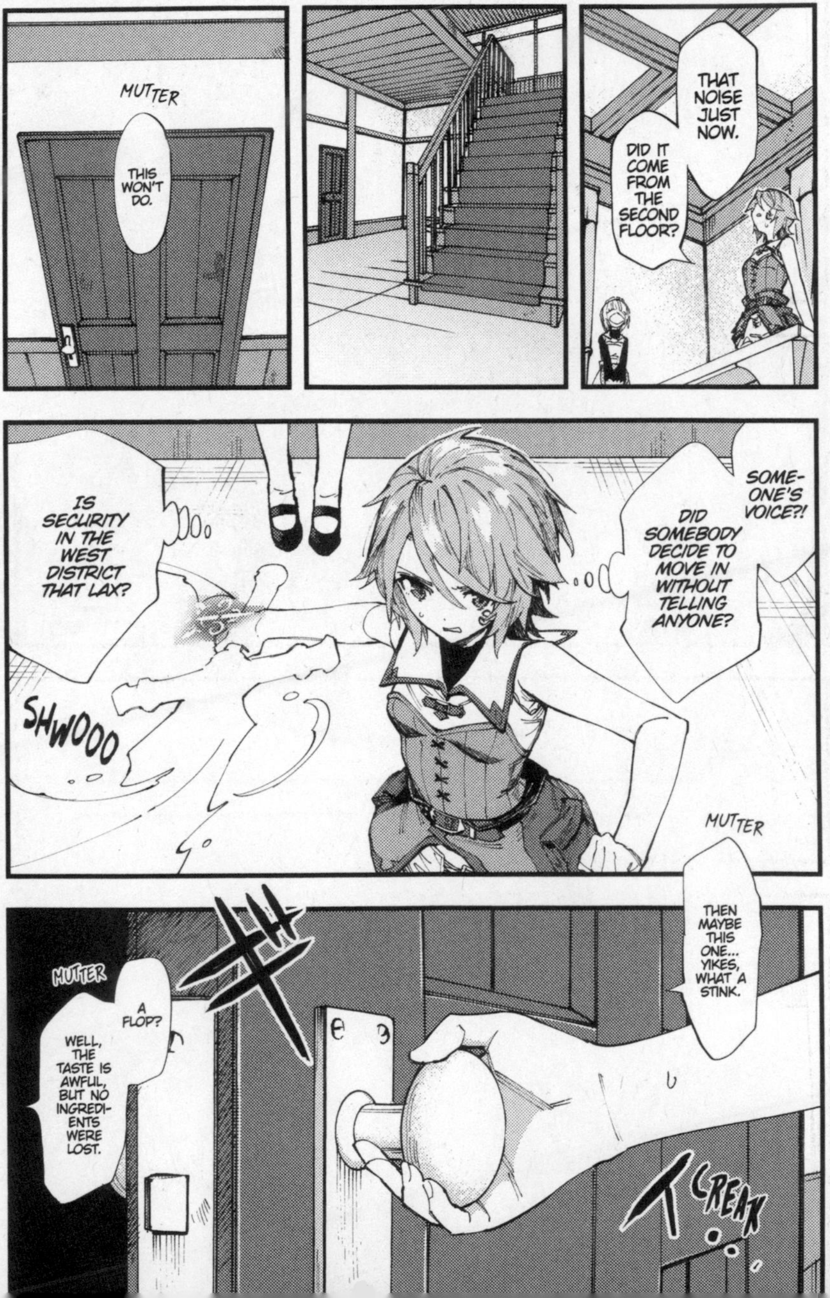
THAT NOISE JUST NOW.
DID IT COME FROM THE SECOND FLOOR?
MUTTER
THIS WON'T DO.
SOME-ONE'S VOICE?!
DID SOMEBODY DECIDE TO MOVE IN WITHOUT TELLING ANYONE?
IS SECURITY IN THE WEST DISTRICT THAT LAX?
SHWOOO
MUTTER
THEN MAYBE THIS ONE... YIKES, WHAT A STINK.
CREAK...
MUTTER
A FLOP?
WELL, THE TASTE IS AWFUL, BUT NO INGREDI-ENTS WERE LOST.

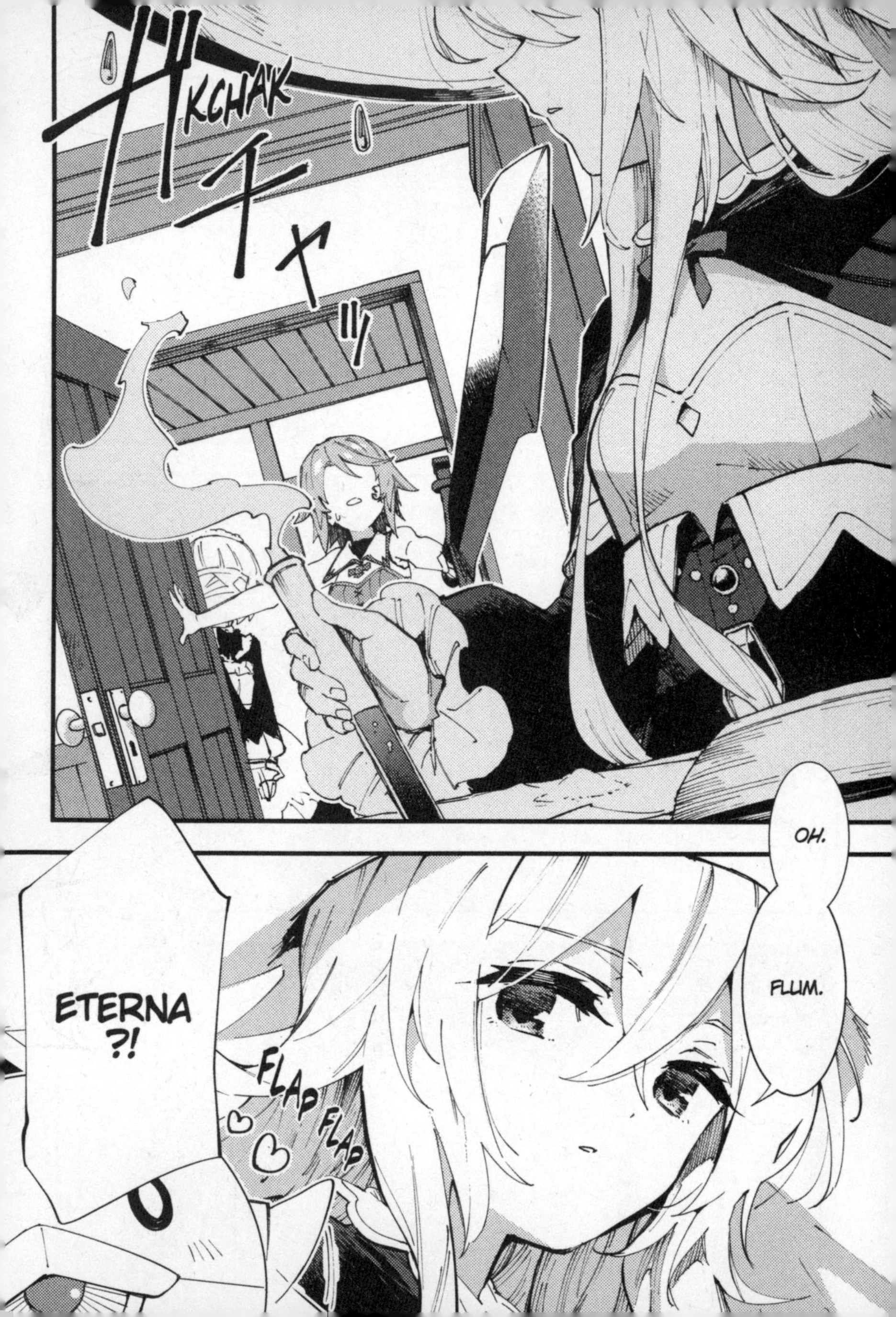
KCHAK
OH.
FLUM.
ETERNA ?!
FLAP FLAP FLAP

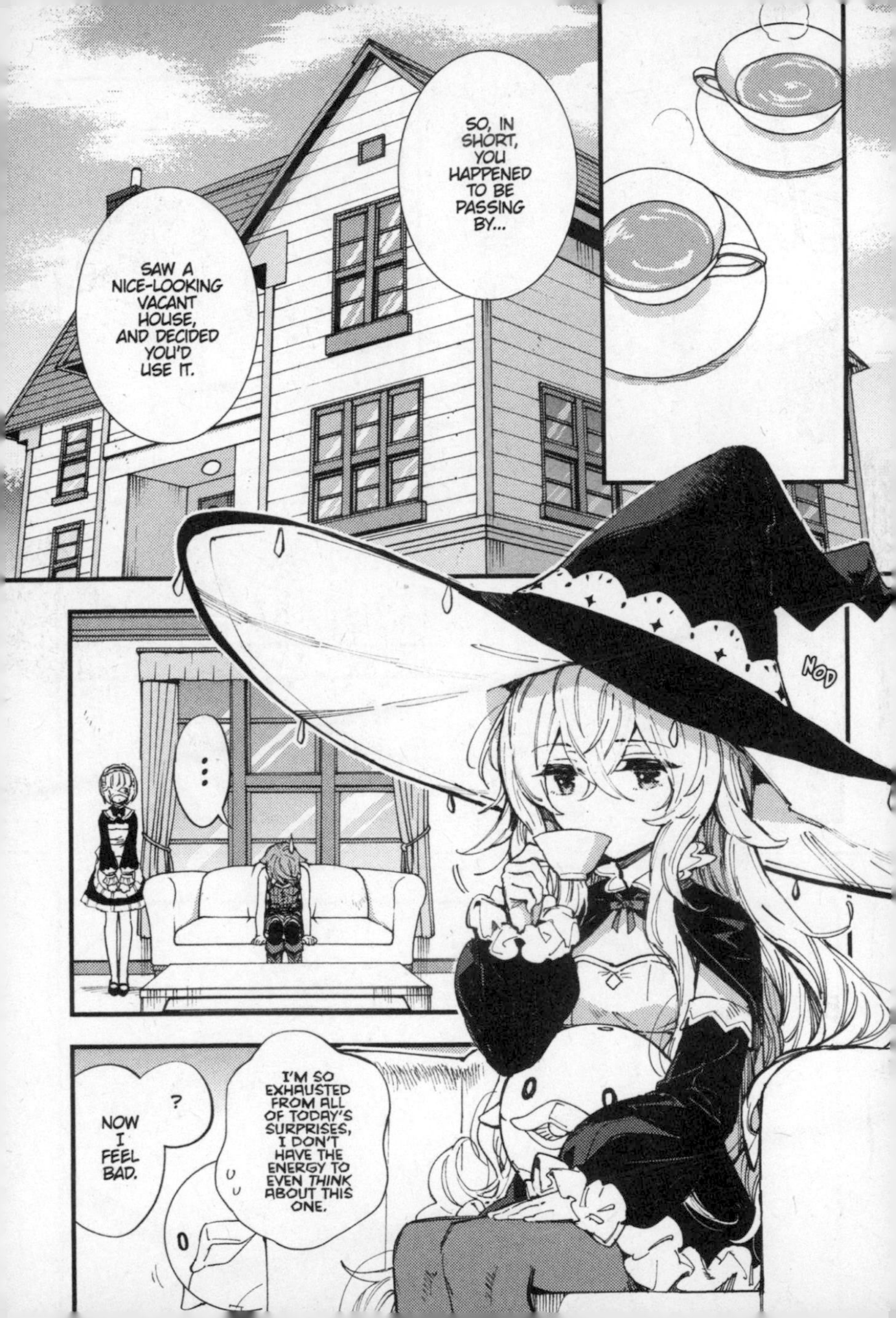
SO, IN SHORT, YOU HAPPENED TO BE PASSING BY...
SAW A NICE-LOOKING VACANT HOUSE, AND DECIDED YOU'D USE IT.
NOD
...
I'M SO EXHAUSTED FROM ALL OF TODAY'S SURPRISES, I DON'T HAVE THE ENERGY TO EVEN *THINK* ABOUT THIS ONE.
?
NOW I FEEL BAD.

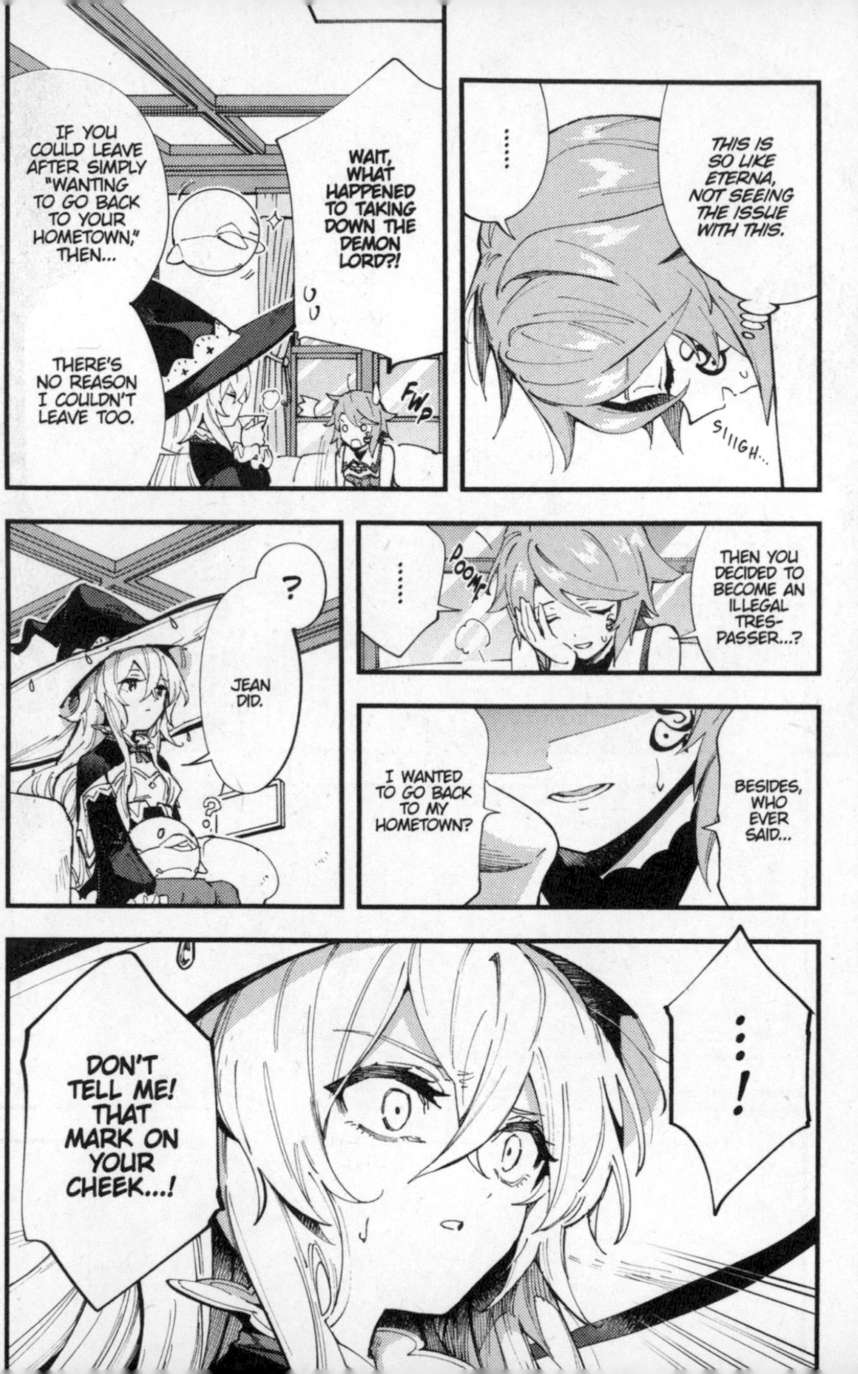

THIS IS SO LIKE ETERNA, NOT SEEING THE ISSUE WITH THIS.
......
SIIIGH...
WAIT, WHAT HAPPENED TO TAKING DOWN THE DEMON LORD?!
IF YOU COULD LEAVE AFTER SIMPLY "WANTING TO GO BACK TO YOUR HOMETOWN," THEN...
FWP
THERE'S NO REASON I COULDN'T LEAVE TOO.
THEN YOU DECIDED TO BECOME AN ILLEGAL TRES-PASSER...?
POOMF
......
BESIDES, WHO EVER SAID...
I WANTED TO GO BACK TO MY HOMETOWN?
?
JEAN DID.
...!
DON'T TELL ME! THAT MARK ON YOUR CHEEK...!

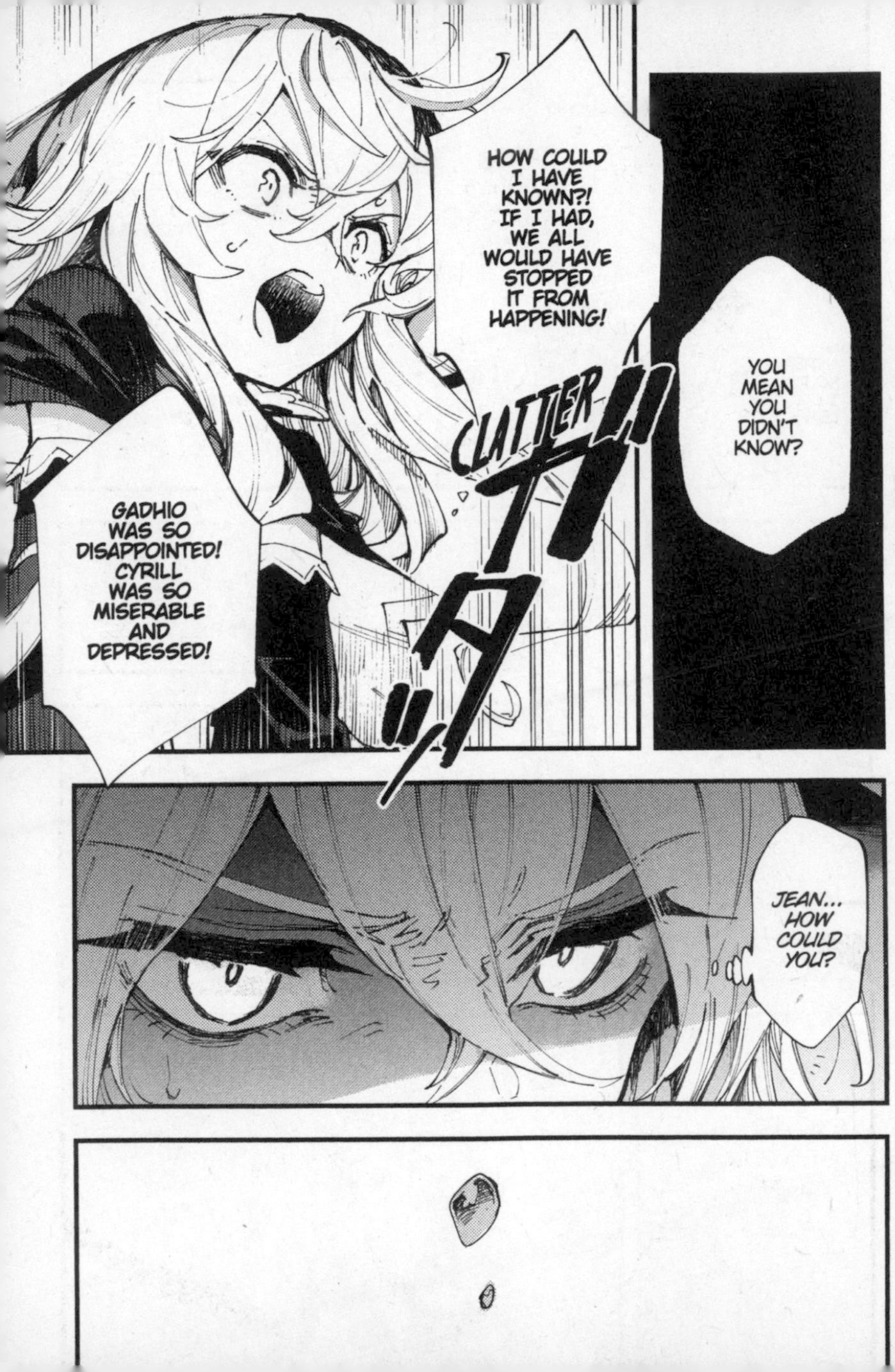
YOU MEAN YOU DIDN'T KNOW?
HOW COULD I HAVE KNOWN?! IF I HAD, WE ALL WOULD HAVE STOPPED IT FROM HAPPENING!
CLATTER
GADHIO WAS SO DISAPPOINTED! CYRILL WAS SO MISERABLE AND DEPRESSED!
JEAN... HOW COULD YOU?

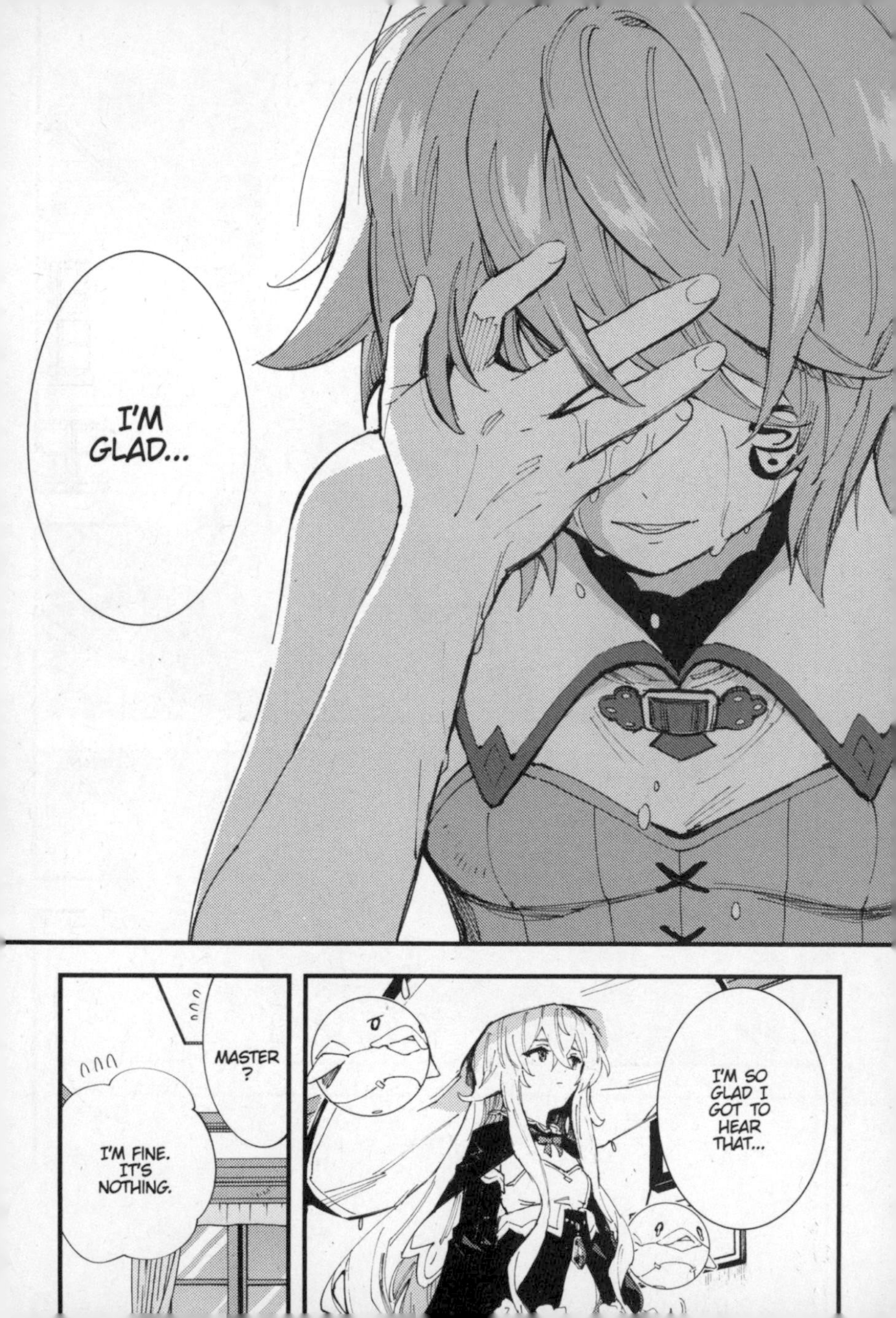
I'M GLAD...
I'M SO GLAD I GOT TO HEAR THAT...
MASTER?
I'M FINE. IT'S NOTHING.

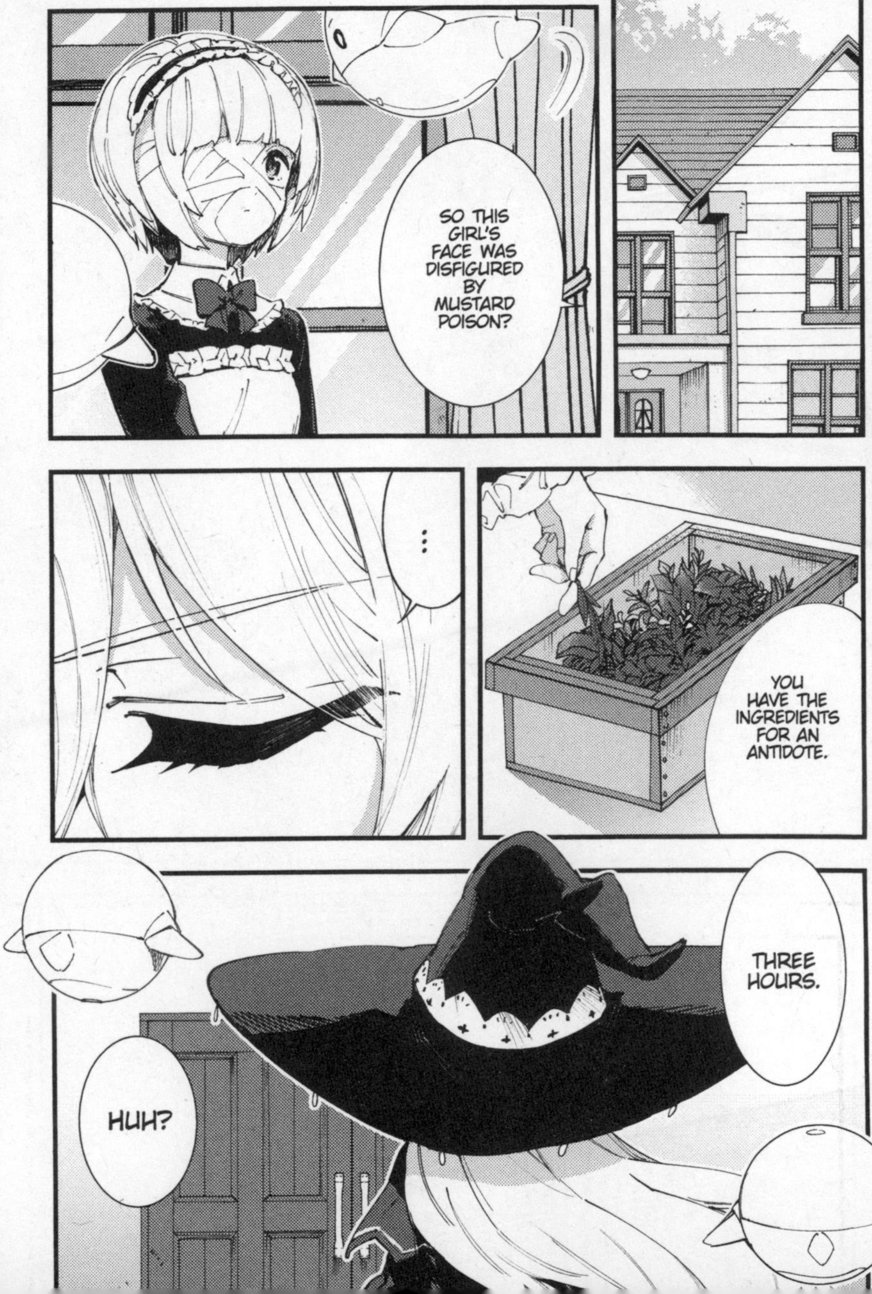
SO THIS GIRL'S FACE WAS DISFIGURED BY MUSTARD POISON?
YOU HAVE THE INGREDIENTS FOR AN ANTIDOTE.
...
THREE HOURS.
HUH?

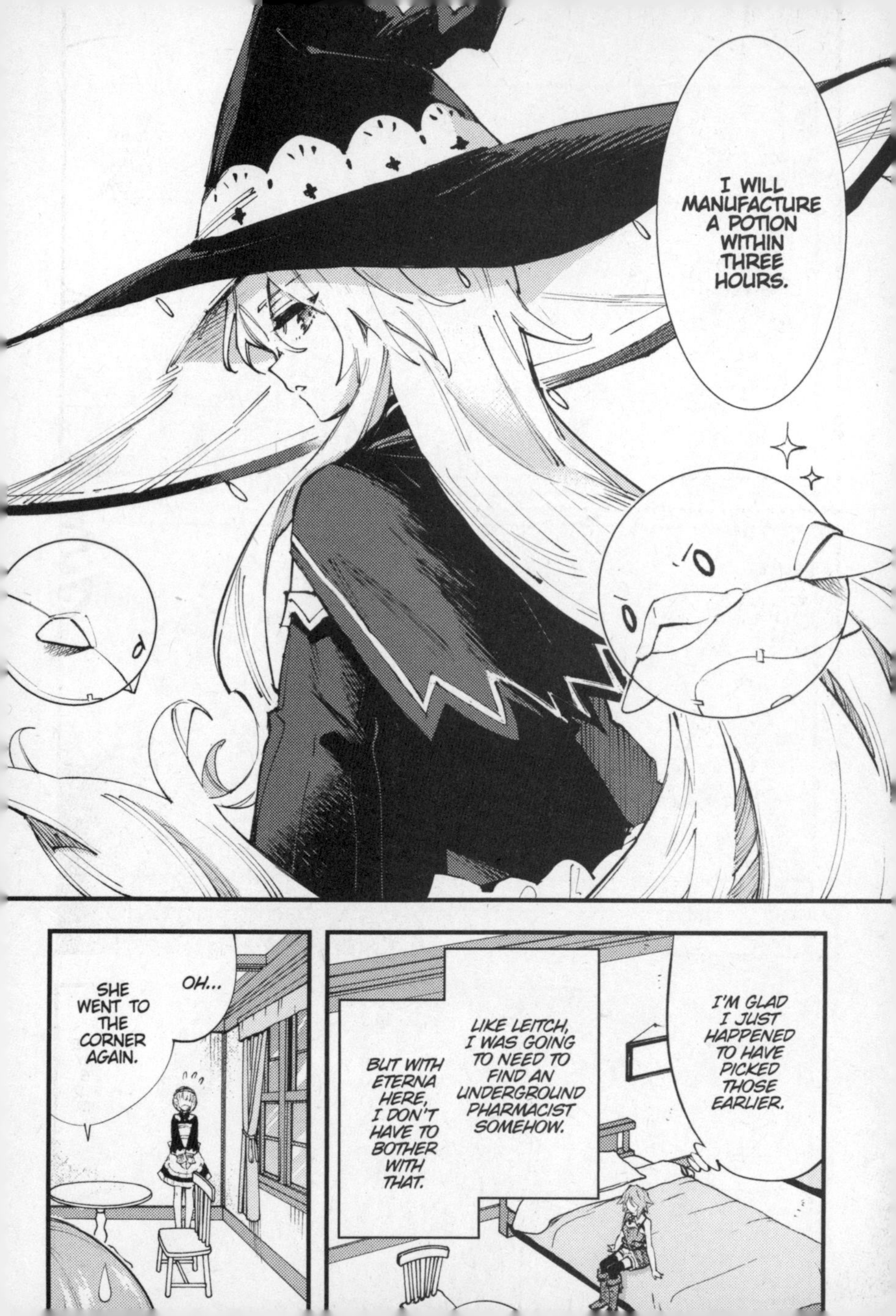
I WILL MANUFACTURE A POTION WITHIN THREE HOURS.
I'M GLAD I JUST HAPPENED TO HAVE PICKED THOSE EARLIER.
LIKE LEITCH, I WAS GOING TO NEED TO FIND AN UNDERGROUND PHARMACIST SOMEHOW.
BUT WITH ETERNA HERE, I DON'T HAVE TO BOTHER WITH THAT.
OH...
SHE WENT TO THE CORNER AGAIN.

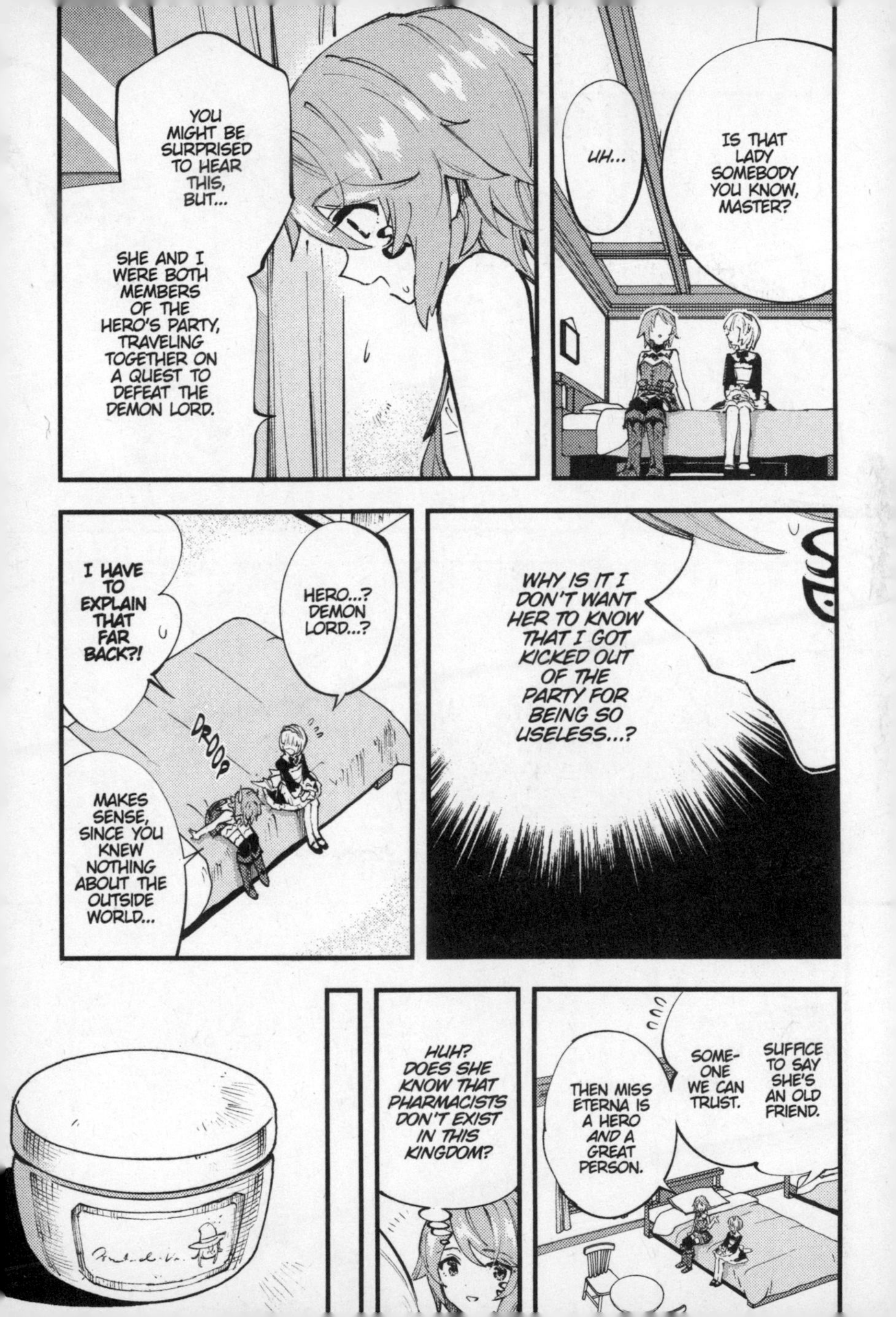
IS THAT LADY SOMEBODY YOU KNOW, MASTER?
UH...
YOU MIGHT BE SURPRISED TO HEAR THIS, BUT...
SHE AND I WERE BOTH MEMBERS OF THE HERO'S PARTY, TRAVELING TOGETHER ON A QUEST TO DEFEAT THE DEMON LORD.
WHY IS IT I DON'T WANT HER TO KNOW THAT I GOT KICKED OUT OF THE PARTY FOR BEING SO USELESS...?
HERO...? DEMON LORD...?
I HAVE TO EXPLAIN THAT FAR BACK?!
DROOP
MAKES SENSE, SINCE YOU KNEW NOTHING ABOUT THE OUTSIDE WORLD...
SUFFICE TO SAY SHE'S AN OLD FRIEND.
SOME-ONE WE CAN TRUST.
THEN MISS ETERNA IS A HERO AND A GREAT PERSON.
HUH? DOES SHE KNOW THAT PHARMACISTS DON'T EXIST IN THIS KINGDOM?

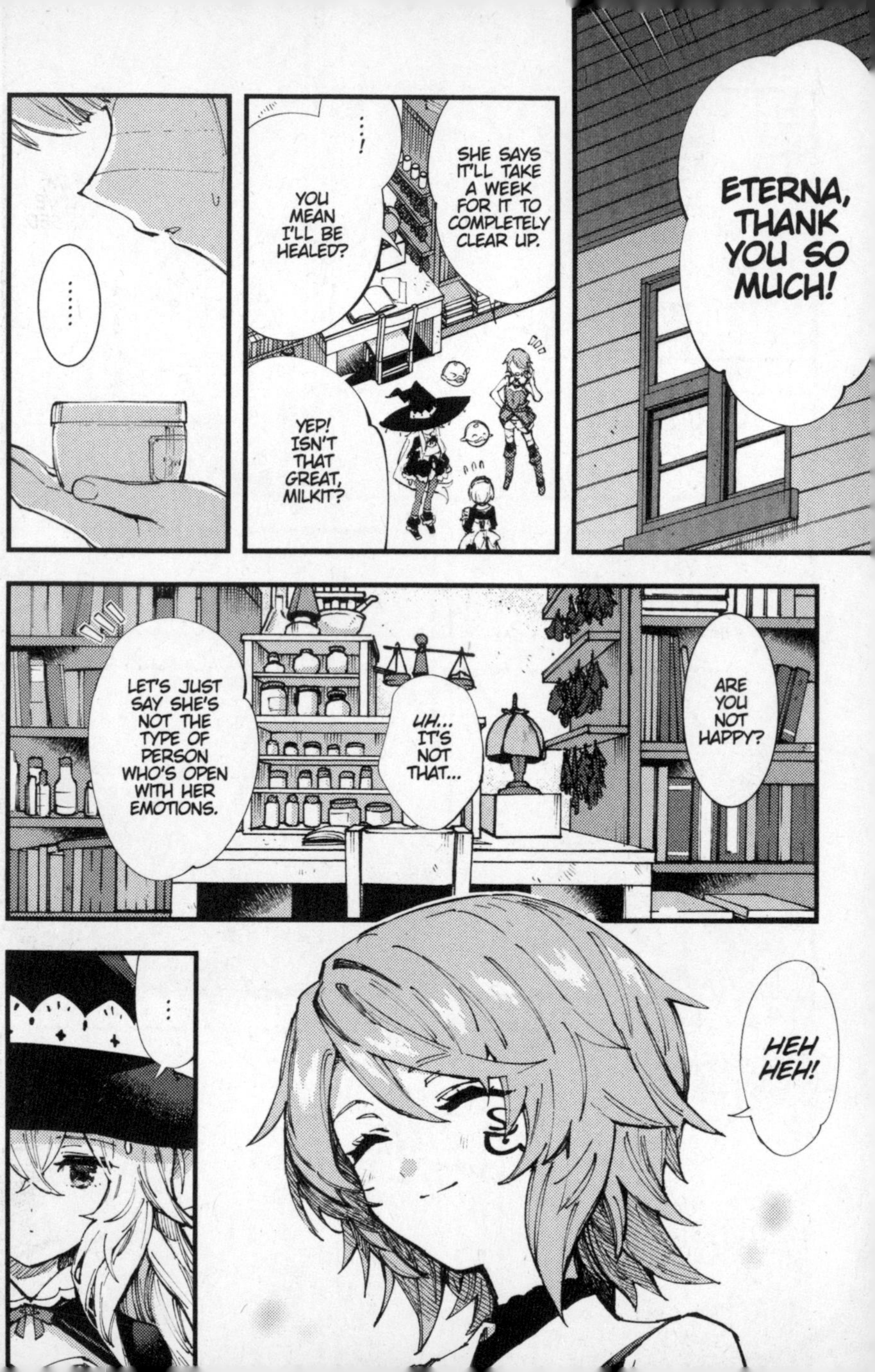
ETERNA, THANK YOU SO MUCH!
SHE SAYS IT'LL TAKE A WEEK FOR IT TO COMPLETELY CLEAR UP.
...!
YOU MEAN I'LL BE HEALED?
YEP! ISN'T THAT GREAT, MILKIT?
......
ARE YOU NOT HAPPY?
UH... IT'S NOT THAT...
LET'S JUST SAY SHE'S NOT THE TYPE OF PERSON WHO'S OPEN WITH HER EMOTIONS.
HEH HEH!
...

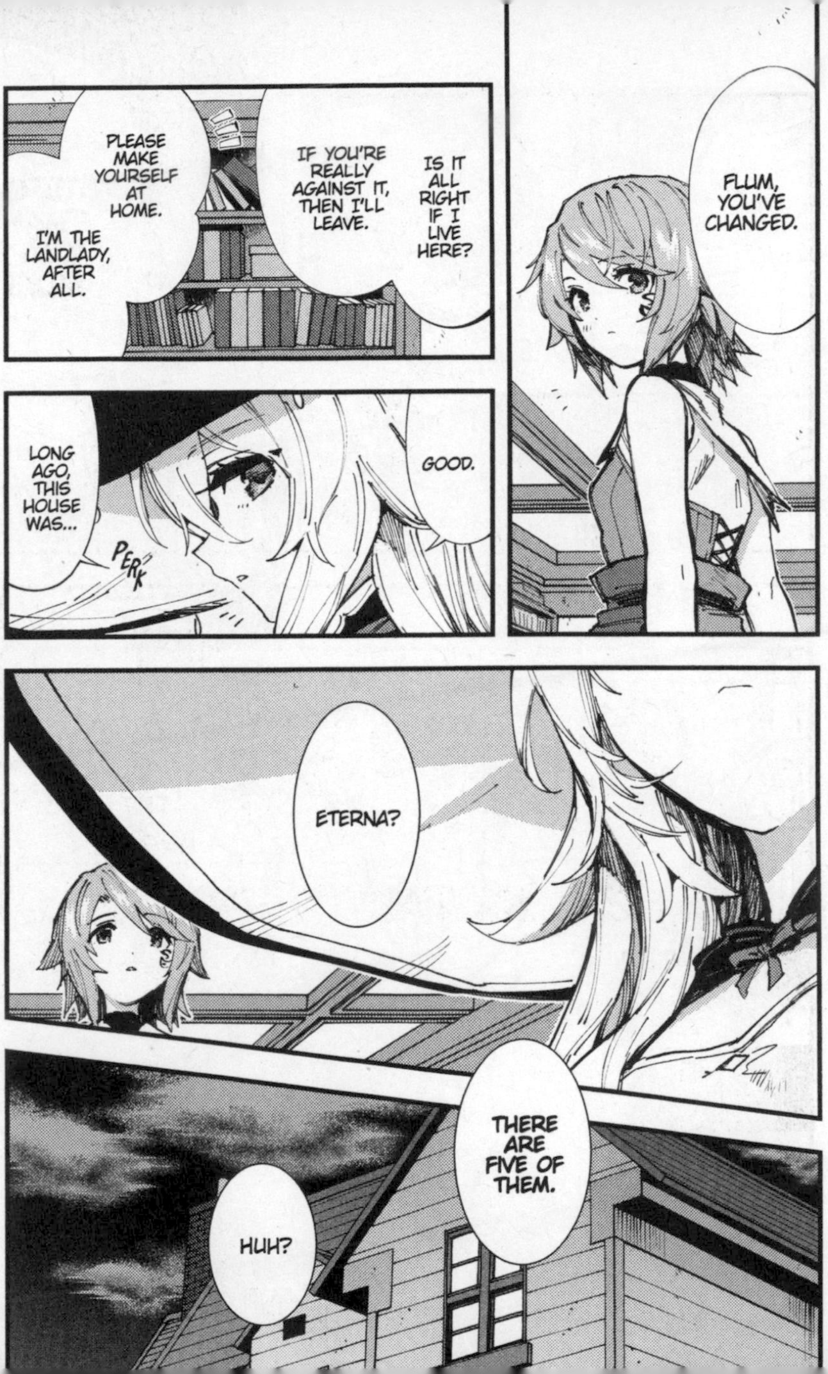
FLUM, YOU'VE CHANGED.
IS IT ALL RIGHT IF I LIVE HERE?
IF YOU'RE REALLY AGAINST IT, THEN I'LL LEAVE.
PLEASE MAKE YOURSELF AT HOME.
I'M THE LANDLADY, AFTER ALL.
GOOD.
LONG AGO, THIS HOUSE WAS...
PERK
ETERNA?
THERE ARE FIVE OF THEM.
HUH?

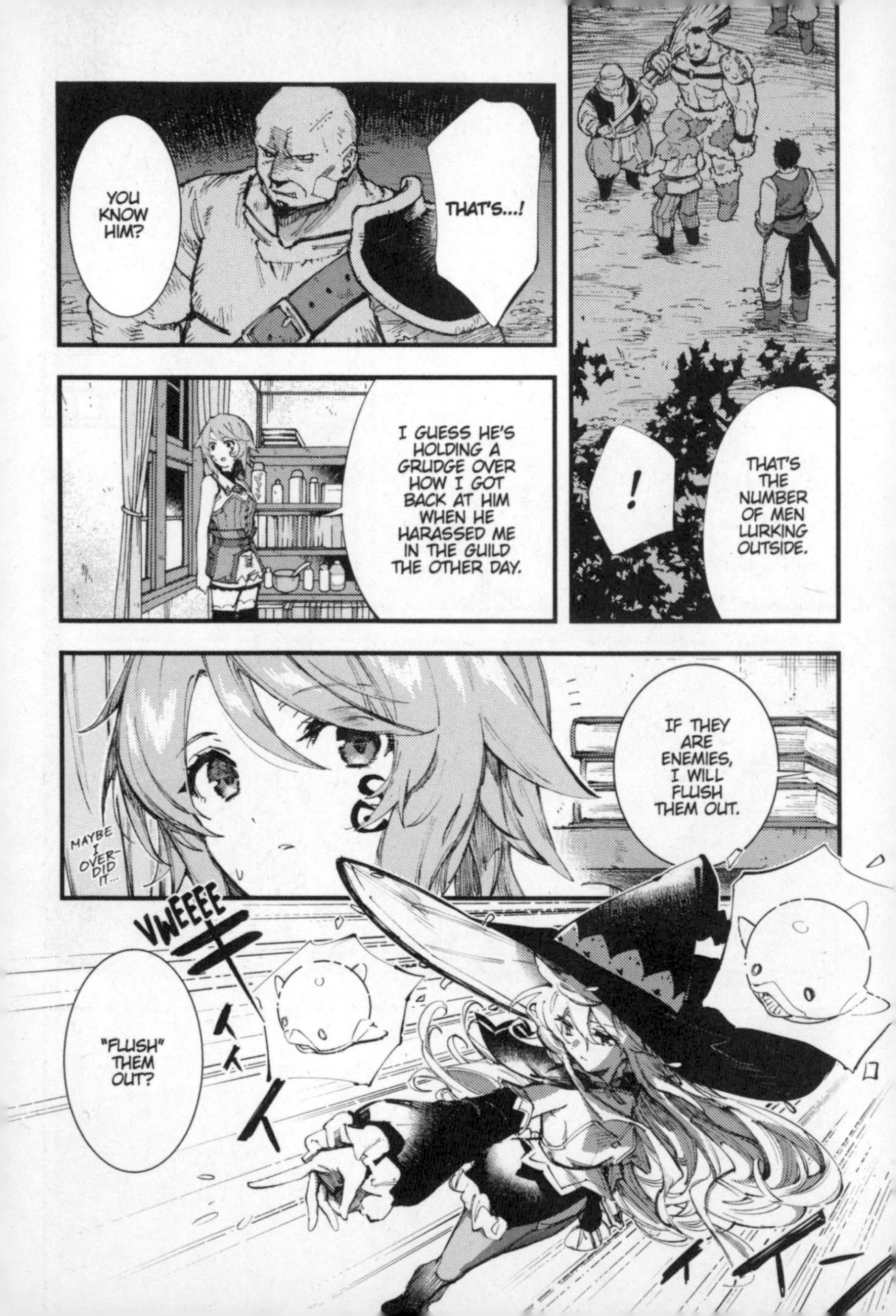
THAT'S THE NUMBER OF MEN LURKING OUTSIDE.
!
THAT'S...!
YOU KNOW HIM?
I GUESS HE'S HOLDING A GRUDGE OVER HOW I GOT BACK AT HIM WHEN HE HARASSED ME IN THE GUILD THE OTHER DAY.
IF THEY ARE ENEMIES, I WILL FLUSH THEM OUT.
MAYBE I OVER-DID IT...
VWEEEE
"FLUSH" THEM OUT?

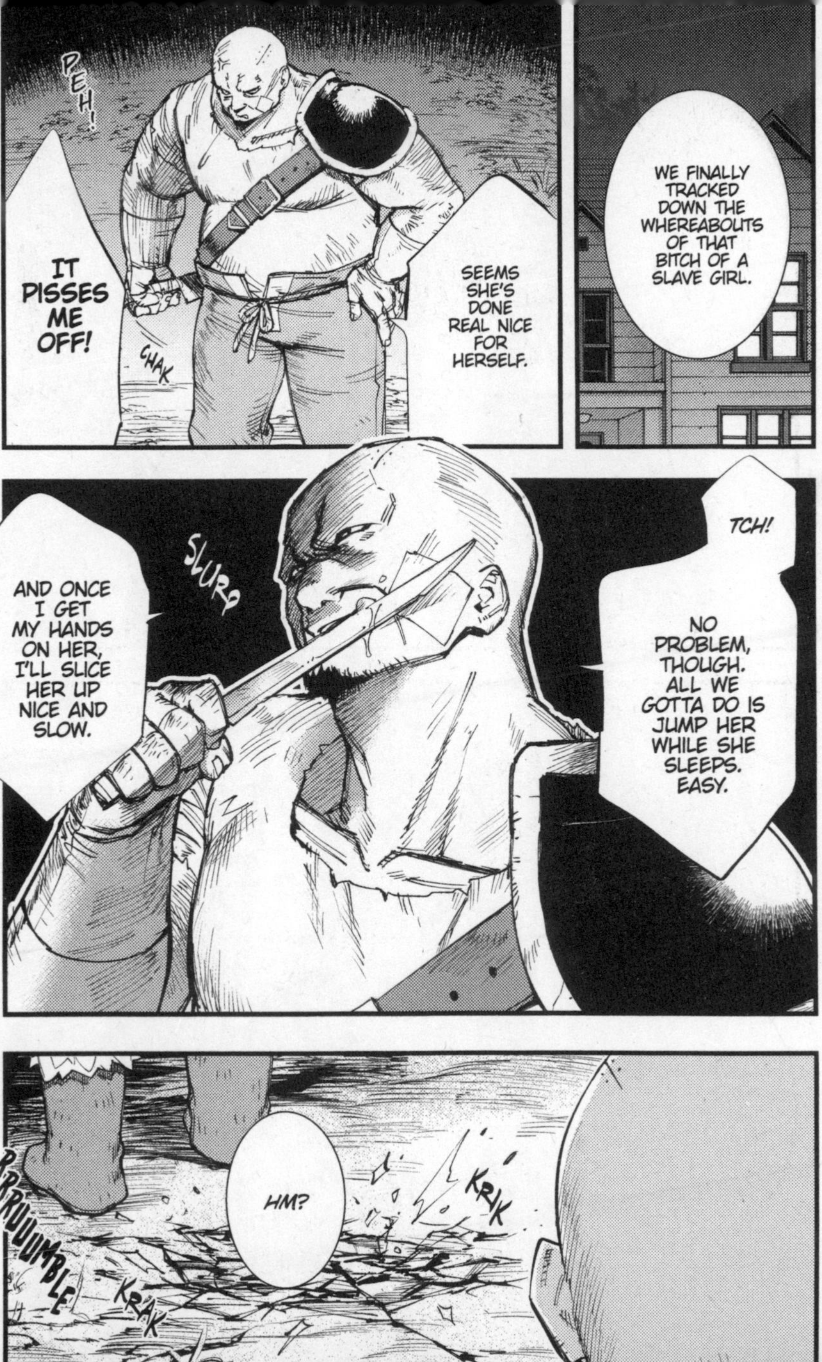
WE FINALLY TRACKED DOWN THE WHEREABOUTS OF THAT BITCH OF A SLAVE GIRL.
SEEMS SHE'S DONE REAL NICE FOR HERSELF.
PEH!
IT PISSES ME OFF!
CHAK
TCH!
NO PROBLEM, THOUGH. ALL WE GOTTA DO IS JUMP HER WHILE SHE SLEEPS. EASY.
SLURP
AND ONCE I GET MY HANDS ON HER, I'LL SLICE HER UP NICE AND SLOW.
KRIK
HM?
KRAK
R-RRUUUMBLE

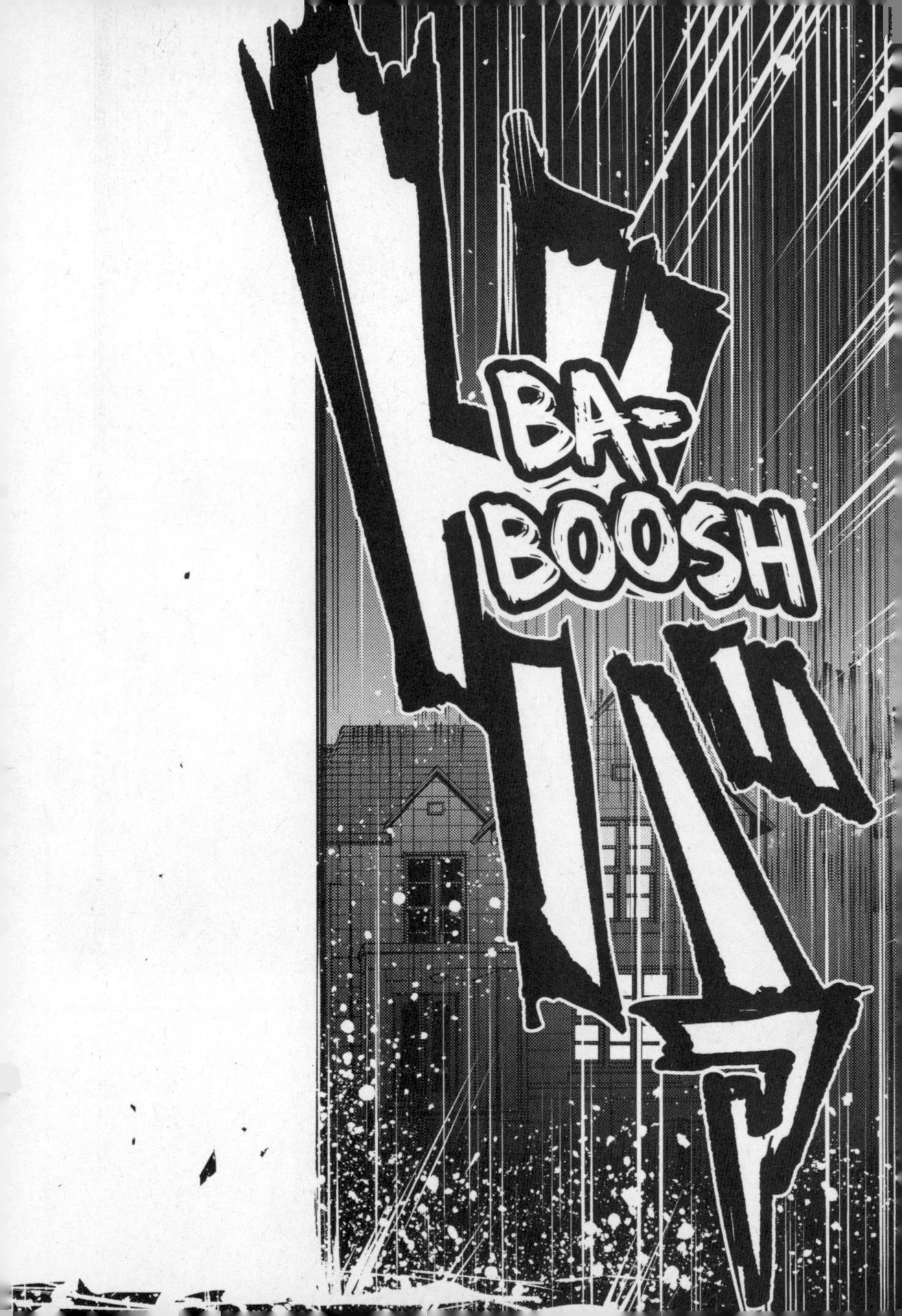
BA-
BOOSH

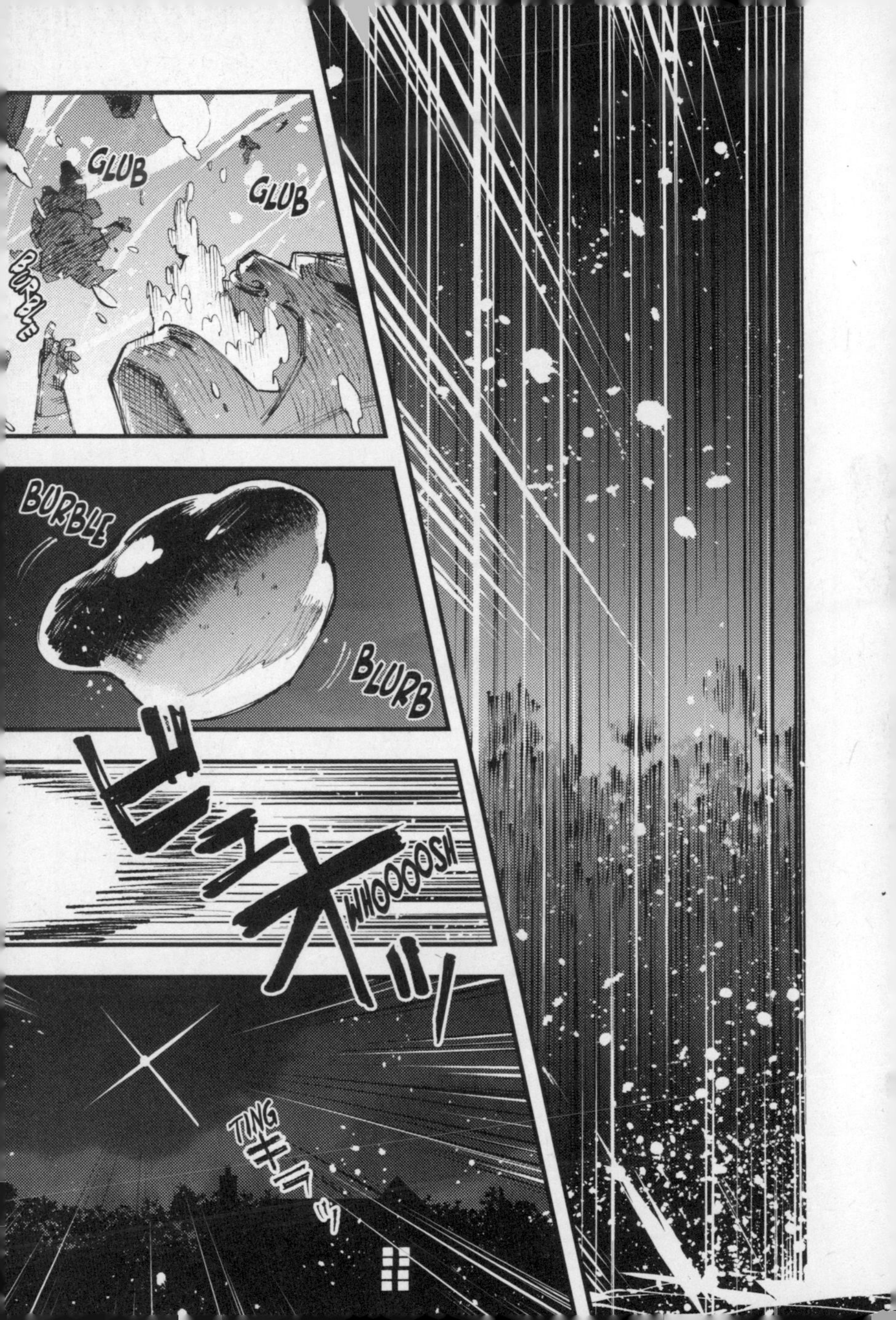
GLUB
GLUB
BURBLE
BURBLE
BLURB
WHOOOOSH
TING

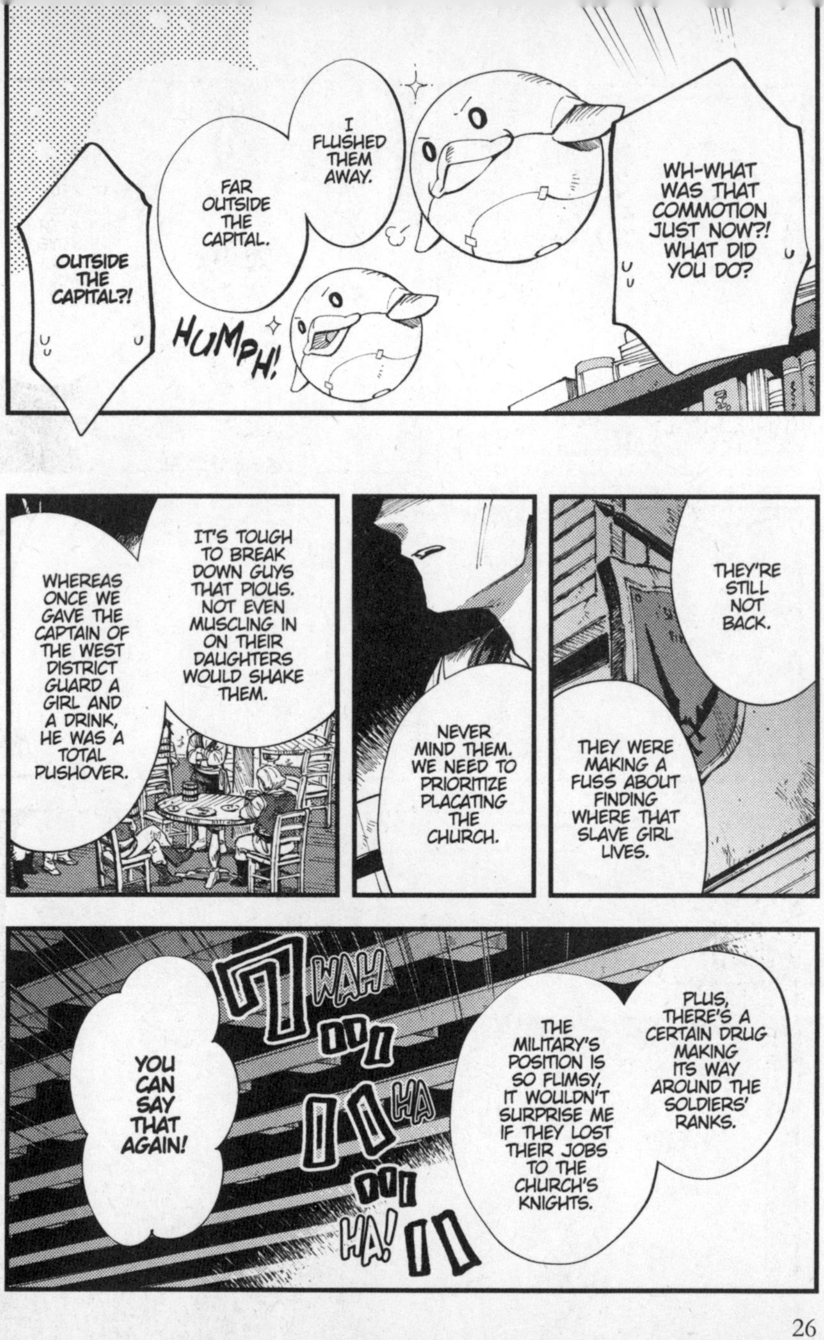
WH-WHAT WAS THAT COMMOTION JUST NOW?! WHAT DID YOU DO?
I FLUSHED THEM AWAY.
FAR OUTSIDE THE CAPITAL.
HUMPH!
OUTSIDE THE CAPITAL?!
THEY'RE STILL NOT BACK.
THEY WERE MAKING A FUSS ABOUT FINDING WHERE THAT SLAVE GIRL LIVES.
NEVER MIND THEM. WE NEED TO PRIORITIZE PLACATING THE CHURCH.
IT'S TOUGH TO BREAK DOWN GUYS THAT PIOUS. NOT EVEN MUSCLING IN ON THEIR DAUGHTERS WOULD SHAKE THEM.
WHEREAS ONCE WE GAVE THE CAPTAIN OF THE WEST DISTRICT GUARD A GIRL AND A DRINK, HE WAS A TOTAL PUSHOVER.
PLUS, THERE'S A CERTAIN DRUG MAKING ITS WAY AROUND THE SOLDIERS' RANKS.
THE MILITARY'S POSITION IS SO FLIMSY, IT WOULDN'T SURPRISE ME IF THEY LOST THEIR JOBS TO THE CHURCH'S KNIGHTS.
WAH HA HA HA!
YOU CAN SAY THAT AGAIN!

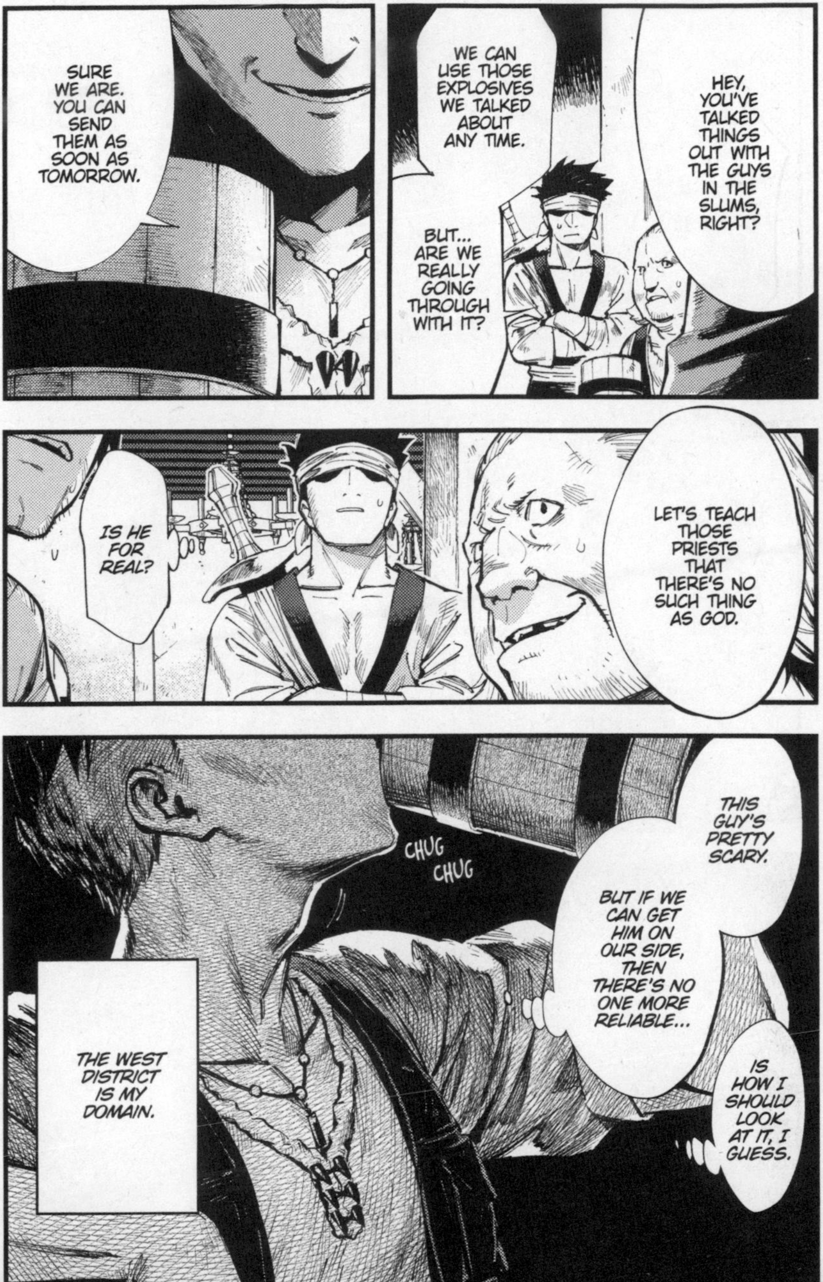
HEY, YOU'VE TALKED THINGS OUT WITH THE GUYS IN THE SLUMS, RIGHT?
WE CAN USE THOSE EXPLOSIVES WE TALKED ABOUT ANY TIME.
BUT... ARE WE REALLY GOING THROUGH WITH IT?
SURE WE ARE. YOU CAN SEND THEM AS SOON AS TOMORROW.
LET'S TEACH THOSE PRIESTS THAT THERE'S NO SUCH THING AS GOD.
IS HE FOR REAL?
THIS GUY'S PRETTY SCARY.
BUT IF WE CAN GET HIM ON OUR SIDE, THEN THERE'S NO ONE MORE RELIABLE...
IS HOW I SHOULD LOOK AT IT, I GUESS.
CHUG CHUG
THE WEST DISTRICT IS MY DOMAIN.

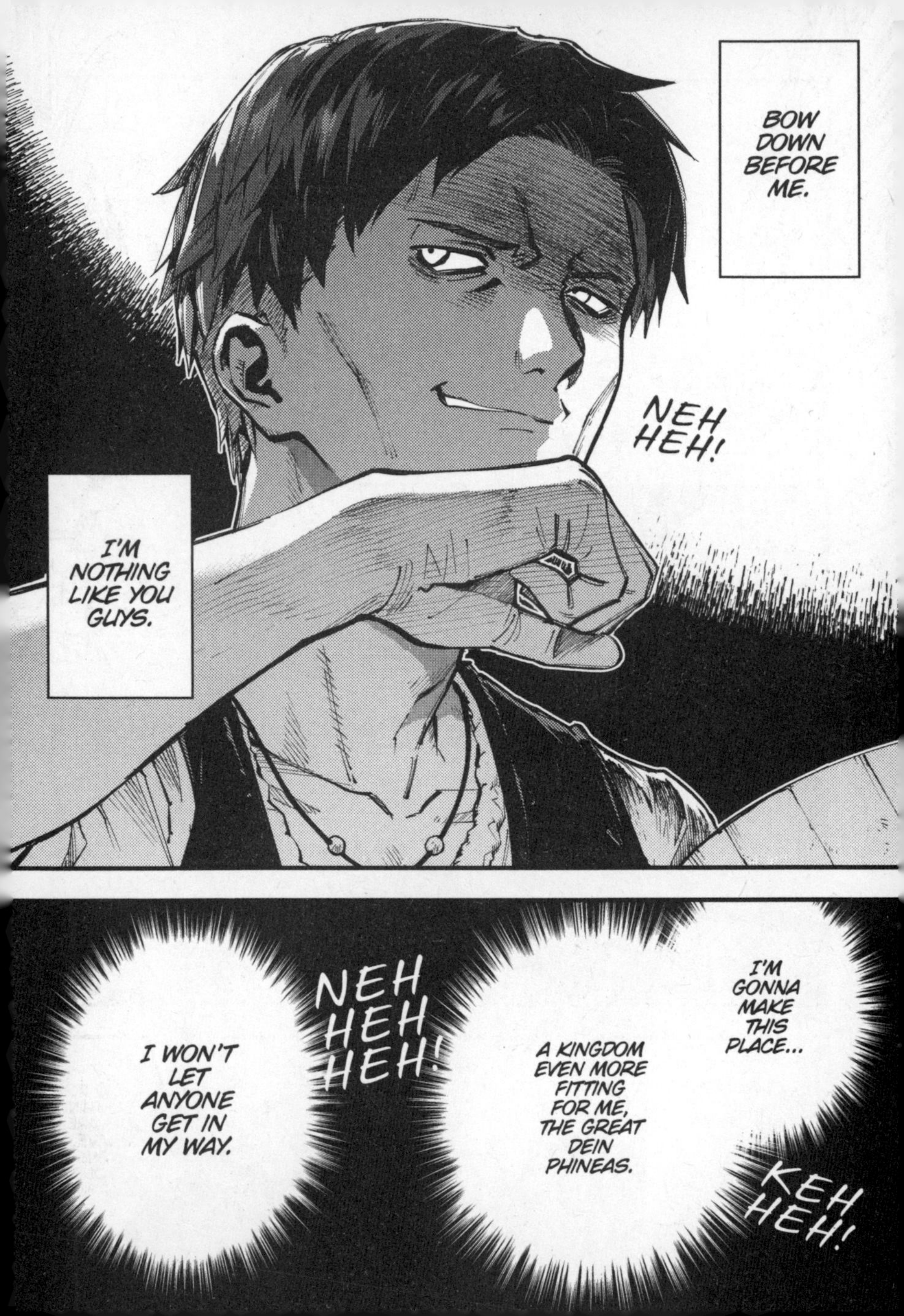
BOW DOWN BEFORE ME.
NEH HEH!
I'M NOTHING LIKE YOU GUYS.
I'M GONNA MAKE THIS PLACE...
A KINGDOM EVEN MORE FITTING FOR ME, THE GREAT DEIN PHINEAS.
KEH HEH!
NEH HEH HEH!
I WON'T LET ANYONE GET IN MY WAY.

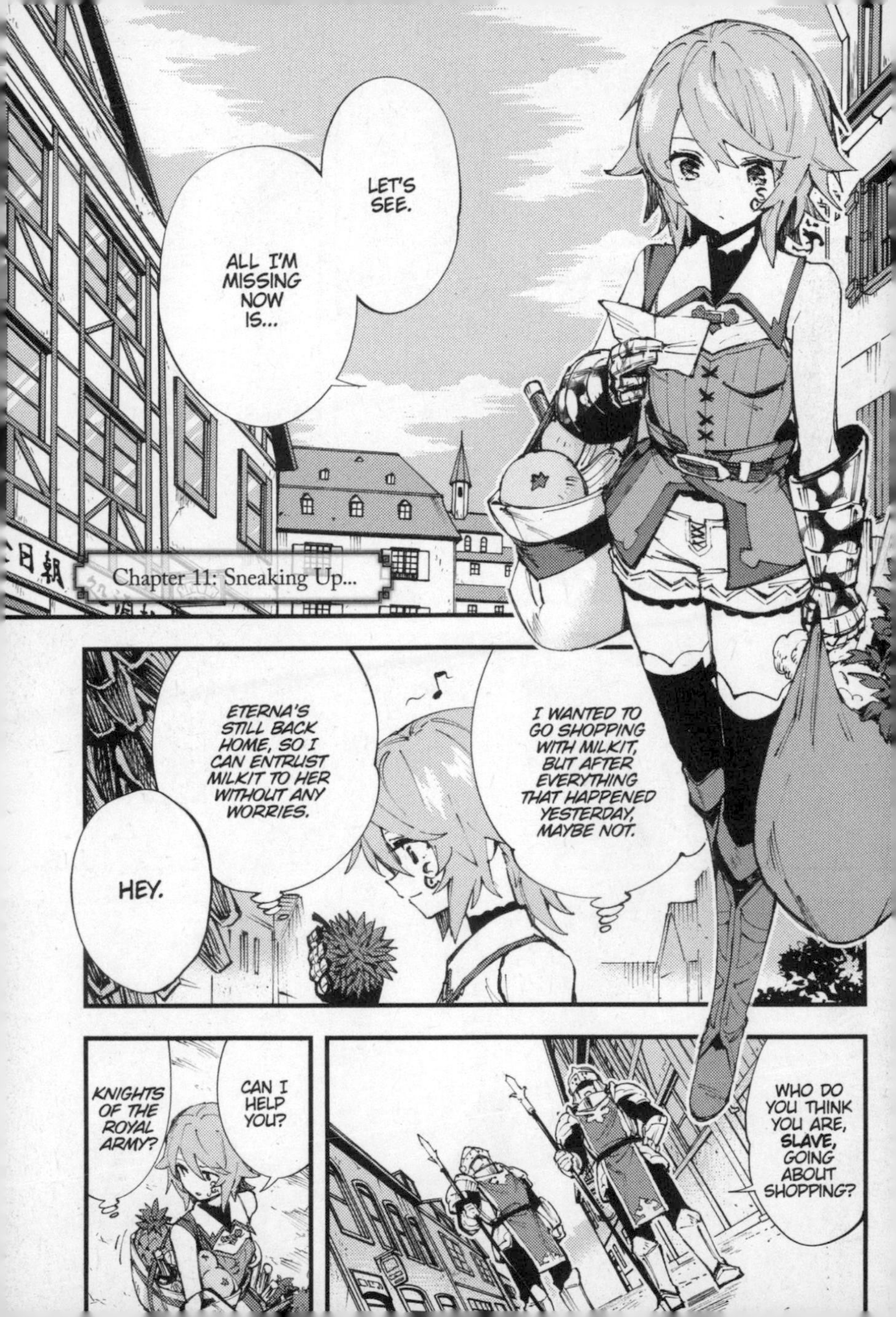
LET'S SEE.
ALL I'M MISSING NOW IS...
Chapter 11: Sneaking Up...
I WANTED TO GO SHOPPING WITH MILKIT, BUT AFTER EVERYTHING THAT HAPPENED YESTERDAY, MAYBE NOT.
ETERNA'S STILL BACK HOME, SO I CAN ENTRUST MILKIT TO HER WITHOUT ANY WORRIES.
HEY.
WHO DO YOU THINK YOU ARE, SLAVE, GOING ABOUT SHOPPING?
CAN I HELP YOU?
KNIGHTS OF THE ROYAL ARMY?

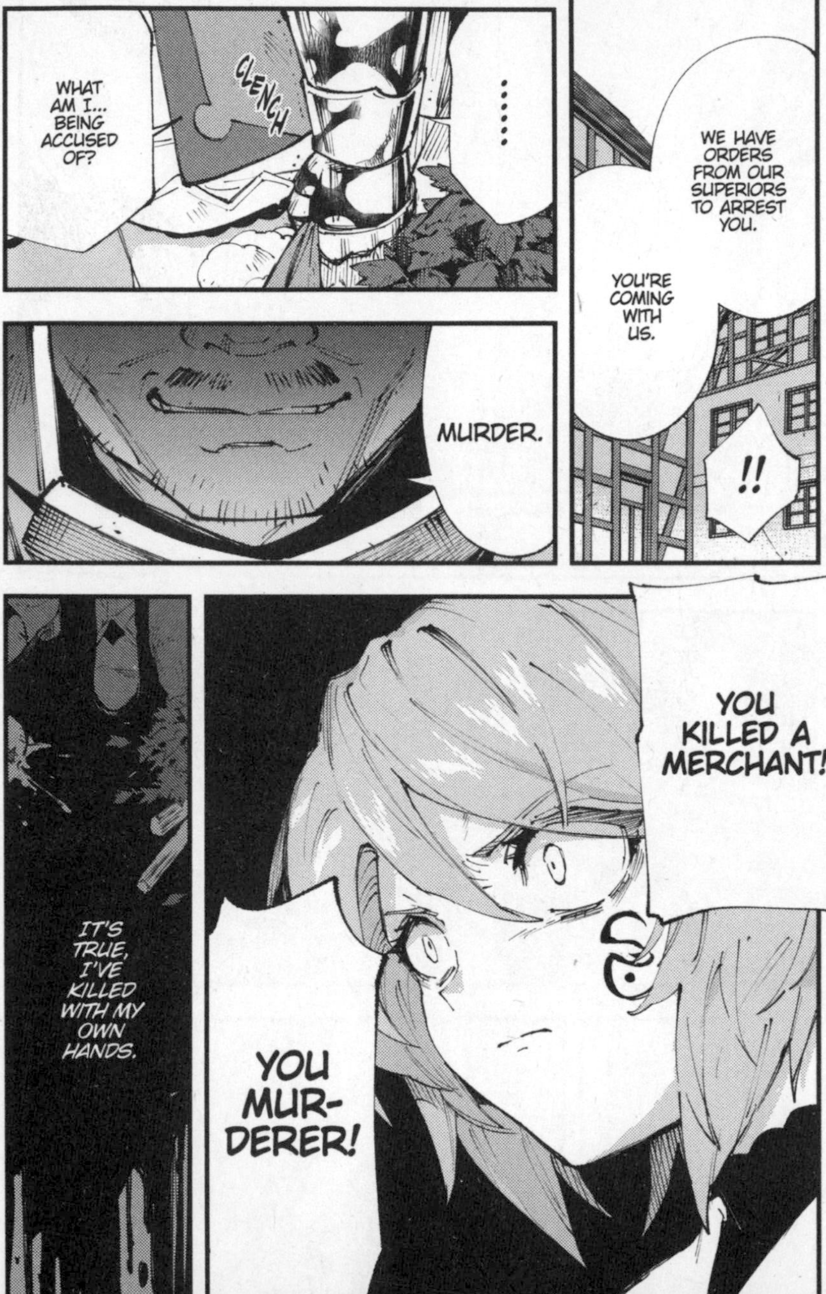
WE HAVE ORDERS FROM OUR SUPERIORS TO ARREST YOU.
YOU'RE COMING WITH US.
!!
......
CLENCH
WHAT AM I... BEING ACCUSED OF?
MURDER.
YOU KILLED A MERCHANT!
YOU MUR-DERER!
IT'S TRUE, I'VE KILLED WITH MY OWN HANDS.

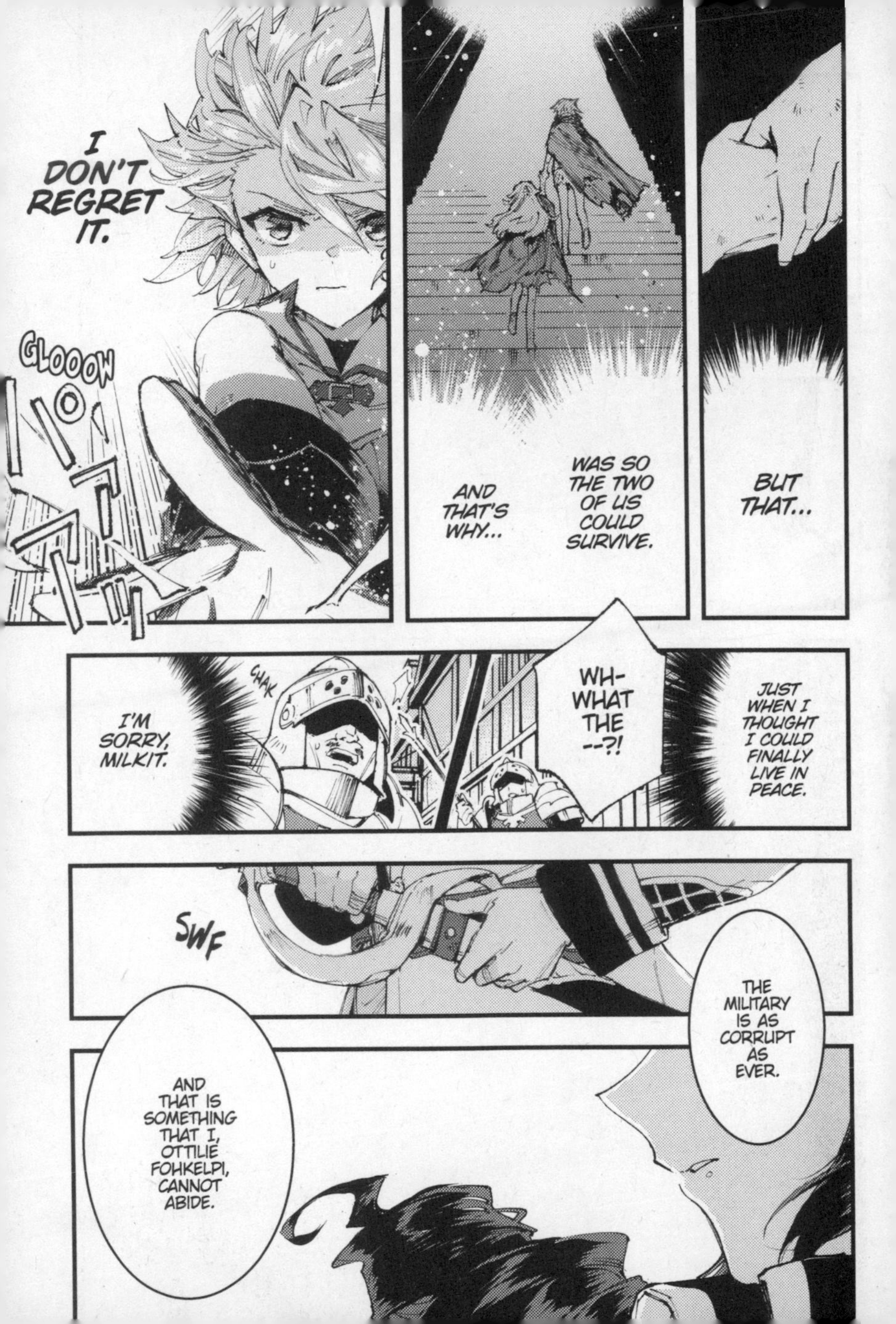
BUT THAT...
WAS SO THE TWO OF US COULD SURVIVE.
AND THAT'S WHY...
I DON'T REGRET IT.
GLOOOW
JUST WHEN I THOUGHT I COULD FINALLY LIVE IN PEACE.
WH-WHAT THE--?!
CHAK
I'M SORRY, MILKIT.
SWF
THE MILITARY IS AS CORRUPT AS EVER.
AND THAT IS SOMETHING THAT I, OTTILIE FOHKELPI, CANNOT ABIDE.

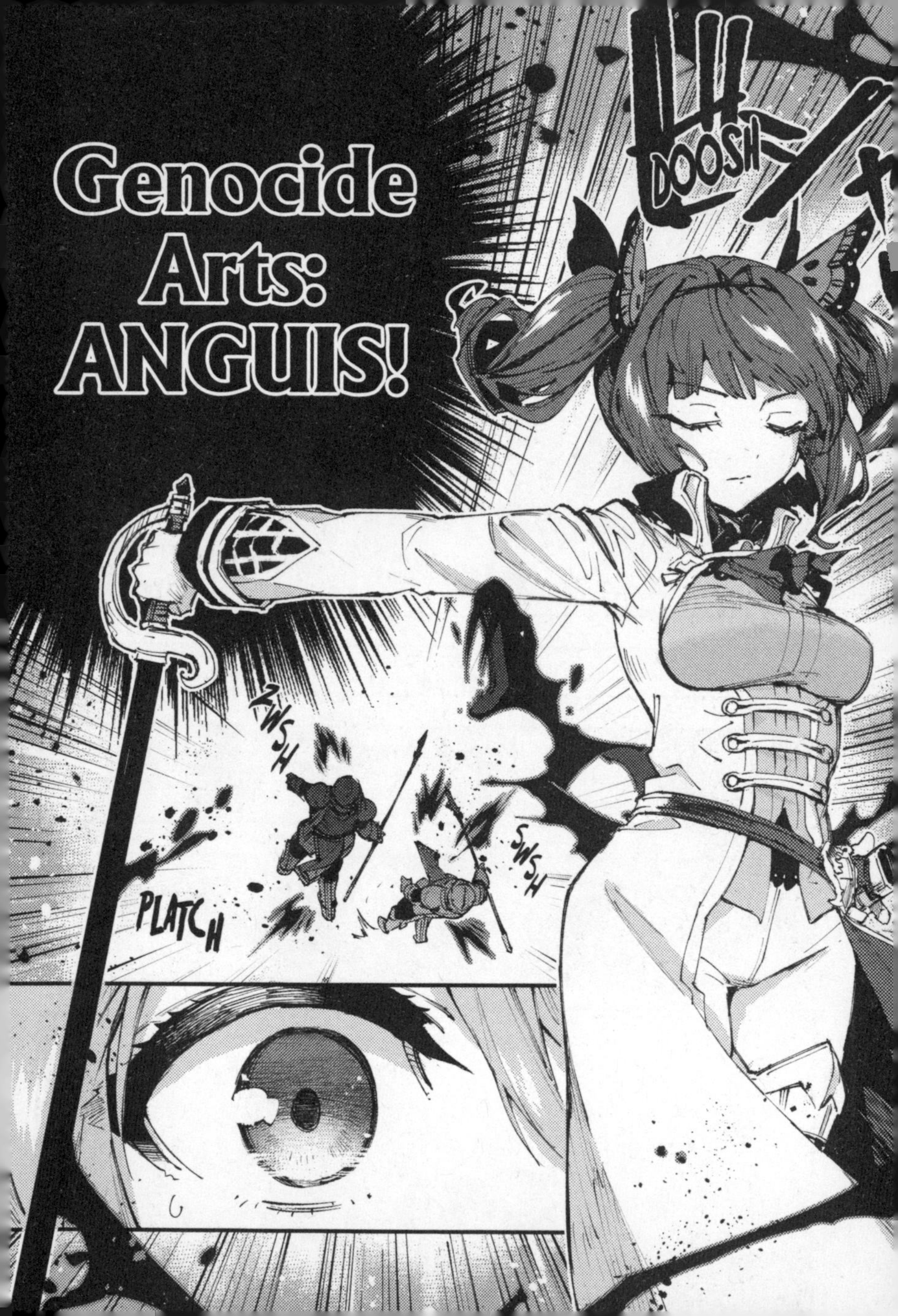
DOOSH
Genocide Arts: ANGUIS!
ZWSH
SWSH
PLATCH

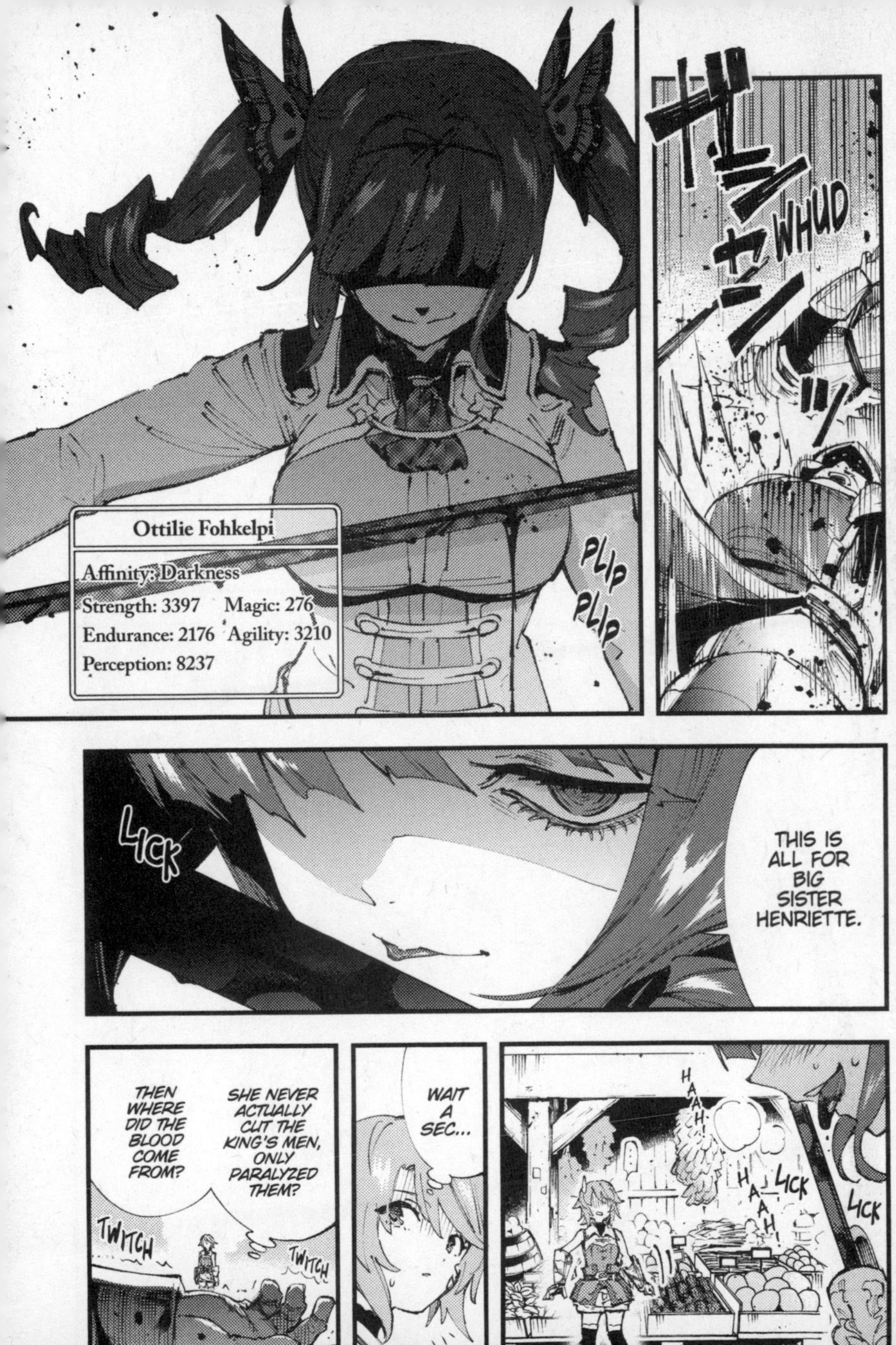
WHUD
Ottilie Fohkelpi
Affinity: Darkness
Strength: 3397 Magic: 276
Endurance: 2176 Agility: 3210
Perception: 8237
PLIP PLIP PLIP
THIS IS ALL FOR BIG SISTER HENRIETTE.
LICK
HAAH! HAAH!
LICK
LICK
WAIT A SEC...
SHE NEVER ACTUALLY CUT THE KING'S MEN, ONLY PARALYZED THEM?
THEN WHERE DID THE BLOOD COME FROM?
TWITCH
TWITCH

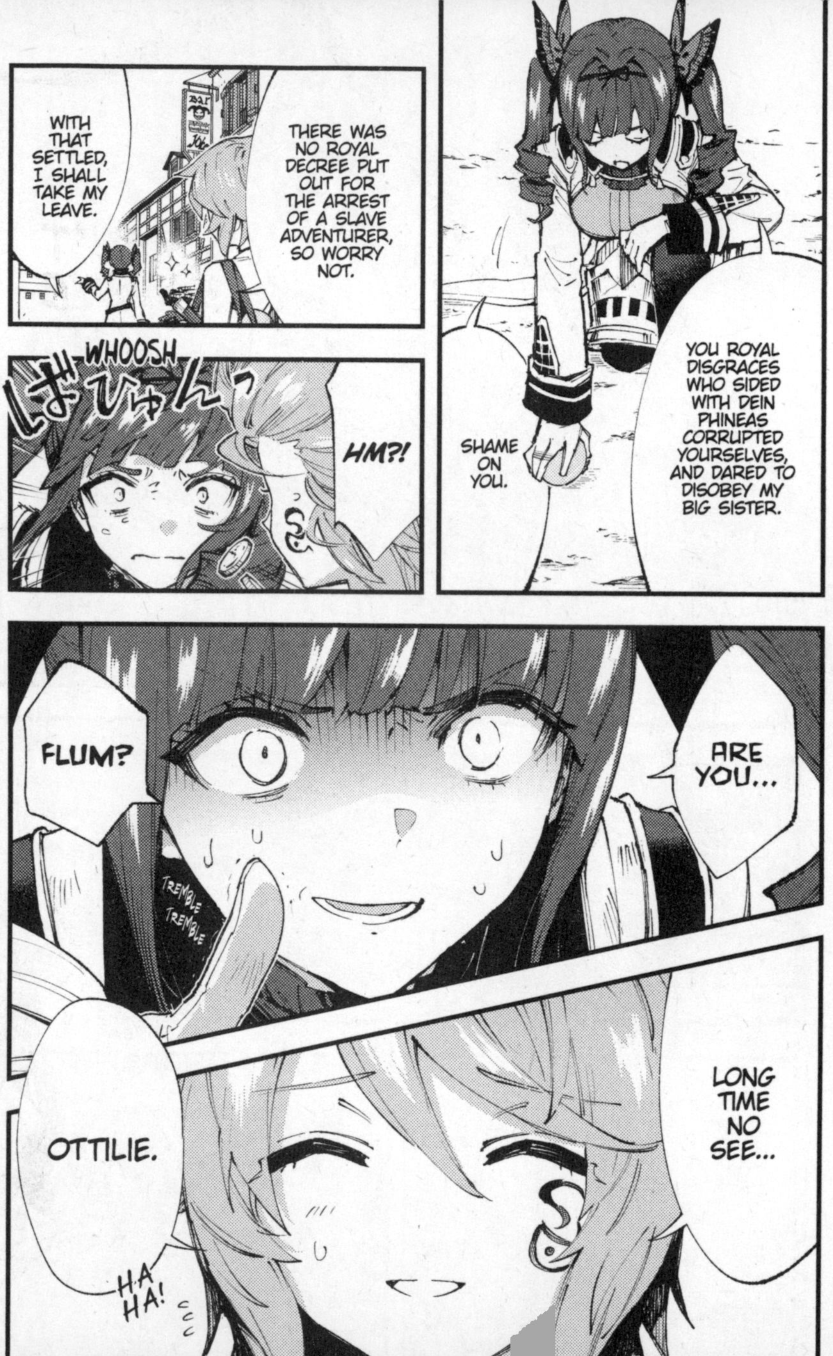
YOU ROYAL DISGRACES WHO SIDED WITH DEIN PHINEAS CORRUPTED YOURSELVES, AND DARED TO DISOBEY MY BIG SISTER.
SHAME ON YOU.
THERE WAS NO ROYAL DECREE PUT OUT FOR THE ARREST OF A SLAVE ADVENTURER, SO WORRY NOT.
WITH THAT SETTLED, I SHALL TAKE MY LEAVE.
WHOOSH
HM?!
ARE YOU...
FLUM?
TREMBLE TREMBLE
LONG TIME NO SEE...
OTTILIE.
HA HA!

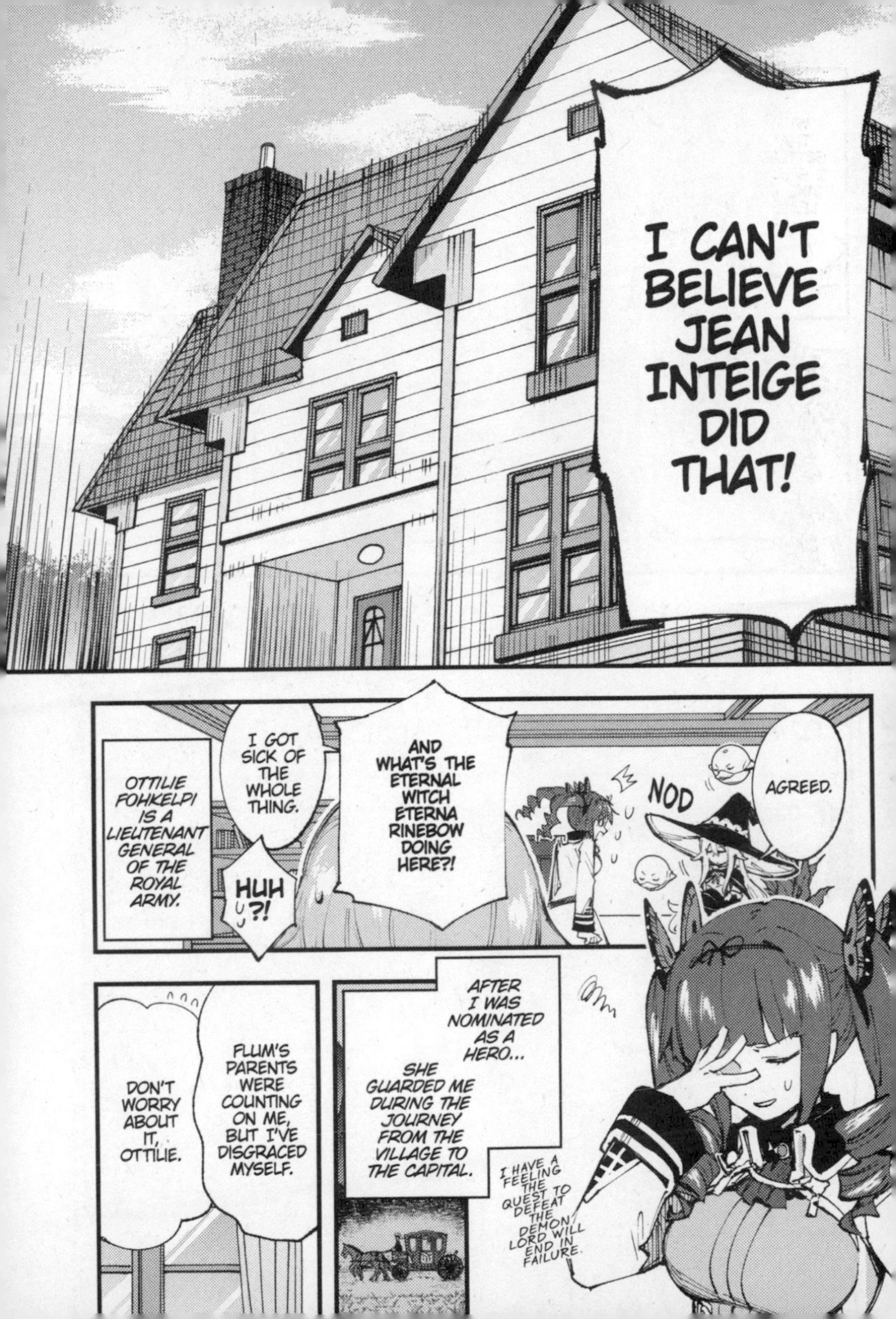
I CAN'T BELIEVE JEAN INTEIGE DID THAT!
AGREED.
NOD
AND WHAT'S THE ETERNAL WITCH ETERNA RINEBOW DOING HERE?!
I GOT SICK OF THE WHOLE THING.
HUH?!
OTTILIE FOHKELPI IS A LIEUTENANT GENERAL OF THE ROYAL ARMY.
I HAVE A FEELING THE QUEST TO DEFEAT THE DEMON LORD WILL END IN FAILURE.
AFTER I WAS NOMINATED AS A HERO...
SHE GUARDED ME DURING THE JOURNEY FROM THE VILLAGE TO THE CAPITAL.
FLUM'S PARENTS WERE COUNTING ON ME, BUT I'VE DISGRACED MYSELF.
DON'T WORRY ABOUT IT, OTTILIE.

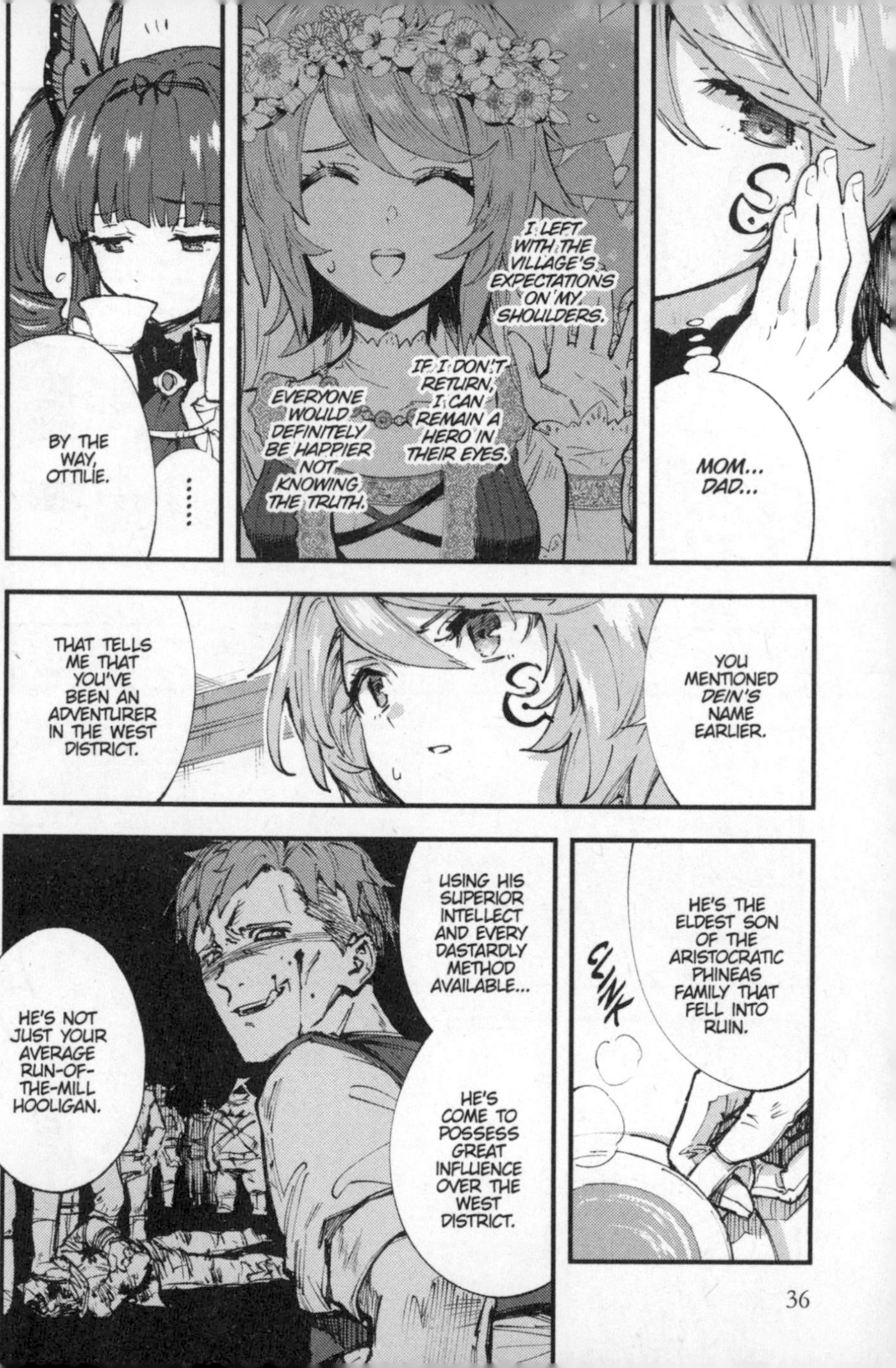
MOM... DAD...
I LEFT WITH THE VILLAGE'S EXPECTATIONS ON MY SHOULDERS.
IF I DON'T RETURN, I CAN REMAIN A HERO IN THEIR EYES.
EVERYONE WOULD DEFINITELY BE HAPPIER NOT KNOWING THE TRUTH.
......
BY THE WAY, OTTILIE.
YOU MENTIONED DEIN'S NAME EARLIER.
THAT TELLS ME THAT YOU'VE BEEN AN ADVENTURER IN THE WEST DISTRICT.
HE'S THE ELDEST SON OF THE ARISTOCRATIC PHINEAS FAMILY THAT FELL INTO RUIN.
CLINK
USING HIS SUPERIOR INTELLECT AND EVERY DASTARDLY METHOD AVAILABLE...
HE'S COME TO POSSESS GREAT INFLUENCE OVER THE WEST DISTRICT.
HE'S NOT JUST YOUR AVERAGE RUN-OF-THE-MILL HOOLIGAN.

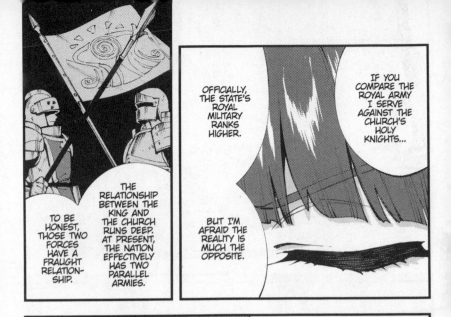

IF YOU COMPARE THE ROYAL ARMY I SERVE AGAINST THE CHURCH'S HOLY KNIGHTS...

OFFICIALLY, THE STATE'S ROYAL MILITARY RANKS HIGHER.

BUT I'M AFRAID THE REALITY IS MUCH THE OPPOSITE.

THE RELATIONSHIP BETWEEN THE KING AND THE CHURCH RUNS DEEP. AT PRESENT, THE NATION EFFECTIVELY HAS TWO PARALLEL ARMIES.

TO BE HONEST, THOSE TWO FORCES HAVE A FRAUGHT RELATIONSHIP.

WHEN YOU ADD THE SHAKY LOYALTIES OF THE RANK-AND-FILE, AND THE CORRUPTION AND WEAKNESS FOSTERED BY DEIN...

MY BIG SISTER DECIDED WE HAD TO STRIKE HARD AND FAST.

YOUR SISTER?

THE GENERAL OF THE ROYAL ARMY.

SQUEEE!

PANT! PANT!

CLATTER

MY BIG SISTER HENRIETTE!

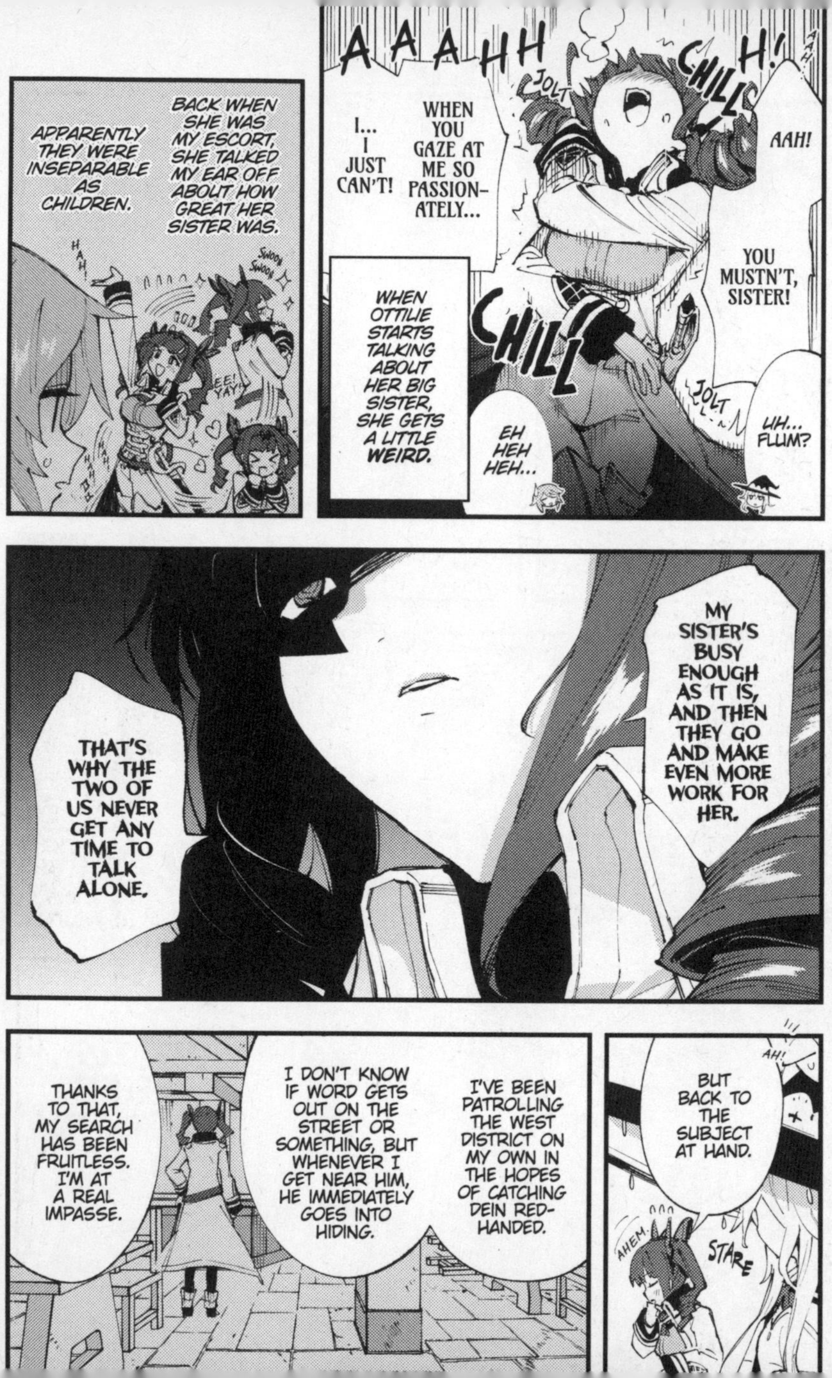
AAAAHH H!
CHILLS
AAH!
WHEN YOU GAZE AT ME SO PASSIONATELY...
I... I JUST CAN'T!
YOU MUSTN'T, SISTER!
CHILL
WHEN OTTILIE STARTS TALKING ABOUT HER BIG SISTER, SHE GETS A LITTLE WEIRD.
UH... FLUM?
JOLT
EH HEH HEH...
BACK WHEN SHE WAS MY ESCORT, SHE TALKED MY EAR OFF ABOUT HOW GREAT HER SISTER WAS.
APPARENTLY THEY WERE INSEPARABLE AS CHILDREN.
SWOON SWOON
EE! YAY!
HAH!
MY SISTER'S BUSY ENOUGH AS IT IS, AND THEN THEY GO AND MAKE EVEN MORE WORK FOR HER.
THAT'S WHY THE TWO OF US NEVER GET ANY TIME TO TALK ALONE.
AH!
BUT BACK TO THE SUBJECT AT HAND.
STARE
AHEM.
I'VE BEEN PATROLLING THE WEST DISTRICT ON MY OWN IN THE HOPES OF CATCHING DEIN RED-HANDED.
I DON'T KNOW IF WORD GETS OUT ON THE STREET OR SOMETHING, BUT WHENEVER I GET NEAR HIM, HE IMMEDIATELY GOES INTO HIDING.
THANKS TO THAT, MY SEARCH HAS BEEN FRUITLESS. I'M AT A REAL IMPASSE.

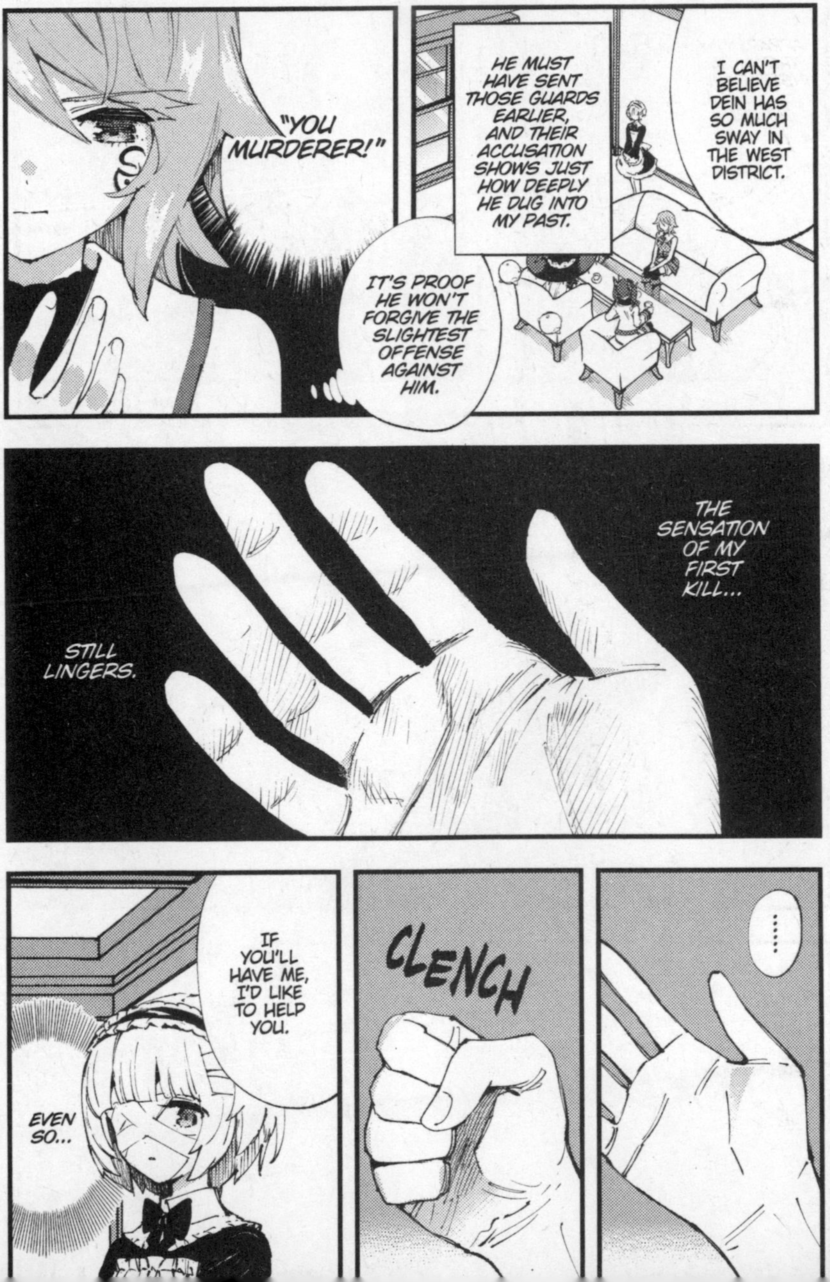
I CAN'T BELIEVE DEIN HAS SO MUCH SWAY IN THE WEST DISTRICT.
HE MUST HAVE SENT THOSE GUARDS EARLIER, AND THEIR ACCUSATION SHOWS JUST HOW DEEPLY HE DUG INTO MY PAST.
IT'S PROOF HE WON'T FORGIVE THE SLIGHTEST OFFENSE AGAINST HIM.
"YOU MURDERER!"
THE SENSATION OF MY FIRST KILL...
STILL LINGERS.
......
CLENCH
IF YOU'LL HAVE ME, I'D LIKE TO HELP YOU.
EVEN SO...

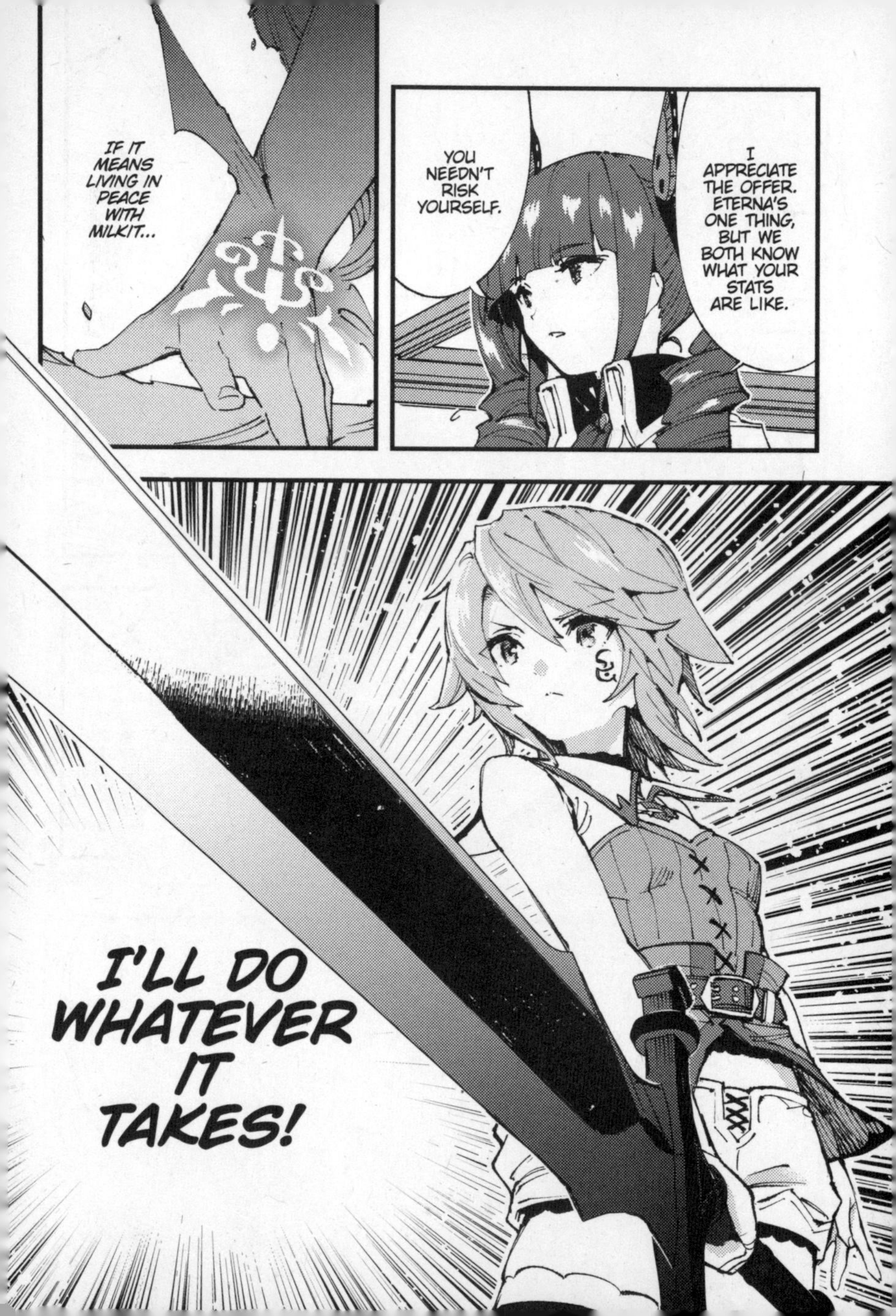
I APPRECIATE THE OFFER. ETERNA'S ONE THING, BUT WE BOTH KNOW WHAT YOUR STATS ARE LIKE.
YOU NEEDN'T RISK YOURSELF.
IF IT MEANS LIVING IN PEACE WITH MILKIT...
I'LL DO WHATEVER IT TAKES!

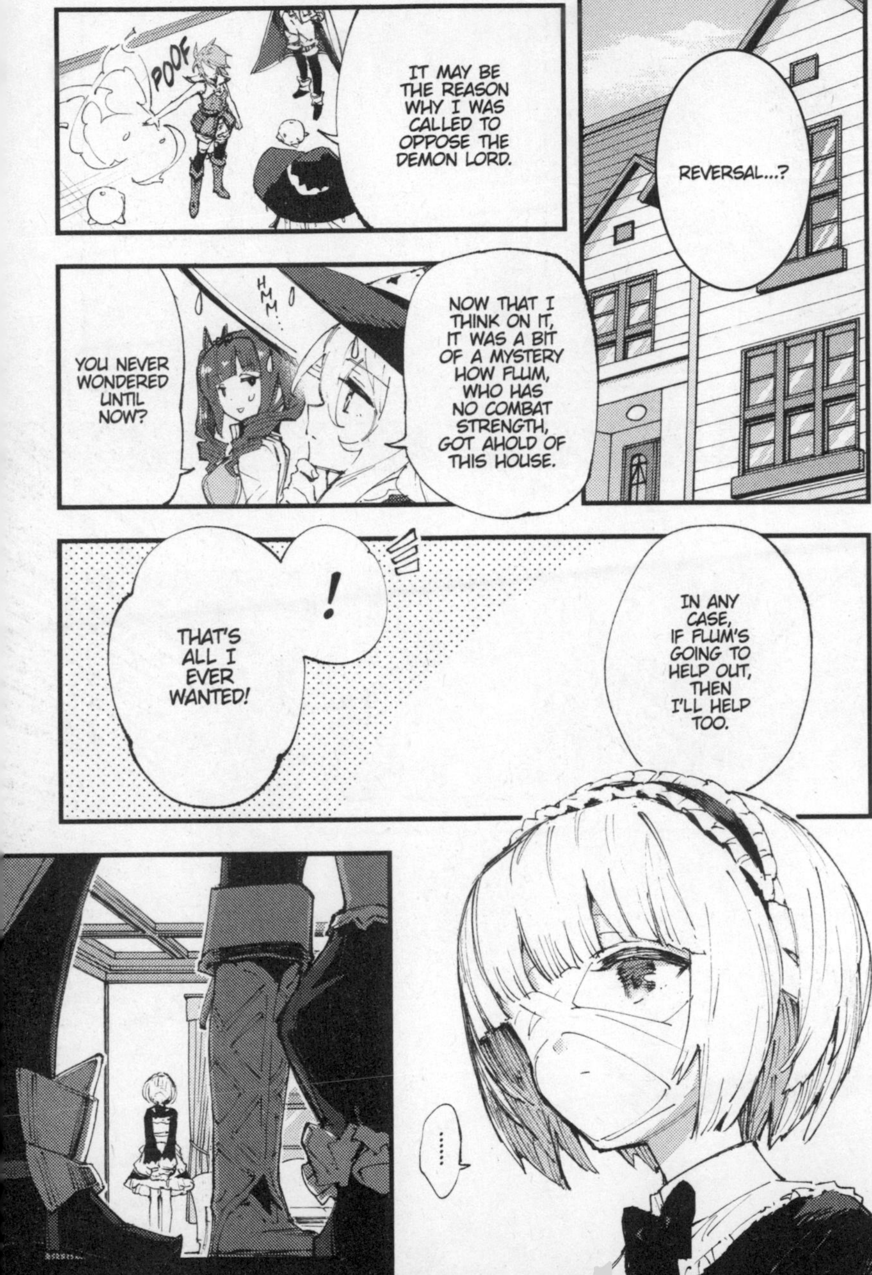
REVERSAL...?
POOF
IT MAY BE THE REASON WHY I WAS CALLED TO OPPOSE THE DEMON LORD.
NOW THAT I THINK ON IT, IT WAS A BIT OF A MYSTERY HOW FLUM, WHO HAS NO COMBAT STRENGTH, GOT AHOLD OF THIS HOUSE.
HMM...
YOU NEVER WONDERED UNTIL NOW?
IN ANY CASE, IF FLUM'S GOING TO HELP OUT, THEN I'LL HELP TOO.
!
THAT'S ALL I EVER WANTED!
......

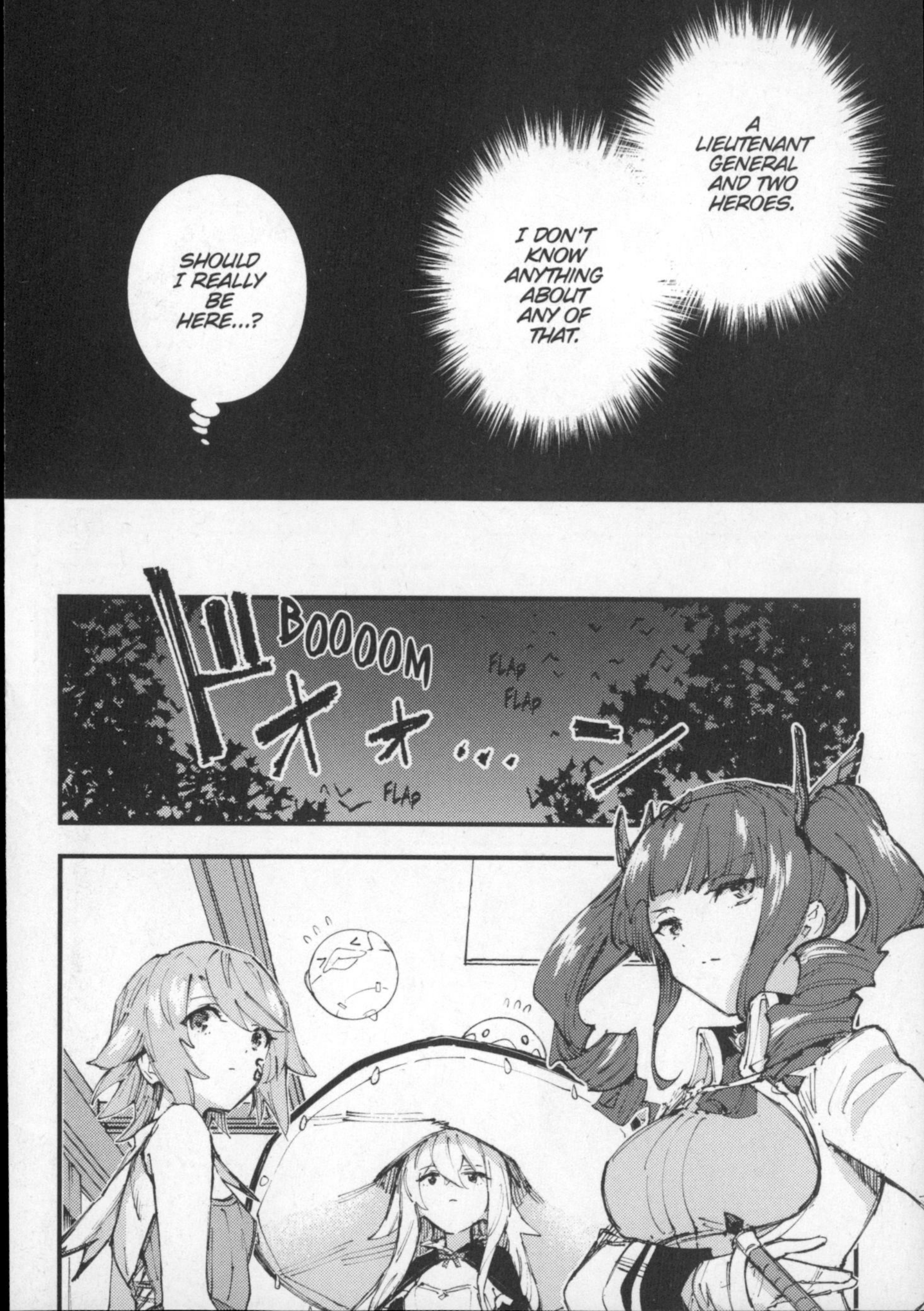
A LIEUTENANT GENERAL AND TWO HEROES.
I DON'T KNOW ANYTHING ABOUT ANY OF THAT.
SHOULD I REALLY BE HERE...?
BOOOOM
FLAP
FLAP
FLAP

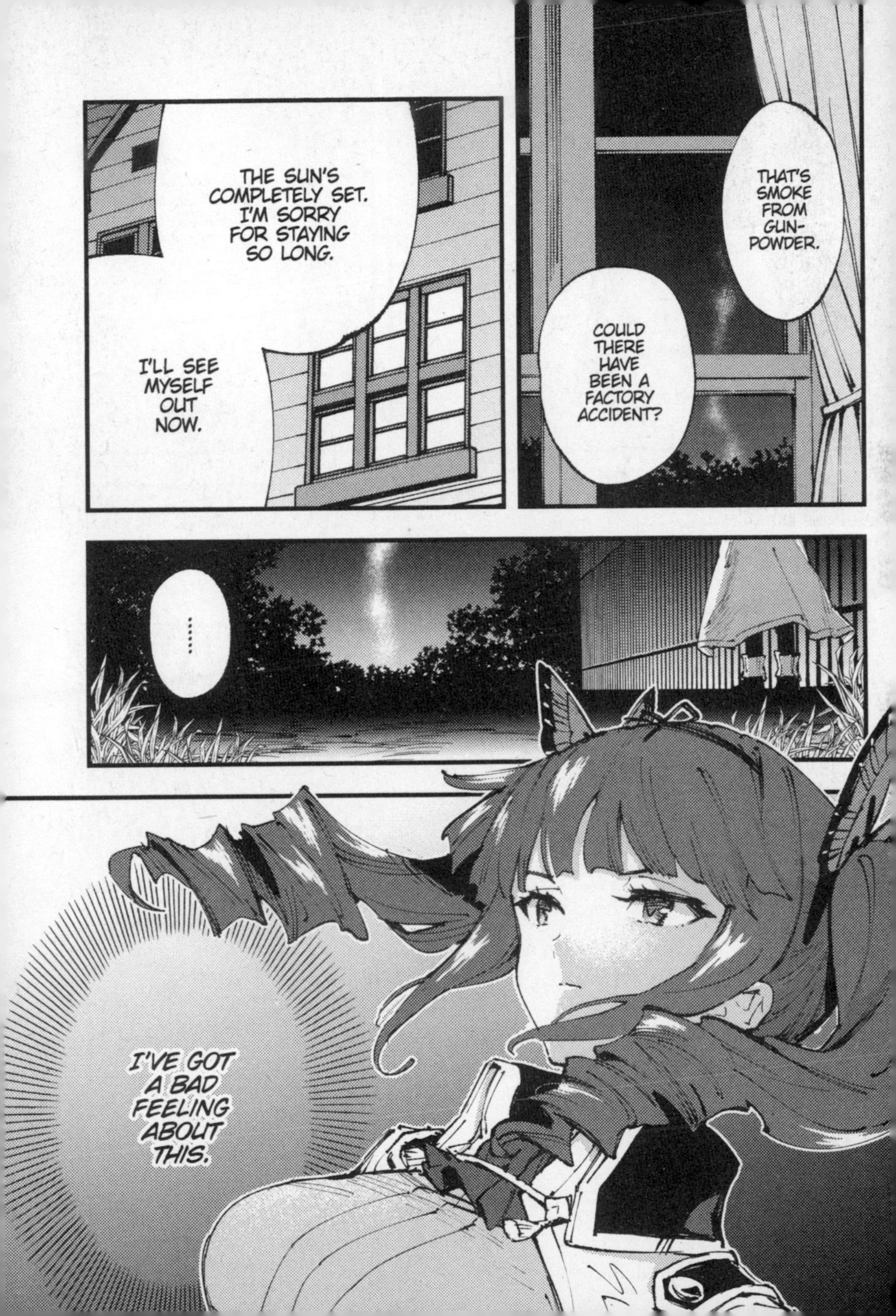
THAT'S SMOKE FROM GUN-POWDER.
COULD THERE HAVE BEEN A FACTORY ACCIDENT?
THE SUN'S COMPLETELY SET. I'M SORRY FOR STAYING SO LONG.
I'LL SEE MYSELF OUT NOW.
……
I'VE GOT A BAD FEELING ABOUT THIS.

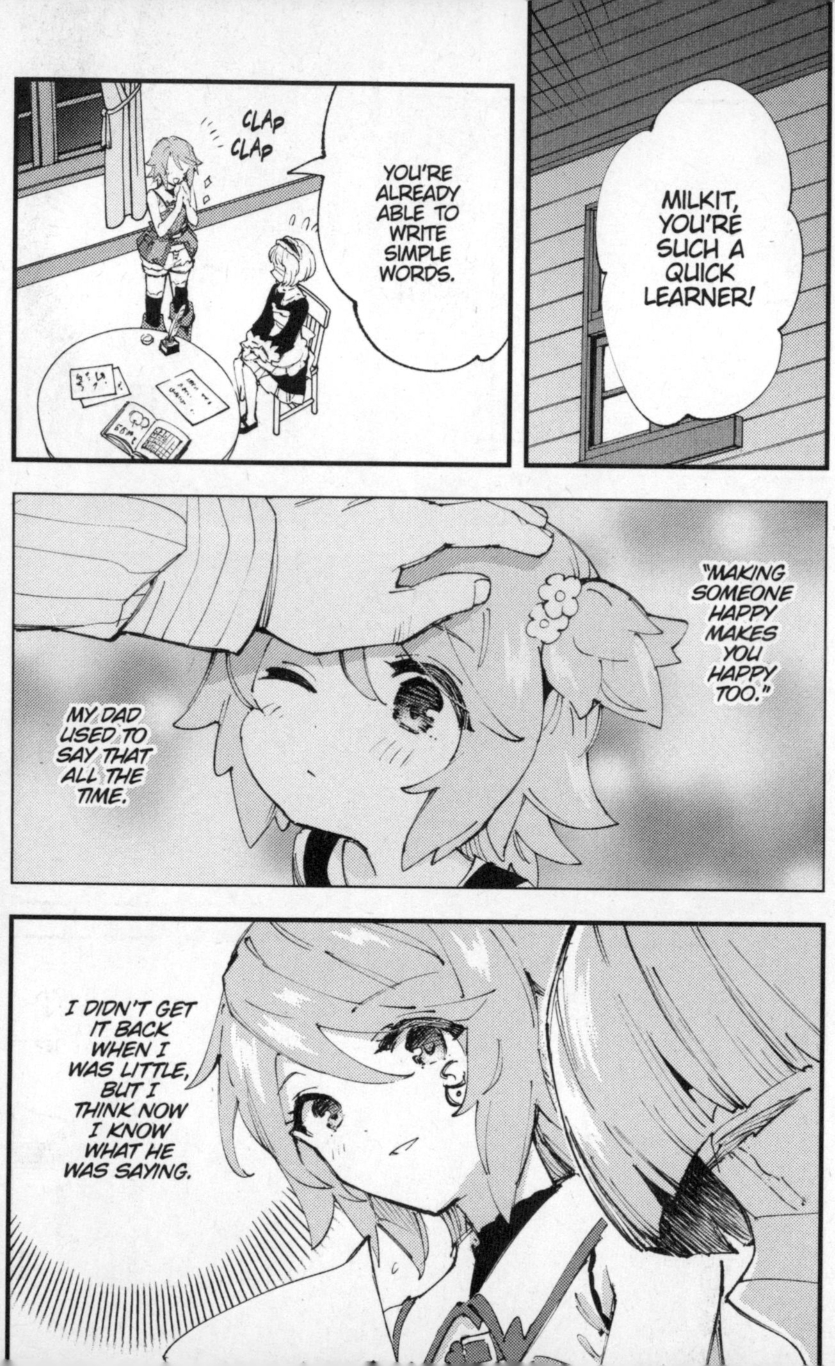
MILKIT, YOU'RE SUCH A QUICK LEARNER!
YOU'RE ALREADY ABLE TO WRITE SIMPLE WORDS.
CLAP CLAP
"MAKING SOMEONE HAPPY MAKES YOU HAPPY TOO."
MY DAD USED TO SAY THAT ALL THE TIME.
I DIDN'T GET IT BACK WHEN I WAS LITTLE, BUT I THINK NOW I KNOW WHAT HE WAS SAYING.

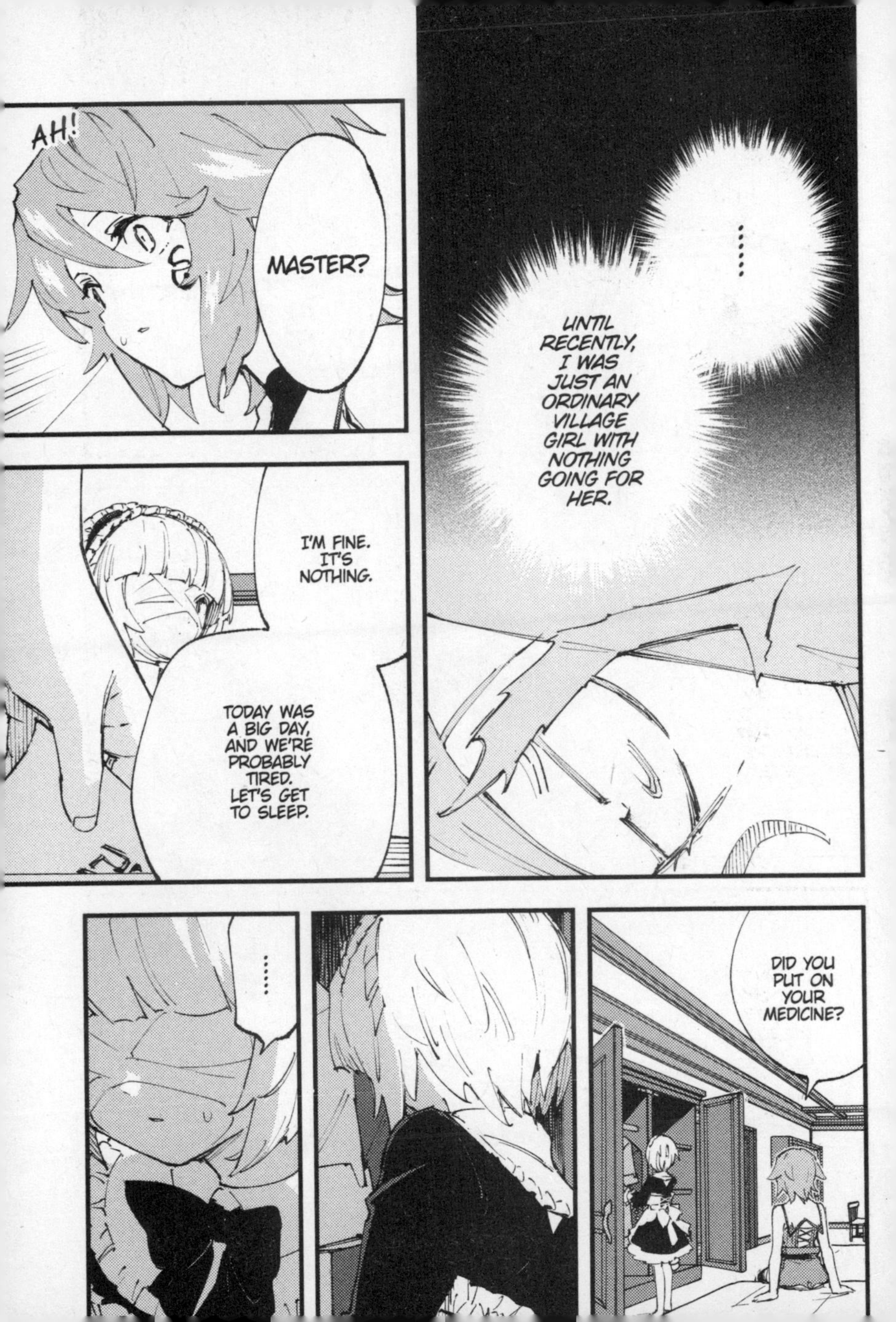
......
UNTIL RECENTLY, I WAS JUST AN ORDINARY VILLAGE GIRL WITH NOTHING GOING FOR HER.
AH!
MASTER?
I'M FINE. IT'S NOTHING.
TODAY WAS A BIG DAY, AND WE'RE PROBABLY TIRED. LET'S GET TO SLEEP.
DID YOU PUT ON YOUR MEDICINE?
......

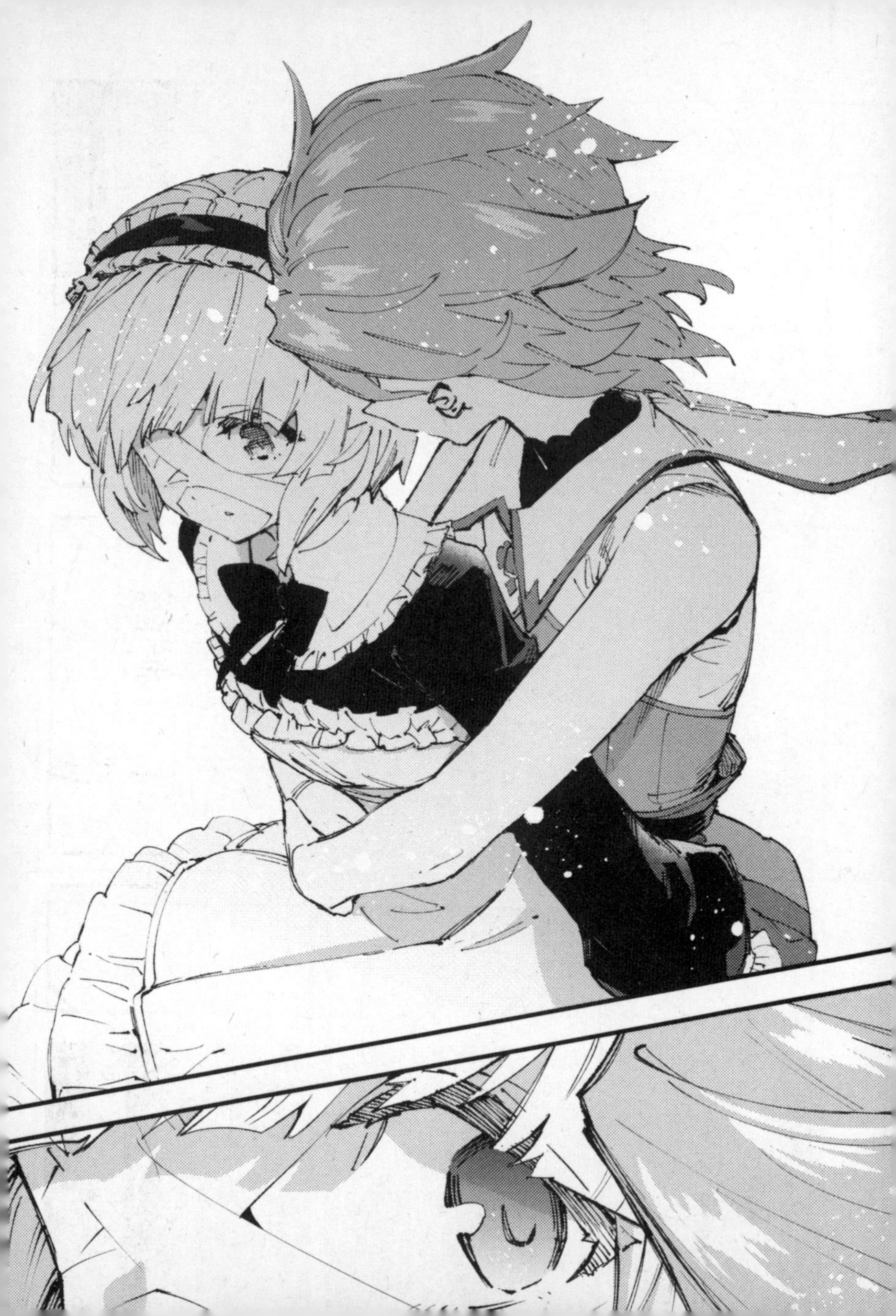

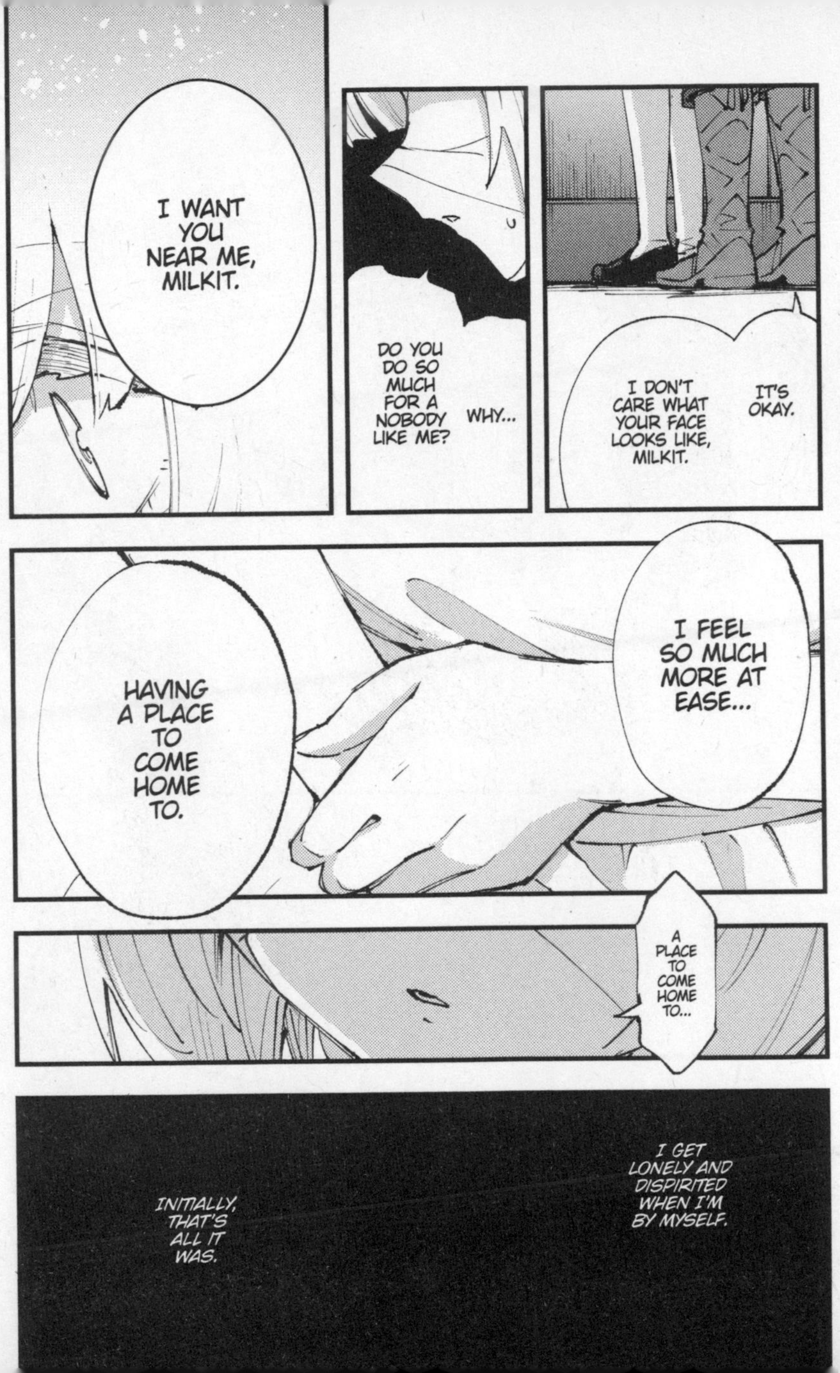
IT'S OKAY.
I DON'T CARE WHAT YOUR FACE LOOKS LIKE, MILKIT.
WHY...
DO YOU DO SO MUCH FOR A NOBODY LIKE ME?
I WANT YOU NEAR ME, MILKIT.
I FEEL SO MUCH MORE AT EASE...
HAVING A PLACE TO COME HOME TO.
A PLACE TO COME HOME TO...
I GET LONELY AND DISPIRITED WHEN I'M BY MYSELF.
INITIALLY, THAT'S ALL IT WAS.

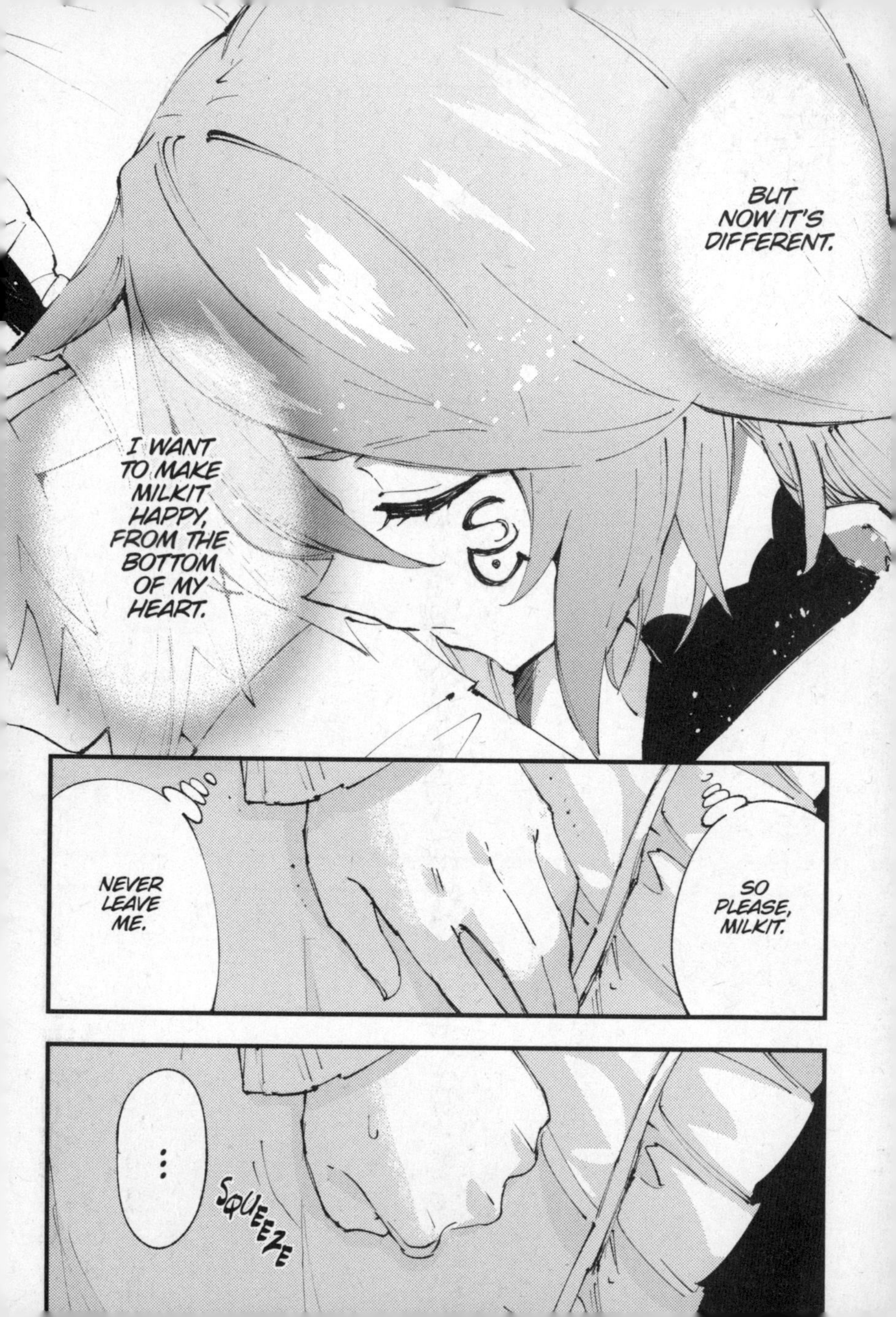
BUT NOW IT'S DIFFERENT.
I WANT TO MAKE MILKIT HAPPY, FROM THE BOTTOM OF MY HEART.
SO PLEASE, MILKIT.
NEVER LEAVE ME.
...
SQUEEZE

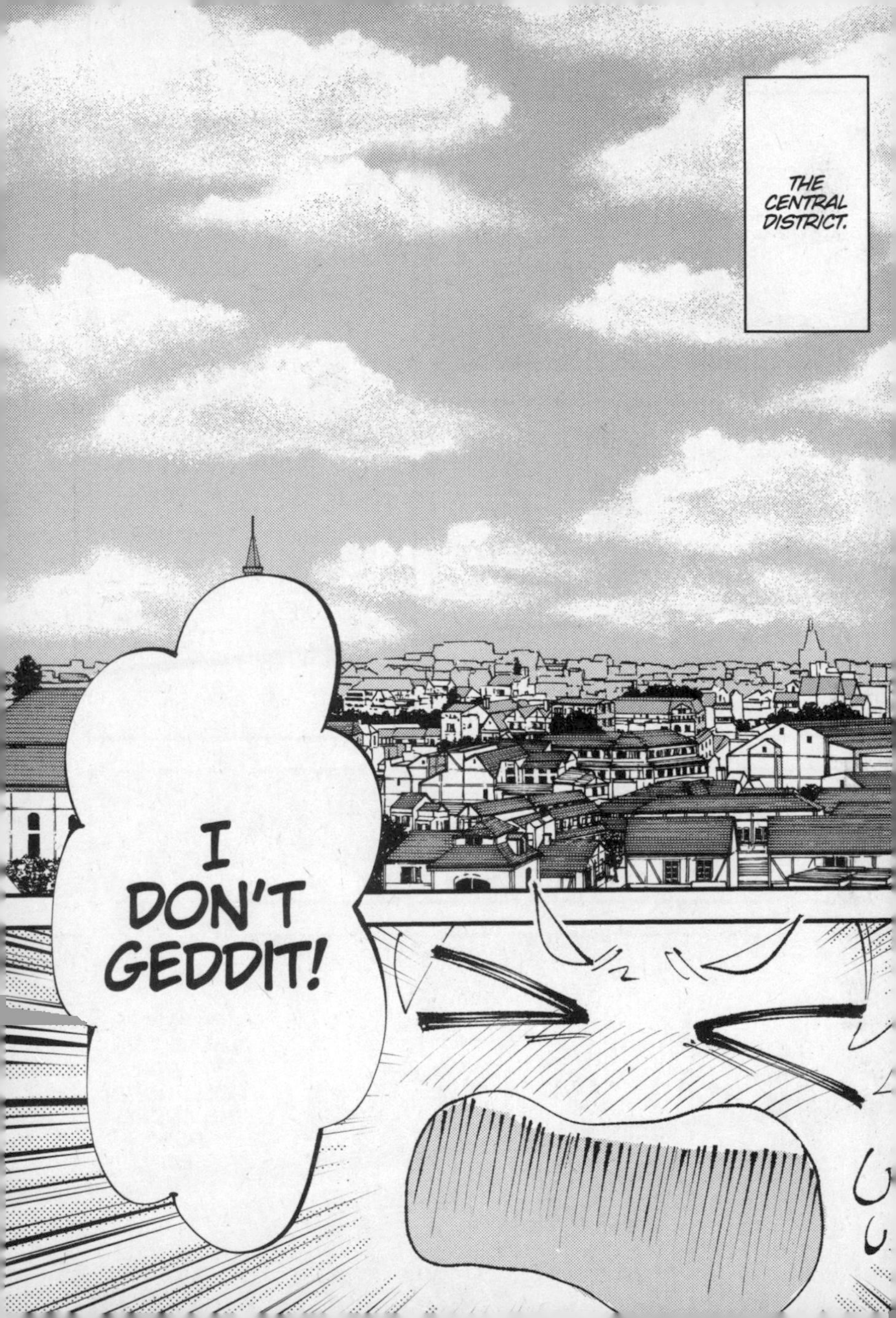
THE CENTRAL DISTRICT.
I DON'T GEDDIT!

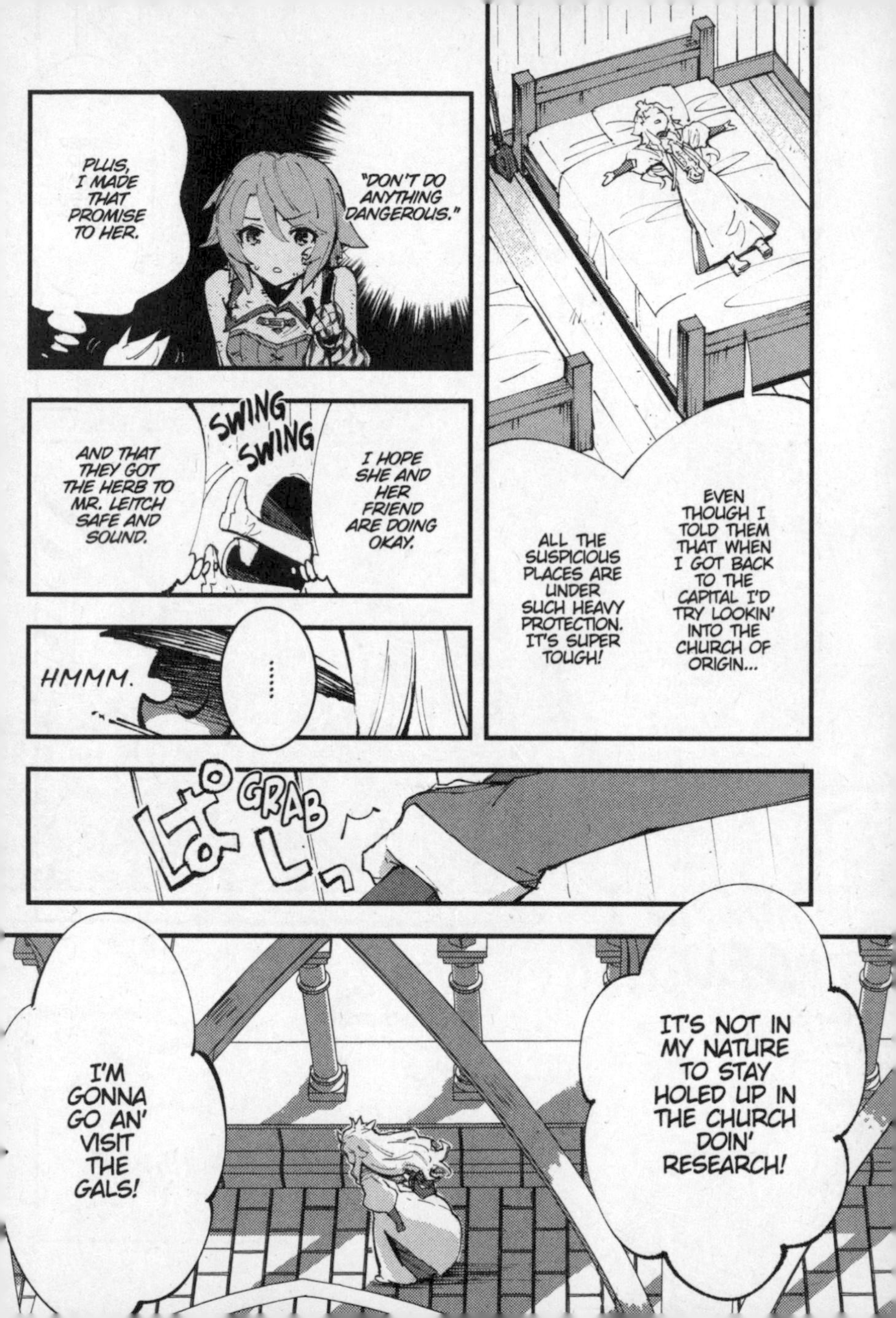
EVEN THOUGH I TOLD THEM THAT WHEN I GOT BACK TO THE CAPITAL I'D TRY LOOKIN' INTO THE CHURCH OF ORIGIN...
ALL THE SUSPICIOUS PLACES ARE UNDER SUCH HEAVY PROTECTION. IT'S SUPER TOUGH!
"DON'T DO ANYTHING DANGEROUS."
PLUS, I MADE THAT PROMISE TO HER.
SWING SWING
I HOPE SHE AND HER FRIEND ARE DOING OKAY.
AND THAT THEY GOT THE HERB TO MR. LEITCH SAFE AND SOUND.
......
HMMM.
GRAB
IT'S NOT IN MY NATURE TO STAY HOLED UP IN THE CHURCH DOIN' RESEARCH!
I'M GONNA GO AN' VISIT THE GALS!

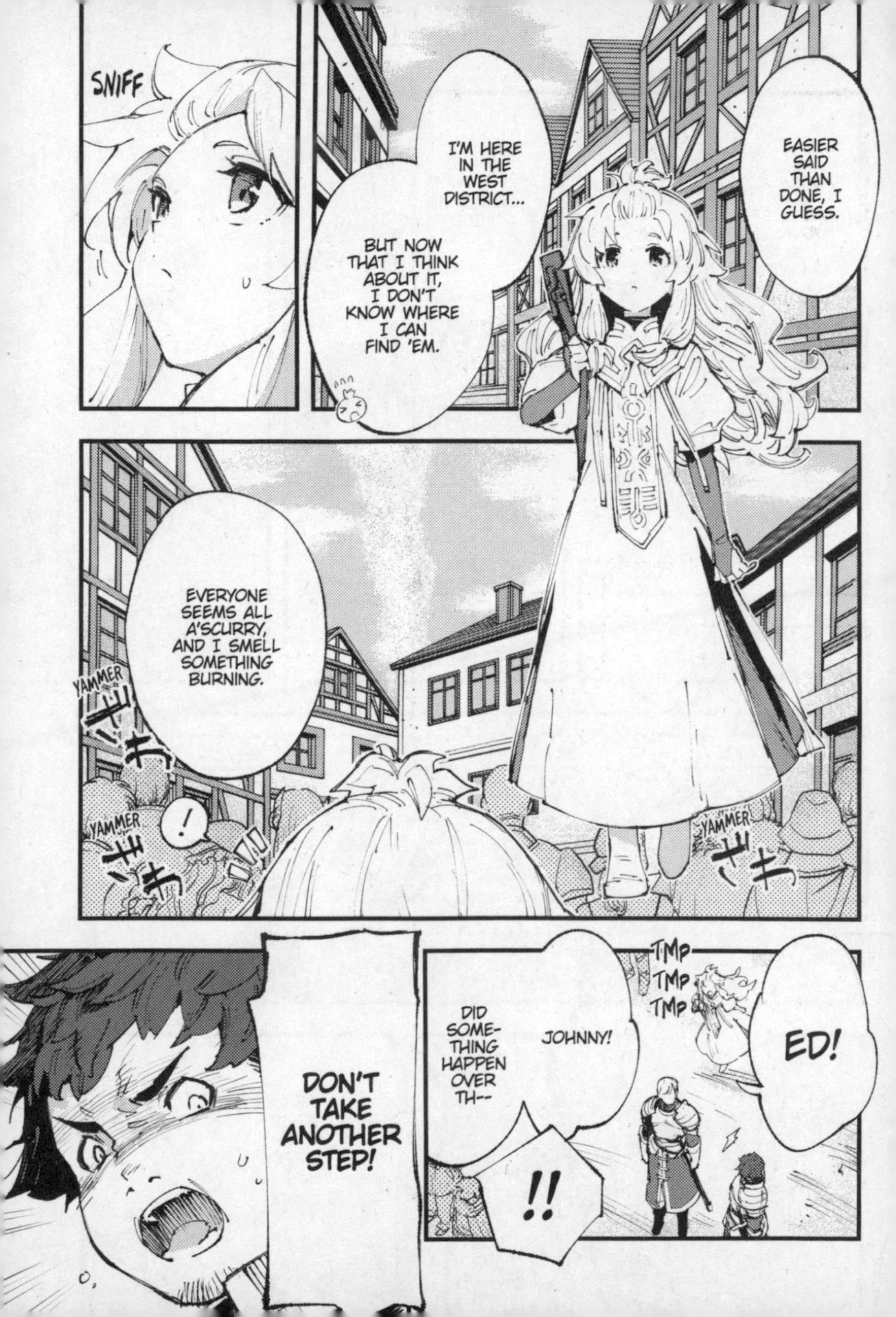
EASIER SAID THAN DONE, I GUESS.
I'M HERE IN THE WEST DISTRICT...
BUT NOW THAT I THINK ABOUT IT, I DON'T KNOW WHERE I CAN FIND 'EM.
SNIFF
EVERYONE SEEMS ALL A'SCURRY, AND I SMELL SOMETHING BURNING.
YAMMER
YAMMER
!
YAMMER
TMP TMP TMP
ED!
JOHNNY!
DID SOME-THING HAPPEN OVER TH--
!!
DON'T TAKE ANOTHER STEP!

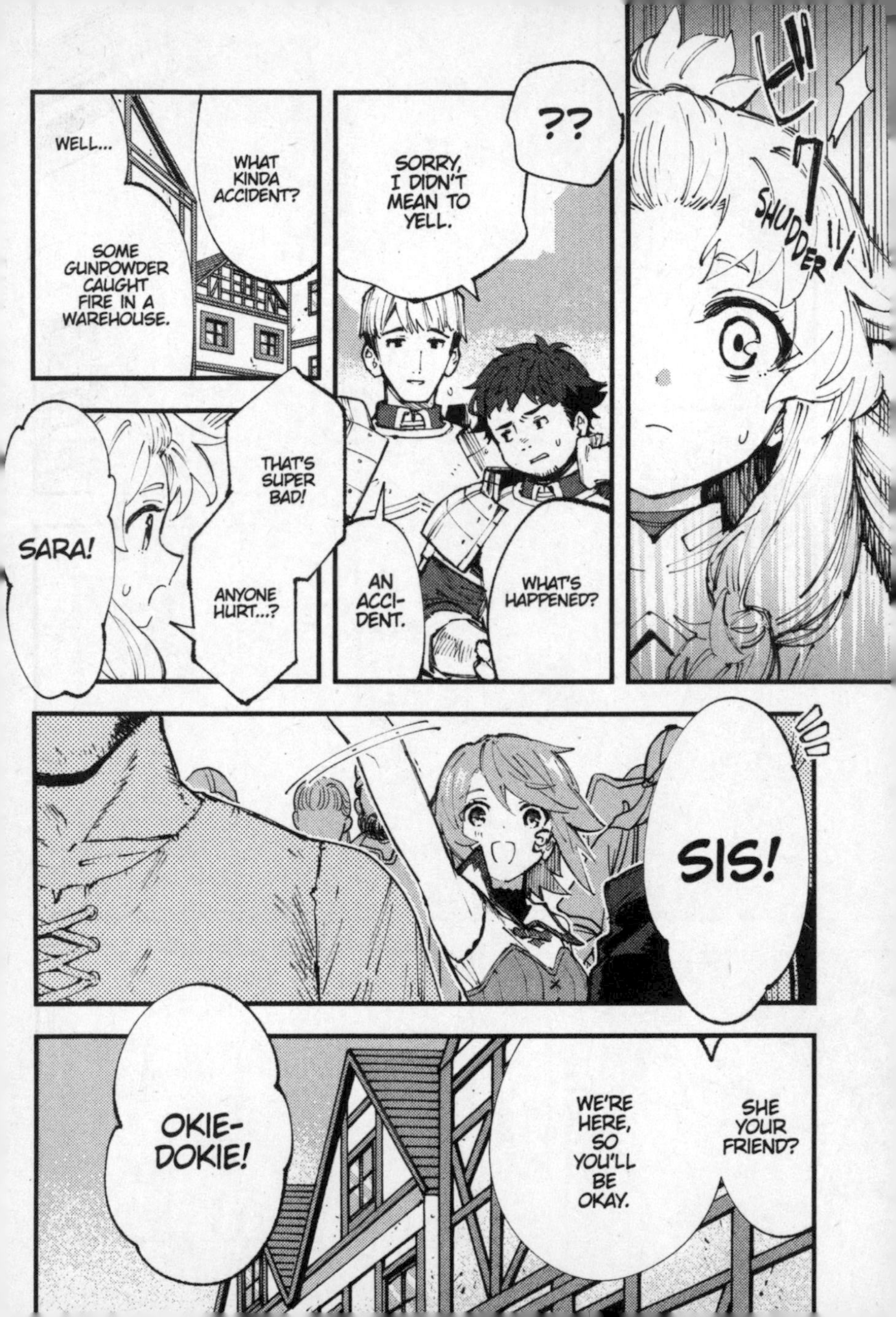
SHUDDER
??
SORRY, I DIDN'T MEAN TO YELL.
WHAT'S HAPPENED?
AN ACCI-DENT.
WHAT KINDA ACCIDENT?
WELL...
SOME GUNPOWDER CAUGHT FIRE IN A WAREHOUSE.
THAT'S SUPER BAD!
ANYONE HURT...?
SARA!
SIS!
SHE YOUR FRIEND?
WE'RE HERE, SO YOU'LL BE OKAY.
OKIE-DOKIE!

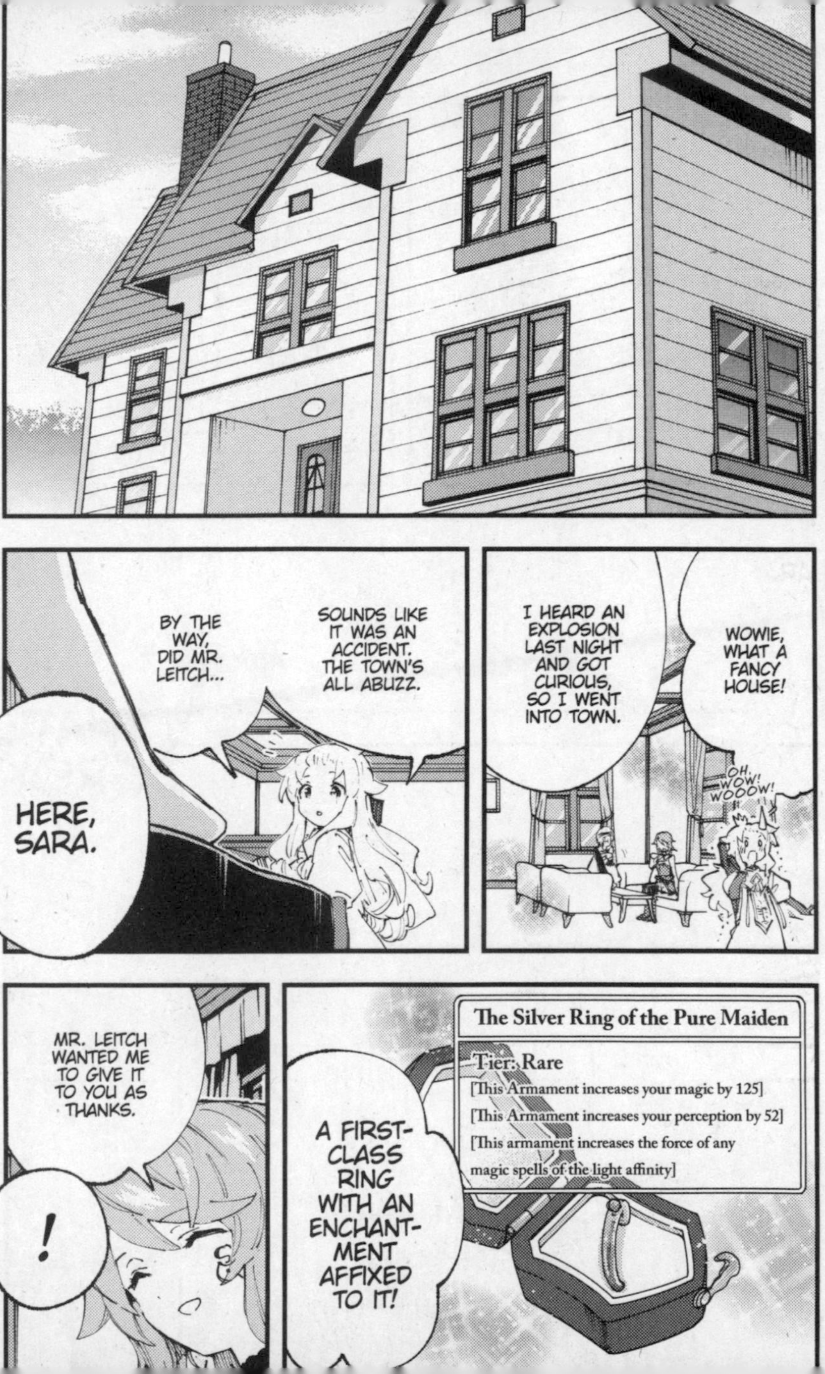
WOWIE, WHAT A FANCY HOUSE!
OH, WOW! WOOOW!
I HEARD AN EXPLOSION LAST NIGHT AND GOT CURIOUS, SO I WENT INTO TOWN.
SOUNDS LIKE IT WAS AN ACCIDENT. THE TOWN'S ALL ABUZZ.
BY THE WAY, DID MR. LEITCH...
HERE, SARA.
The Silver Ring of the Pure Maiden
Tier: Rare
[This Armament increases your magic by 125]
[This Armament increases your perception by 52]
[This armament increases the force of any magic spells of the light affinity]
A FIRST-CLASS RING WITH AN ENCHANTMENT AFFIXED TO IT!
MR. LEITCH WANTED ME TO GIVE IT TO YOU AS THANKS.
!

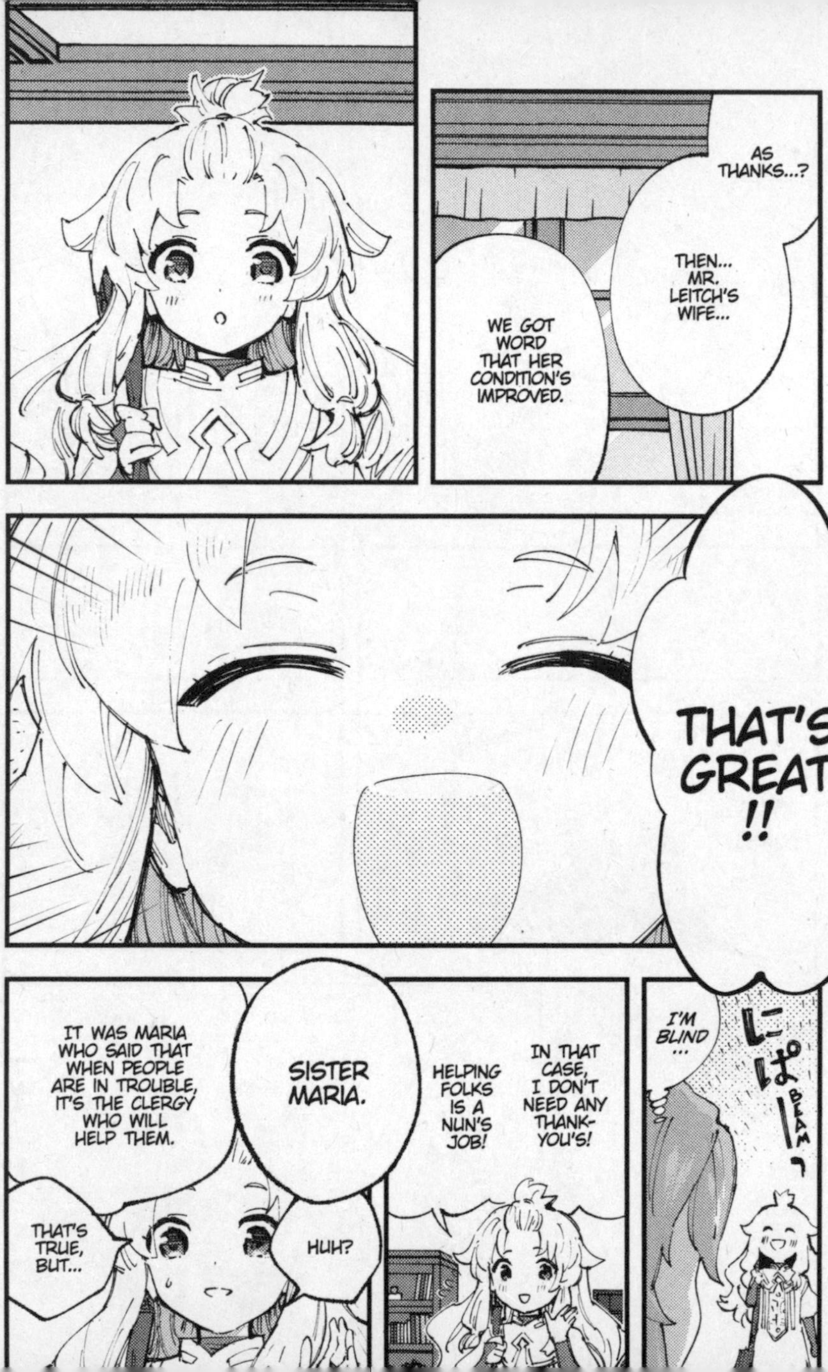
AS THANKS...?
THEN... MR. LEITCH'S WIFE...
WE GOT WORD THAT HER CONDITION'S IMPROVED.
THAT'S GREAT!!
I'M BLIND...
にぱー
BEAM
IN THAT CASE, I DON'T NEED ANY THANK-YOU'S!
HELPING FOLKS IS A NUN'S JOB!
SISTER MARIA.
IT WAS MARIA WHO SAID THAT WHEN PEOPLE ARE IN TROUBLE, IT'S THE CLERGY WHO WILL HELP THEM.
HUH?
THAT'S TRUE, BUT...

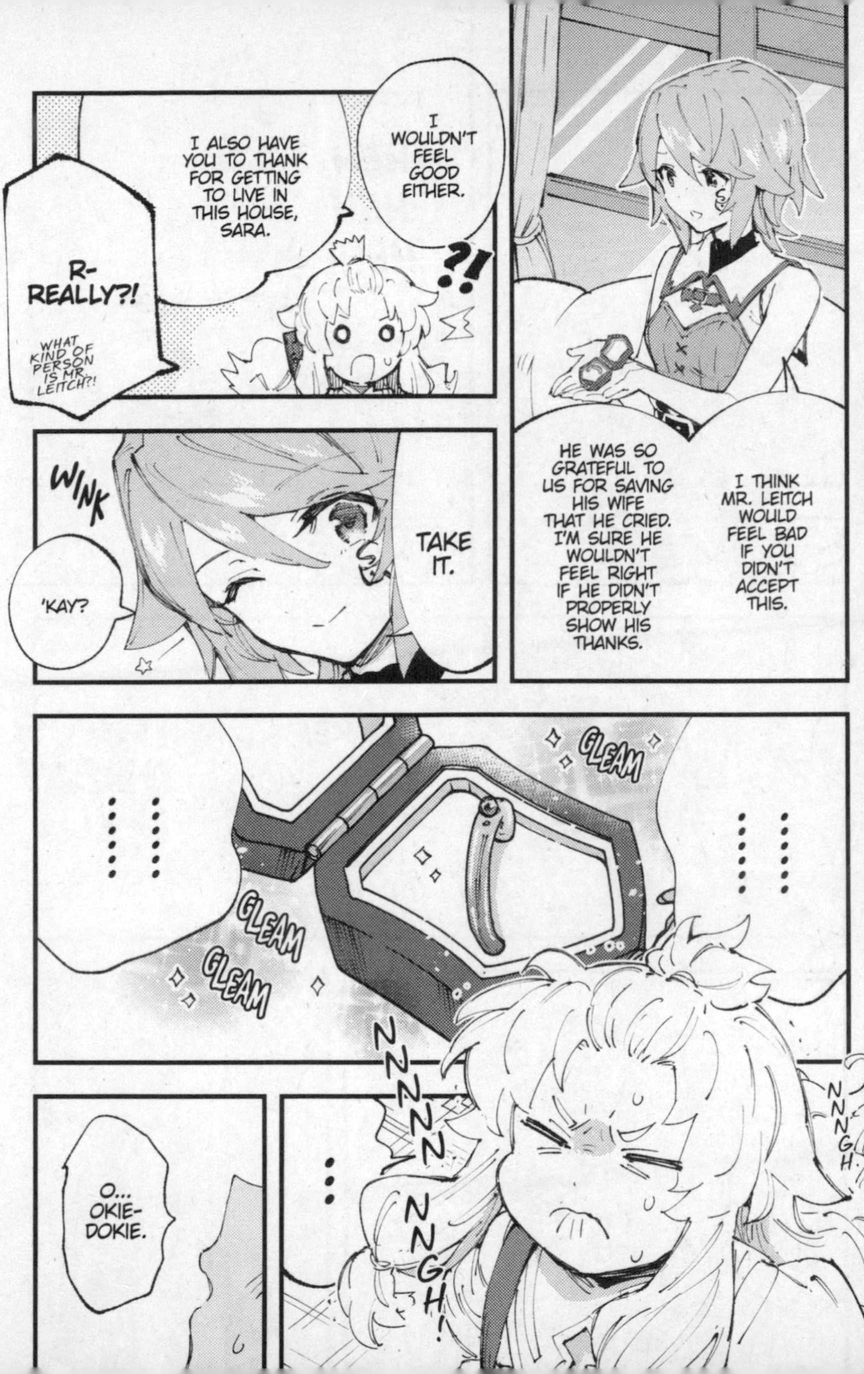
I THINK MR. LEITCH WOULD FEEL BAD IF YOU DIDN'T ACCEPT THIS.
HE WAS SO GRATEFUL TO US FOR SAVING HIS WIFE THAT HE CRIED. I'M SURE HE WOULDN'T FEEL RIGHT IF HE DIDN'T PROPERLY SHOW HIS THANKS.
I WOULDN'T FEEL GOOD EITHER.
I ALSO HAVE YOU TO THANK FOR GETTING TO LIVE IN THIS HOUSE, SARA.
?!
R-REALLY?!
WHAT KIND OF PERSON IS MR. LEITCH?!
TAKE IT.
WINK
'KAY?
......
GLEAM
GLEAM
GLEAM
......
NNNNGH!
NNNNN
NNGH!
...
O... OKIE-DOKIE.

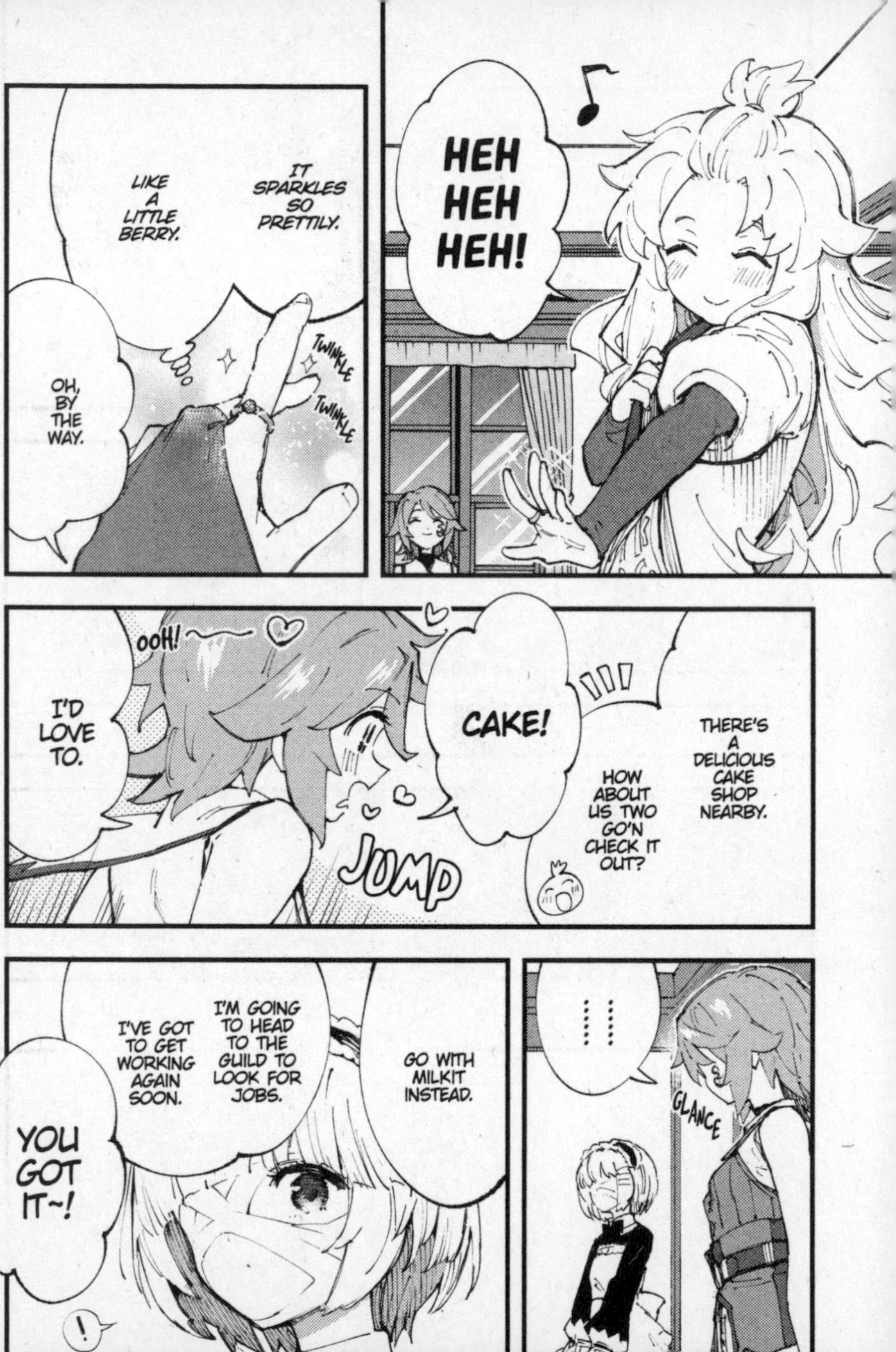
HEH HEH HEH!
IT SPARKLES SO PRETTILY.
LIKE A LITTLE BERRY.
TWINKLE
TWINKLE
OH, BY THE WAY.
THERE'S A DELICIOUS CAKE SHOP NEARBY.
HOW ABOUT US TWO GO'N CHECK IT OUT?
!!!
CAKE!
JUMP
OOH!~
I'D LOVE TO.
......
GLANCE
GO WITH MILKIT INSTEAD.
I'M GOING TO HEAD TO THE GUILD TO LOOK FOR JOBS.
I'VE GOT TO GET WORKING AGAIN SOON.
YOU GOT IT~!
!

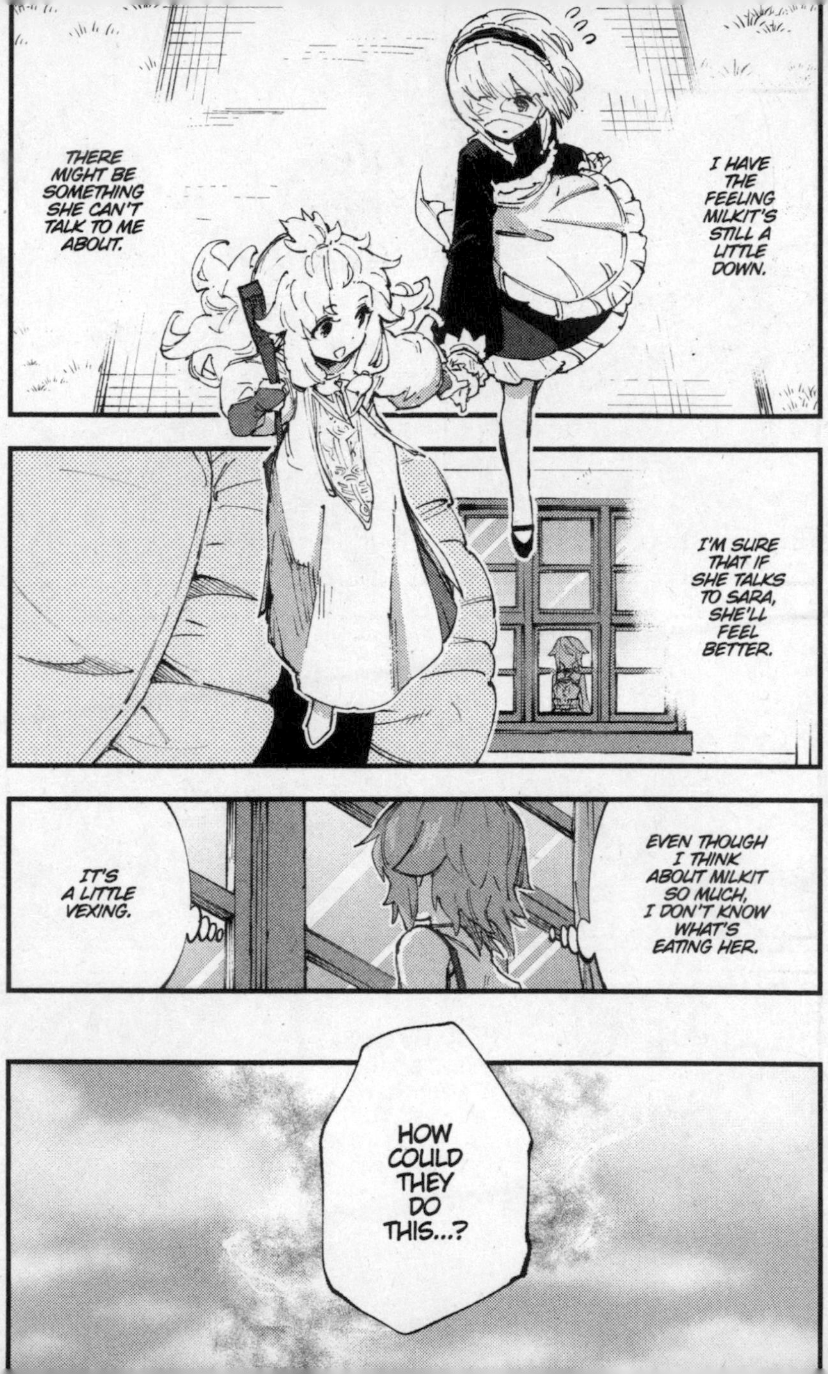
I HAVE THE FEELING MILKIT'S STILL A LITTLE DOWN.
THERE MIGHT BE SOMETHING SHE CAN'T TALK TO ME ABOUT.
I'M SURE THAT IF SHE TALKS TO SARA, SHE'LL FEEL BETTER.
EVEN THOUGH I THINK ABOUT MILKIT SO MUCH, I DON'T KNOW WHAT'S EATING HER.
IT'S A LITTLE VEXING.
HOW COULD THEY DO THIS...?

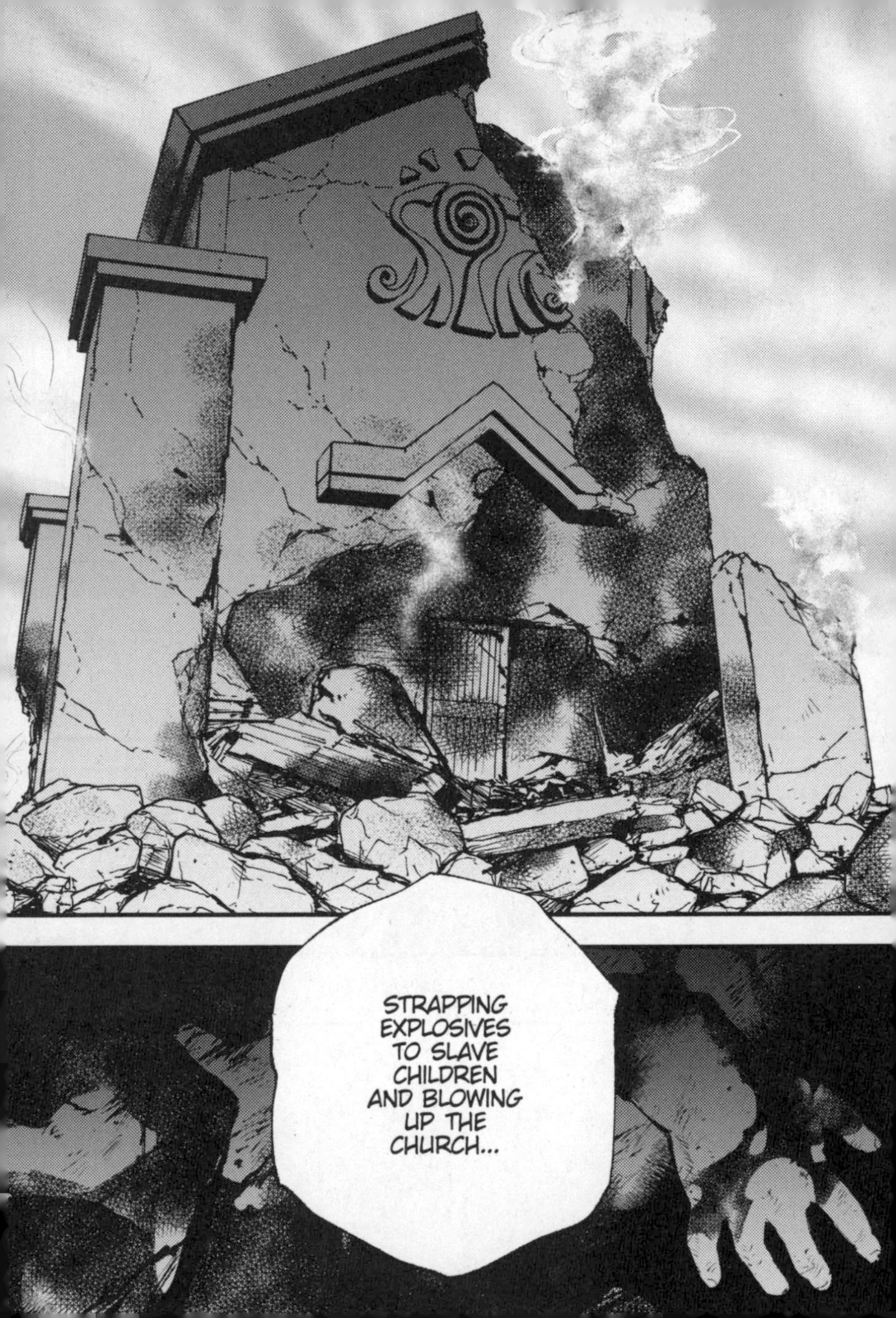
STRAPPING EXPLOSIVES TO SLAVE CHILDREN AND BLOWING UP THE CHURCH...

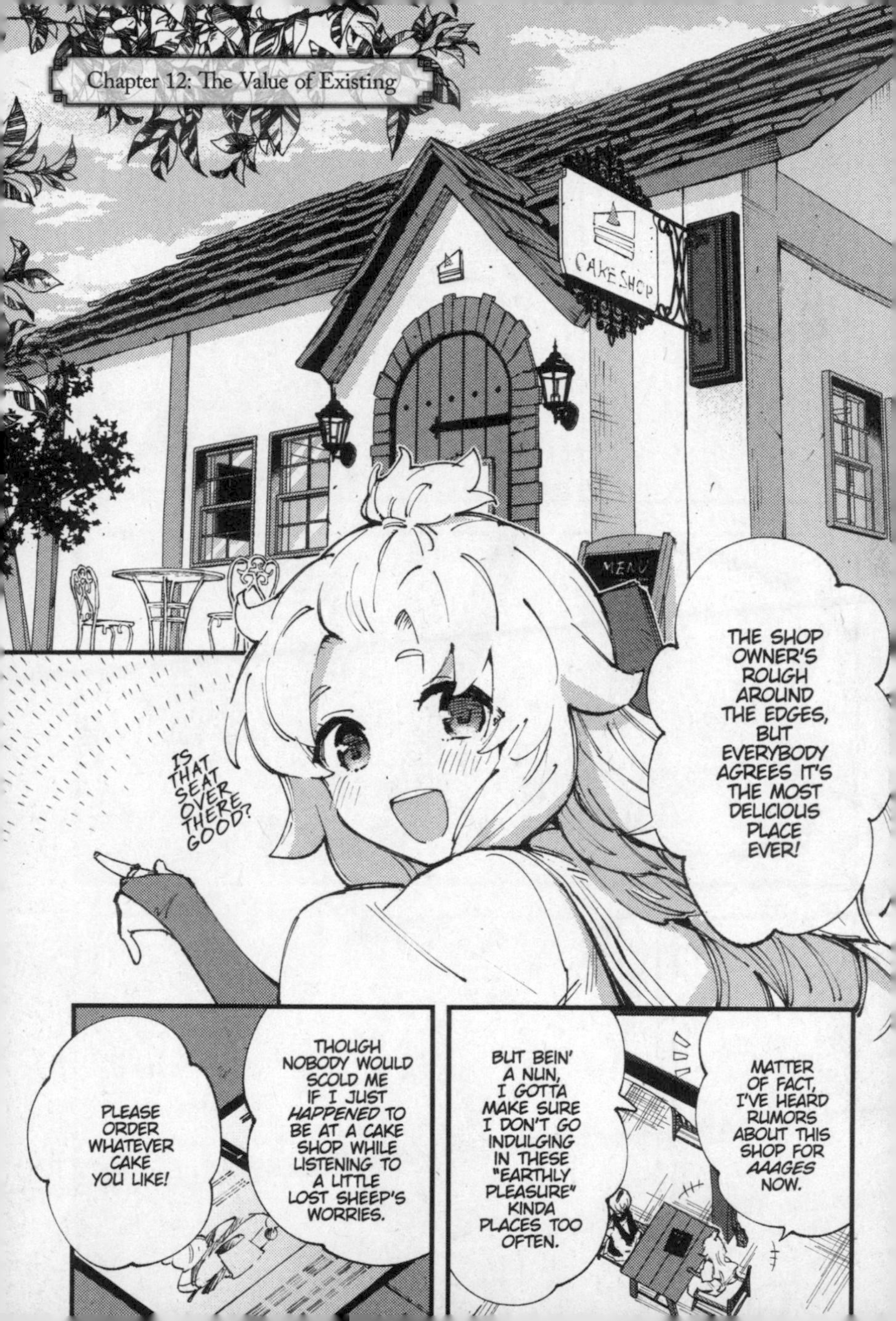
Chapter 12: The Value of Existing
CAKE SHOP
MENU
THE SHOP OWNER'S ROUGH AROUND THE EDGES, BUT EVERYBODY AGREES IT'S THE MOST DELICIOUS PLACE EVER!
IS THAT SEAT OVER THERE GOOD?
MATTER OF FACT, I'VE HEARD RUMORS ABOUT THIS SHOP FOR *AAAGES* NOW.
BUT BEIN' A NUN, I GOTTA MAKE SURE I DON'T GO INDULGING IN THESE "EARTHLY PLEASURE" KINDA PLACES TOO OFTEN.
THOUGH NOBODY WOULD SCOLD ME IF I JUST *HAPPENED* TO BE AT A CAKE SHOP WHILE LISTENING TO A LITTLE LOST SHEEP'S WORRIES.
PLEASE ORDER WHATEVER CAKE YOU LIKE!

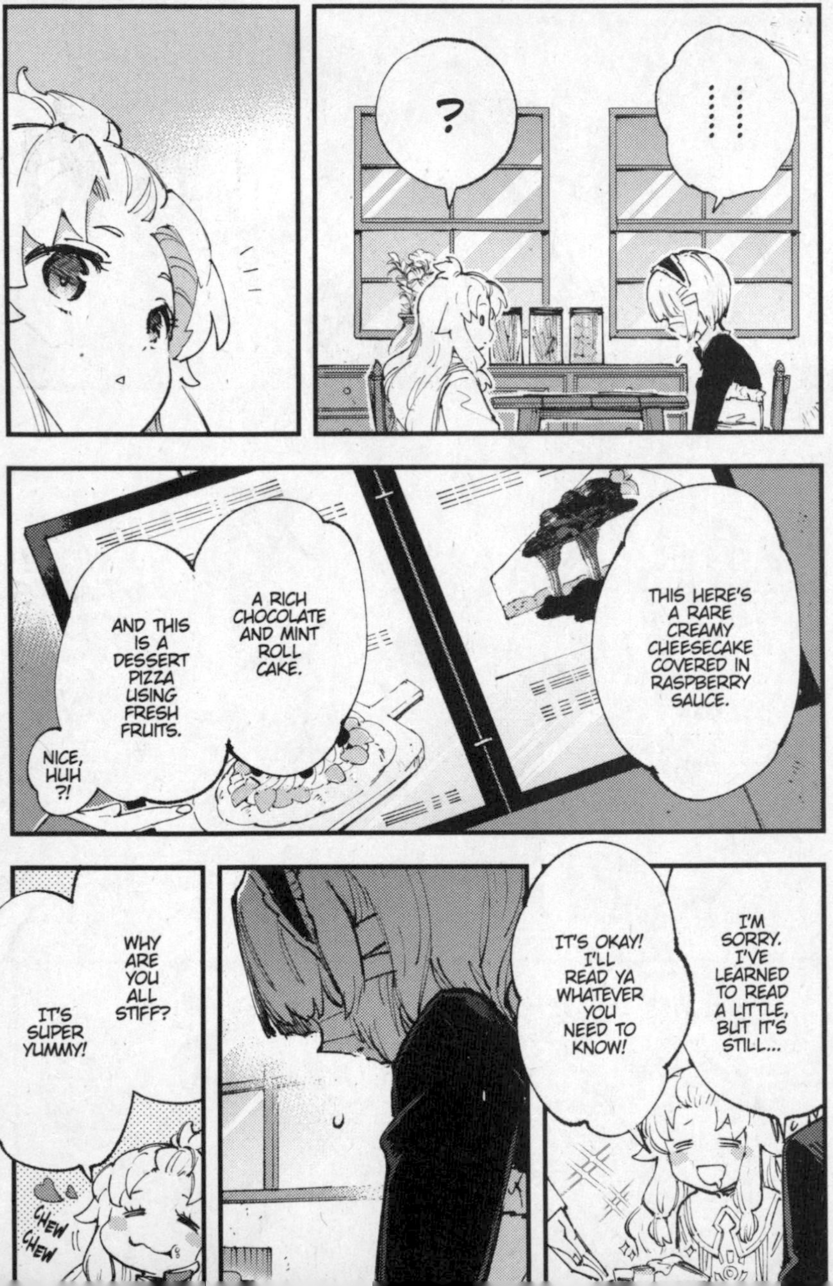
......
?
THIS HERE'S A RARE CREAMY CHEESECAKE COVERED IN RASPBERRY SAUCE.
A RICH CHOCOLATE AND MINT ROLL CAKE.
AND THIS IS A DESSERT PIZZA USING FRESH FRUITS.
NICE, HUH?!
I'M SORRY. I'VE LEARNED TO READ A LITTLE, BUT IT'S STILL...
IT'S OKAY! I'LL READ YA WHATEVER YOU NEED TO KNOW!
WHY ARE YOU ALL STIFF?
IT'S SUPER YUMMY!
CHEW CHEW

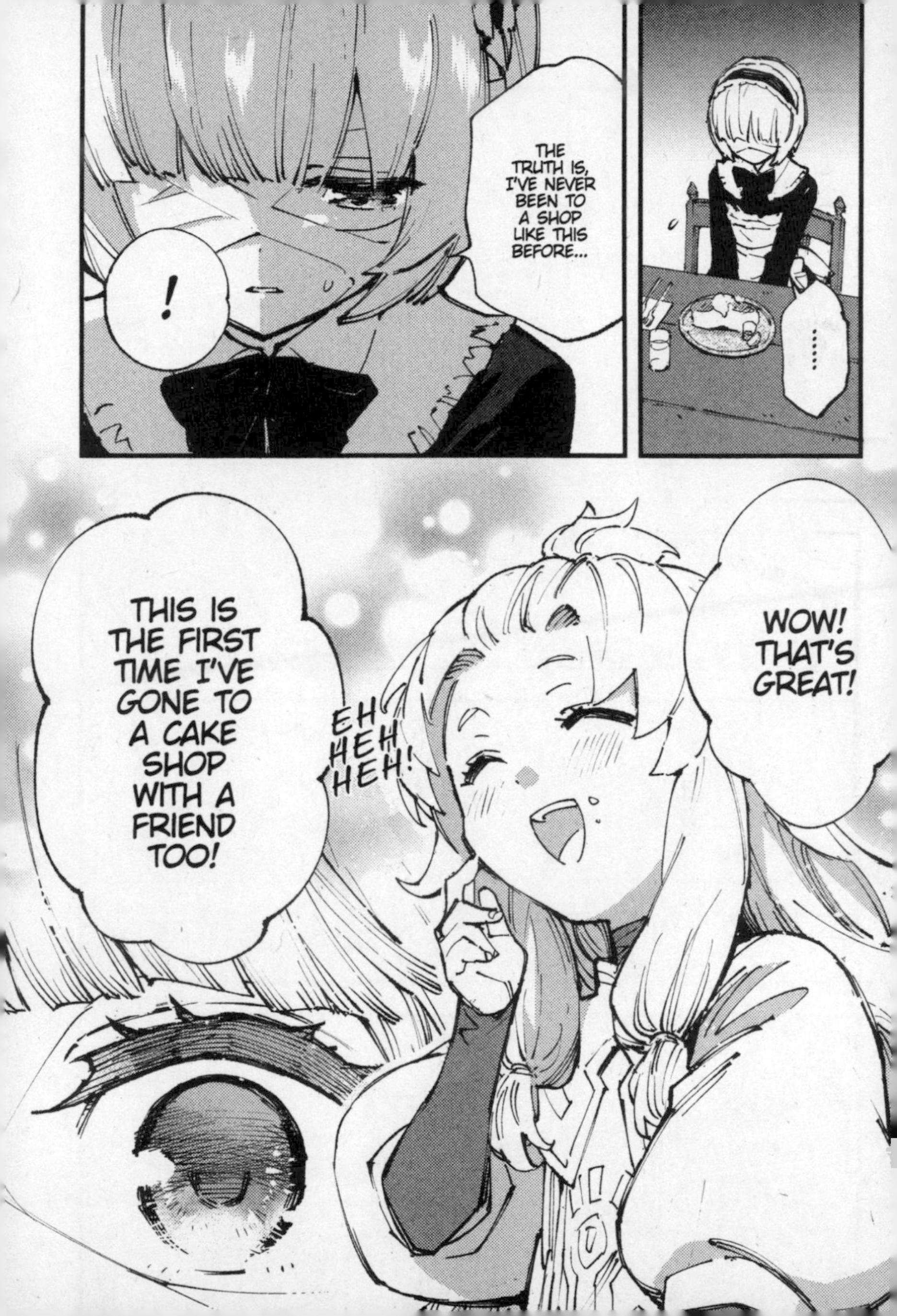
......
THE TRUTH IS, I'VE NEVER BEEN TO A SHOP LIKE THIS BEFORE...
!
WOW! THAT'S GREAT!
EH HEH HEH!
THIS IS THE FIRST TIME I'VE GONE TO A CAKE SHOP WITH A FRIEND TOO!

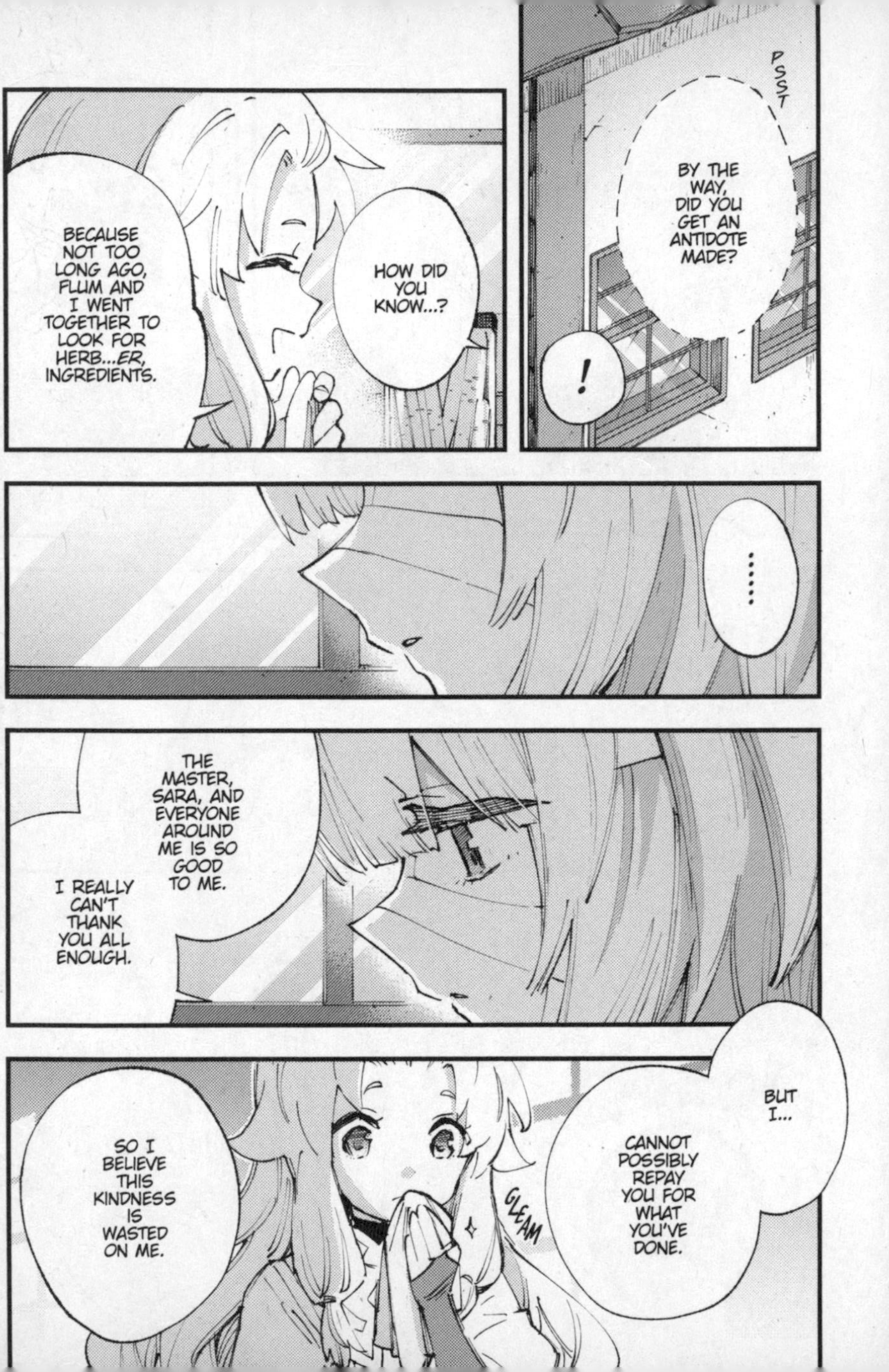
PSST
BY THE WAY, DID YOU GET AN ANTIDOTE MADE?
!
HOW DID YOU KNOW...?
BECAUSE NOT TOO LONG AGO, FLUM AND I WENT TOGETHER TO LOOK FOR HERB...*ER*, INGREDIENTS.
......
THE MASTER, SARA, AND EVERYONE AROUND ME IS SO GOOD TO ME.
I REALLY CAN'T THANK YOU ALL ENOUGH.
BUT I...
CANNOT POSSIBLY REPAY YOU FOR WHAT YOU'VE DONE.
GLEAM
SO I BELIEVE THIS KINDNESS IS WASTED ON ME.

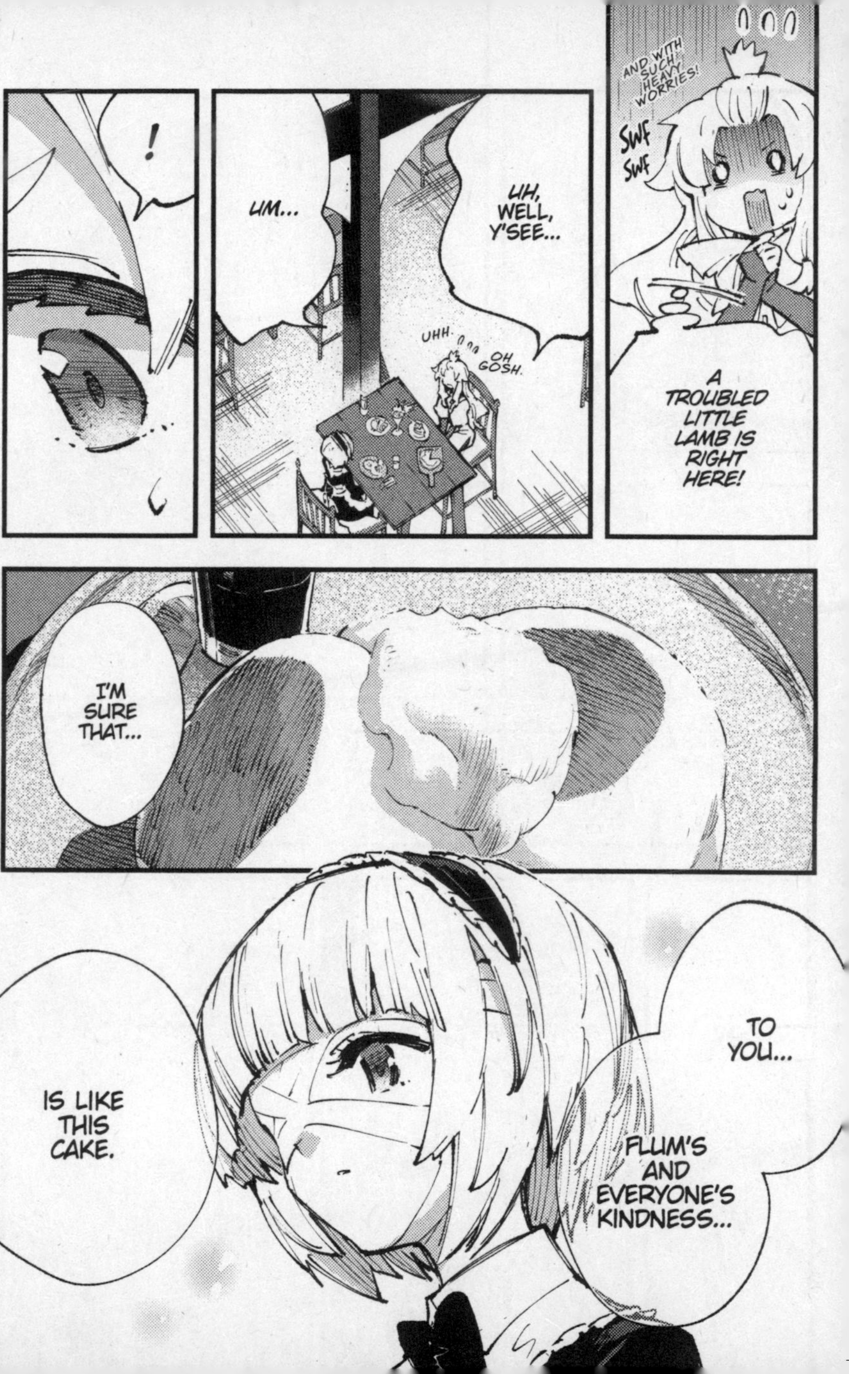
AND WITH SUCH HEAVY WORRIES!
SWF SWF
A TROUBLED LITTLE LAMB IS RIGHT HERE!
UH, WELL, Y'SEE...
UHH.
OH GOSH.
UM...
!
I'M SURE THAT...
TO YOU...
FLUM'S AND EVERYONE'S KINDNESS...
IS LIKE THIS CAKE.

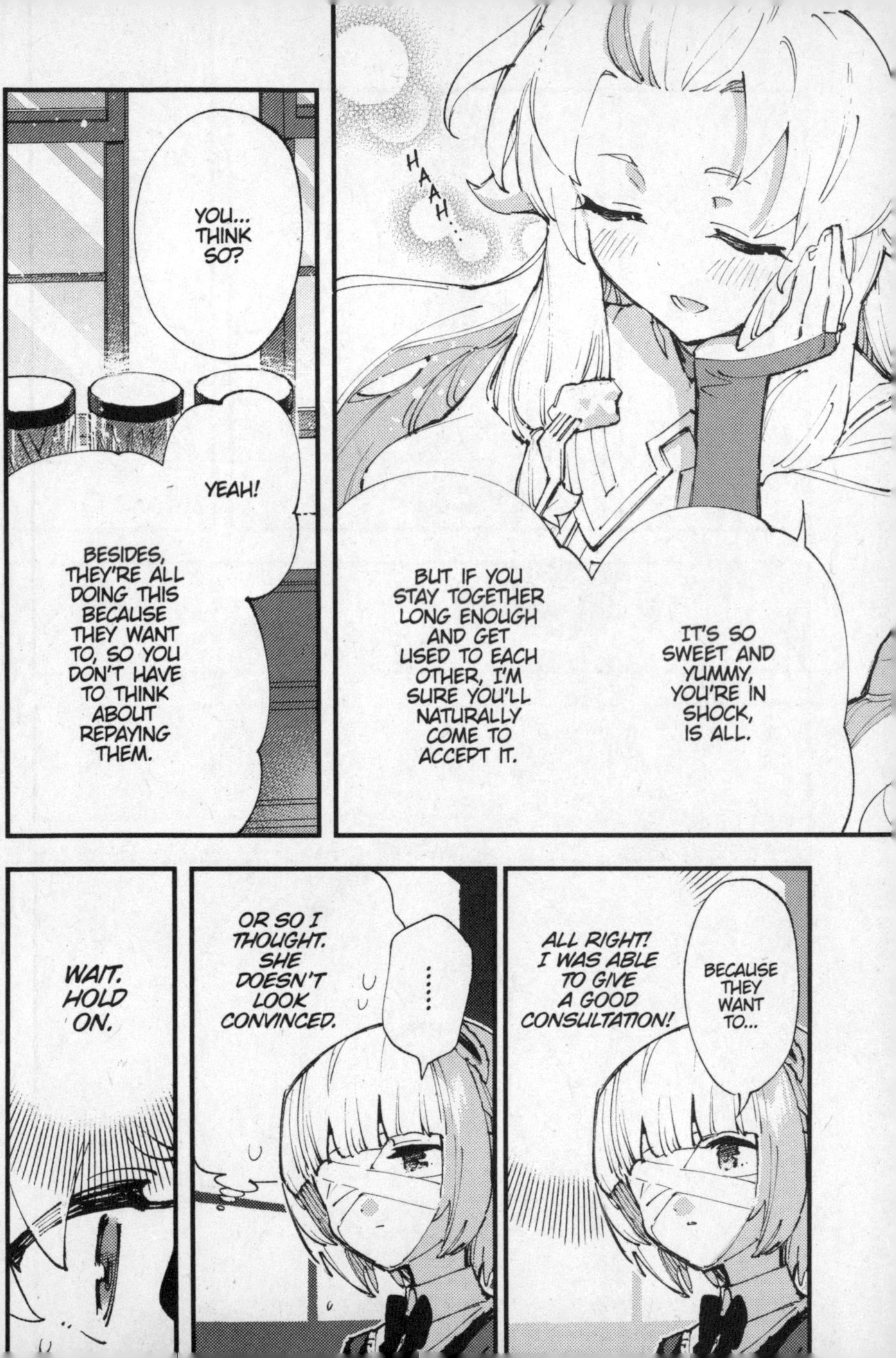
HAAAH...
IT'S SO SWEET AND YUMMY, YOU'RE IN SHOCK, IS ALL.
BUT IF YOU STAY TOGETHER LONG ENOUGH AND GET USED TO EACH OTHER, I'M SURE YOU'LL NATURALLY COME TO ACCEPT IT.
YOU... THINK SO?
YEAH!
BESIDES, THEY'RE ALL DOING THIS BECAUSE THEY WANT TO, SO YOU DON'T HAVE TO THINK ABOUT REPAYING THEM.
BECAUSE THEY WANT TO...
ALL RIGHT! I WAS ABLE TO GIVE A GOOD CONSULTATION!
......
OR SO I THOUGHT. SHE DOESN'T LOOK CONVINCED.
WAIT. HOLD ON.

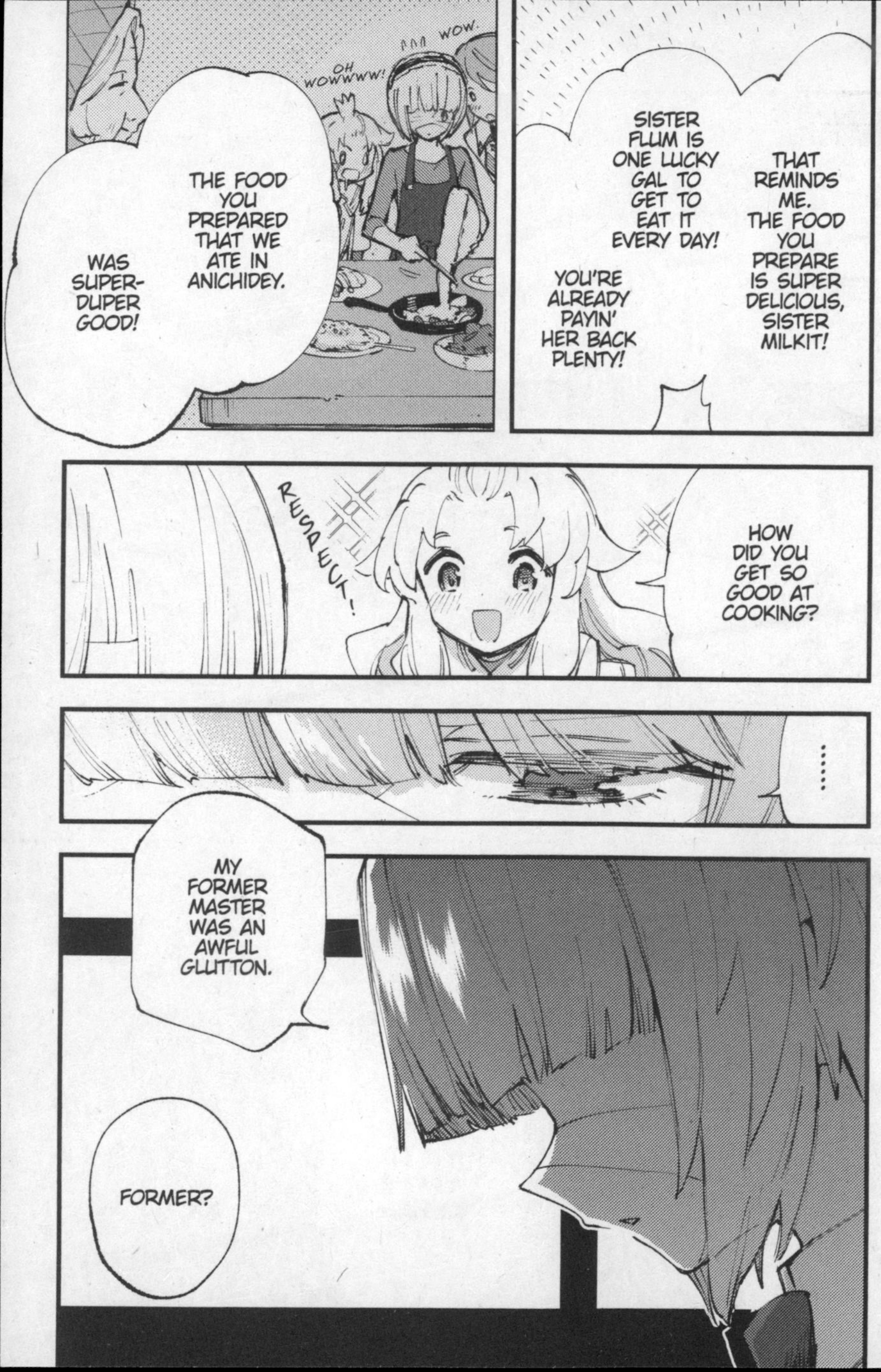
THAT REMINDS ME. THE FOOD YOU PREPARE IS SUPER DELICIOUS, SISTER MILKIT!
SISTER FLUM IS ONE LUCKY GAL TO GET TO EAT IT EVERY DAY!
YOU'RE ALREADY PAYIN' HER BACK PLENTY!
WOW.
OH WOWWWWW!
THE FOOD YOU PREPARED THAT WE ATE IN ANICHIDEY.
WAS SUPER-DUPER GOOD!
HOW DID YOU GET SO GOOD AT COOKING?
RESPECT!
......
MY FORMER MASTER WAS AN AWFUL GLUTTON.
FORMER?

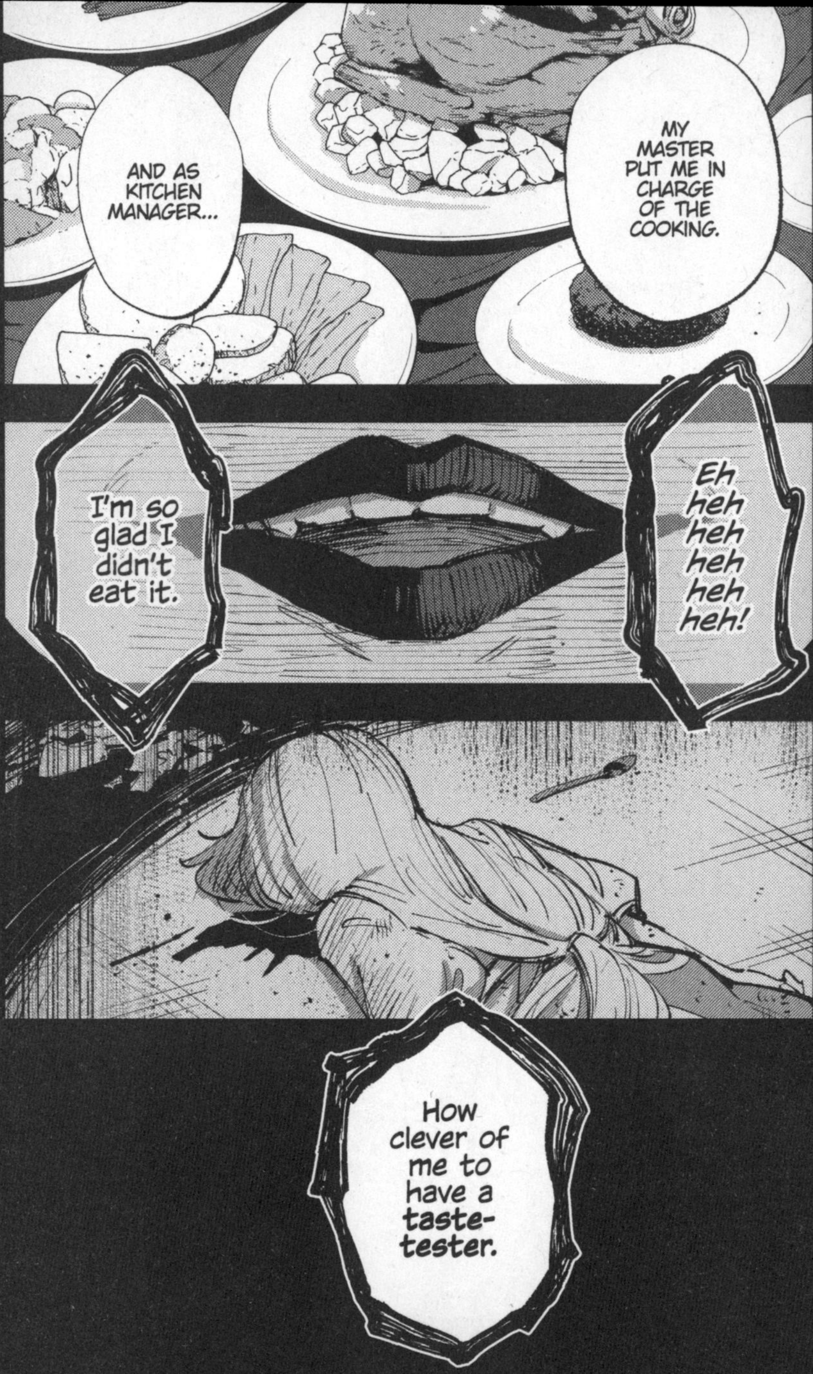
MY MASTER PUT ME IN CHARGE OF THE COOKING.
AND AS KITCHEN MANAGER...
Eh heh heh heh heh heh!
I'm so glad I didn't eat it.
How clever of me to have a taste-tester.

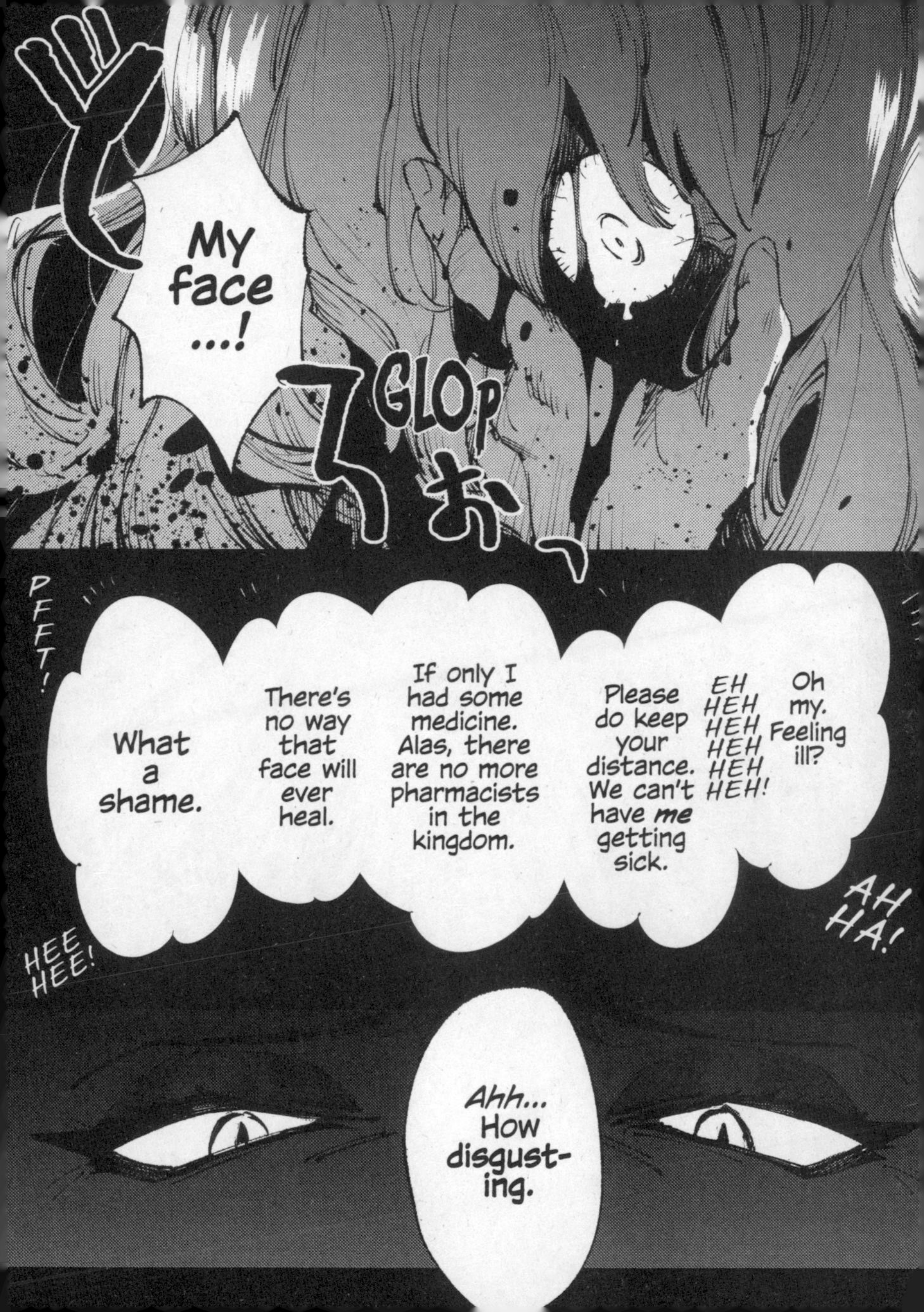
My face ...!
GLOP
AH HA!
Oh my. Feeling ill?
EH HEH HEH HEH HEH HEH!
Please do keep your distance. We can't have *me* getting sick.
If only I had some medicine. Alas, there are no more pharmacists in the kingdom.
There's no way that face will ever heal.
What a shame.
PFFT!
HEE HEE!
Ahh... How disgust-ing.

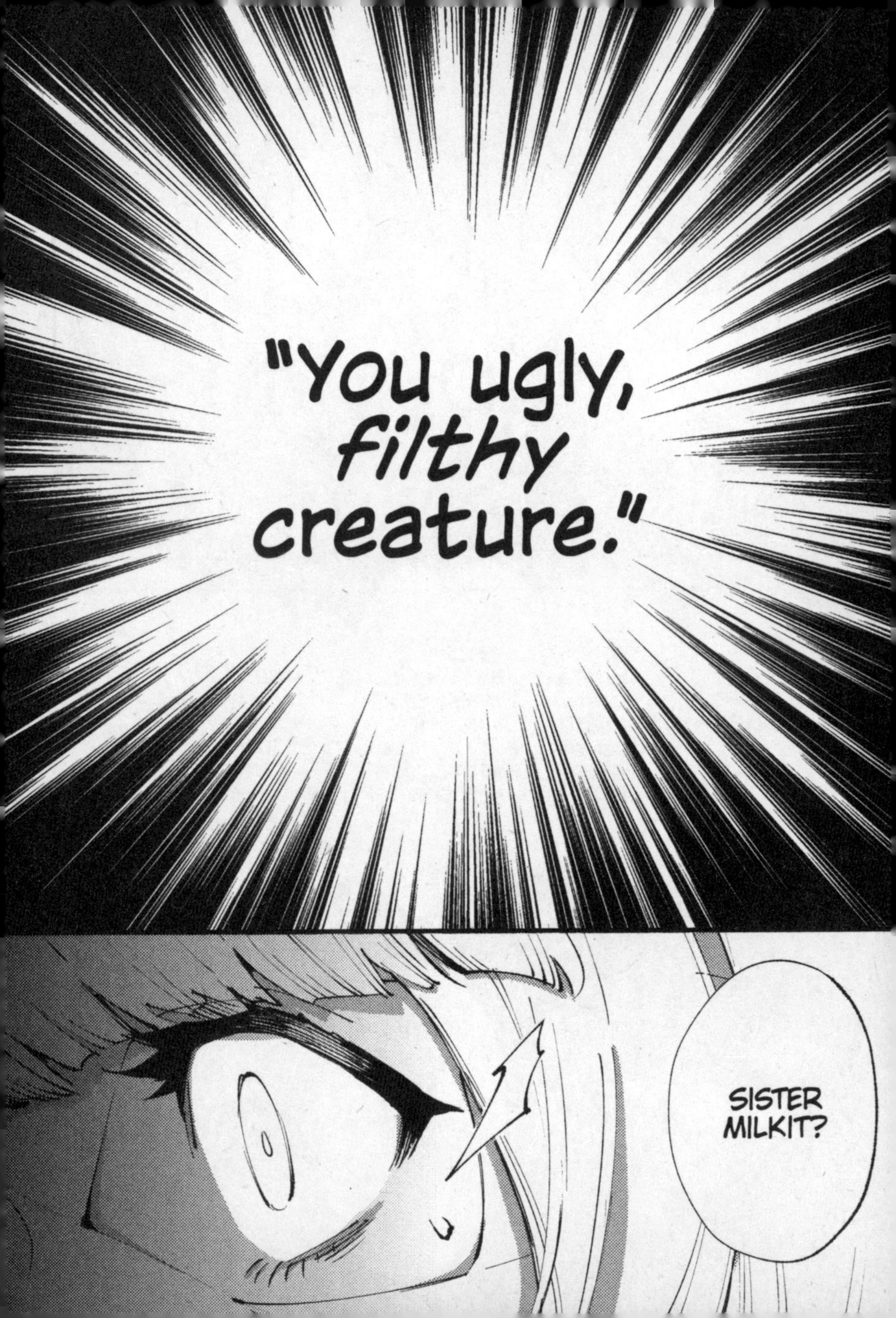
"You ugly, *filthy* creature."
SISTER MILKIT?

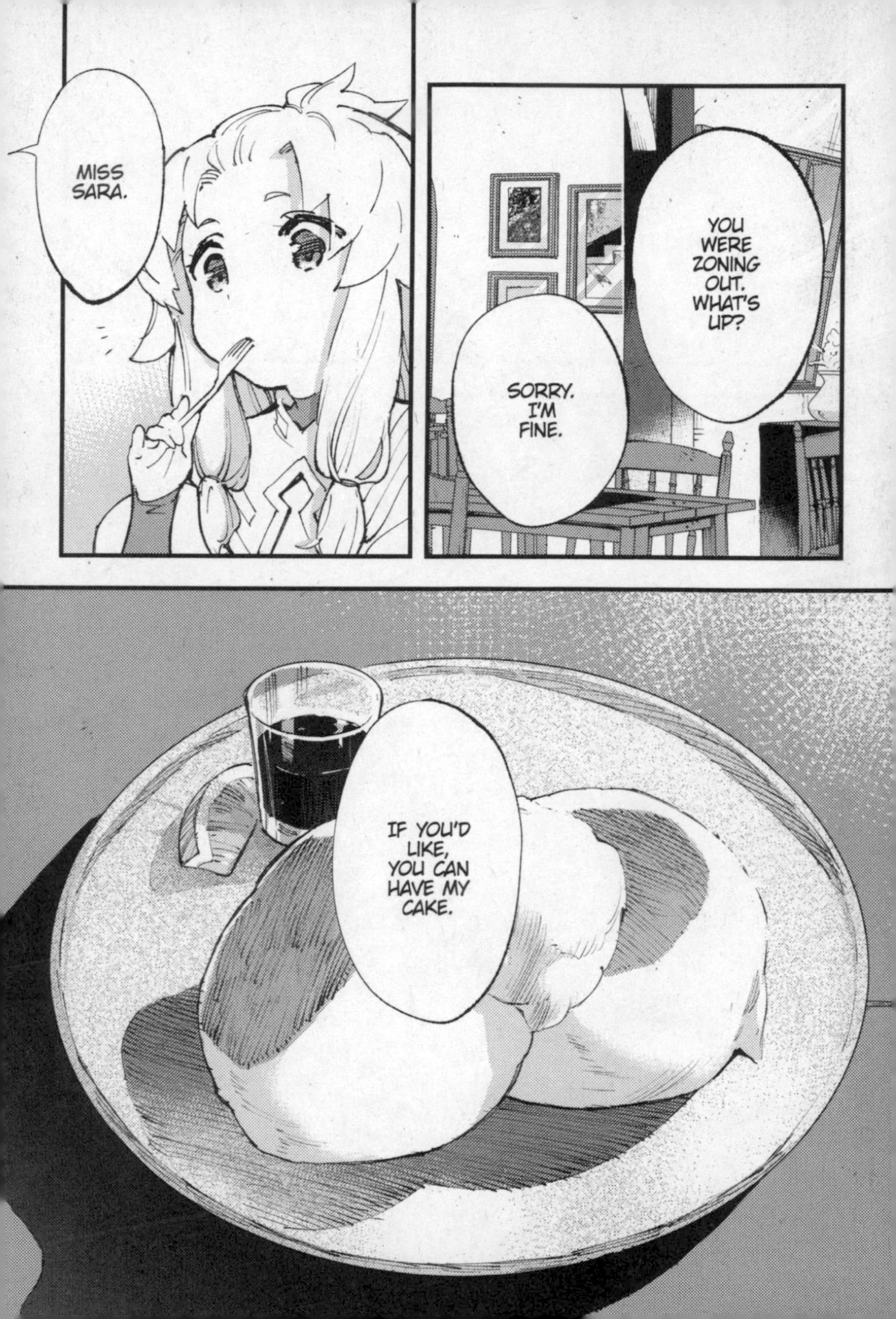
YOU WERE ZONING OUT. WHAT'S UP?
SORRY. I'M FINE.
MISS SARA.
IF YOU'D LIKE, YOU CAN HAVE MY CAKE.

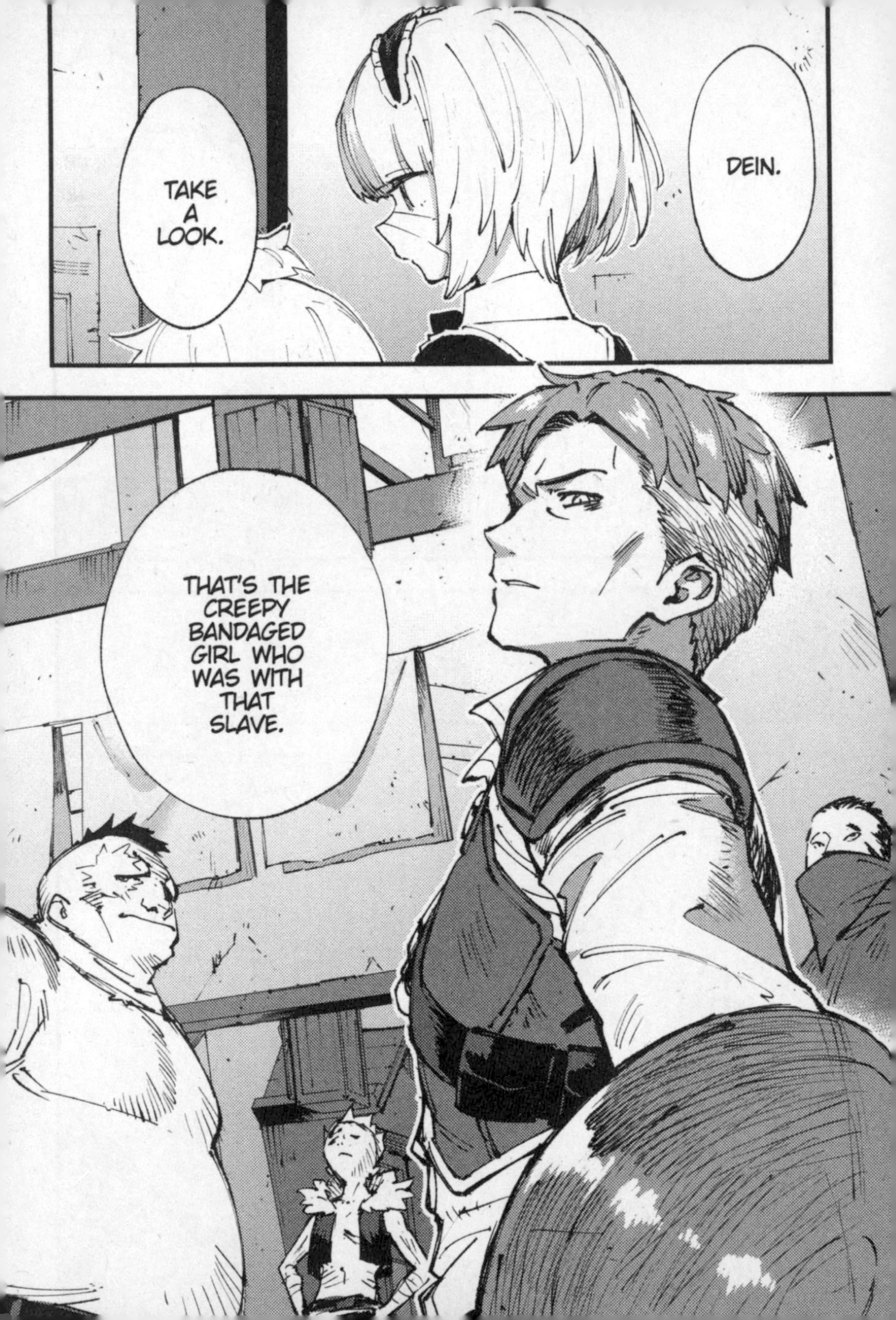
DEIN.
TAKE A LOOK.
THAT'S THE CREEPY BANDAGED GIRL WHO WAS WITH THAT SLAVE.

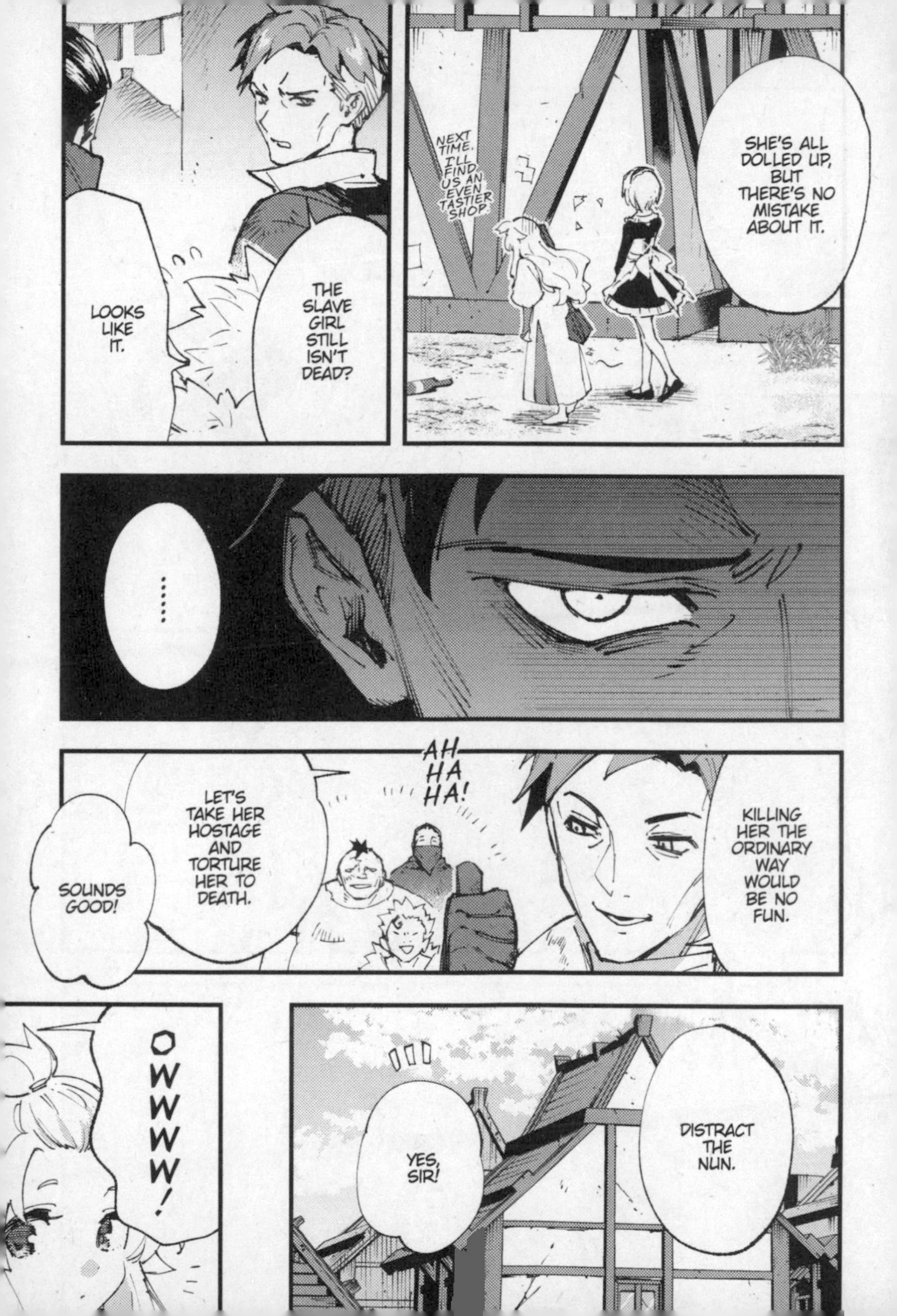
SHE'S ALL DOLLED UP, BUT THERE'S NO MISTAKE ABOUT IT.
NEXT TIME, I'LL FIND US AN EVEN TASTIER SHOP.
THE SLAVE GIRL STILL ISN'T DEAD?
LOOKS LIKE IT.
......
KILLING HER THE ORDINARY WAY WOULD BE NO FUN.
AH HA HA!
LET'S TAKE HER HOSTAGE AND TORTURE HER TO DEATH.
SOUNDS GOOD!
DISTRACT THE NUN.
YES, SIR!
OWWWW!

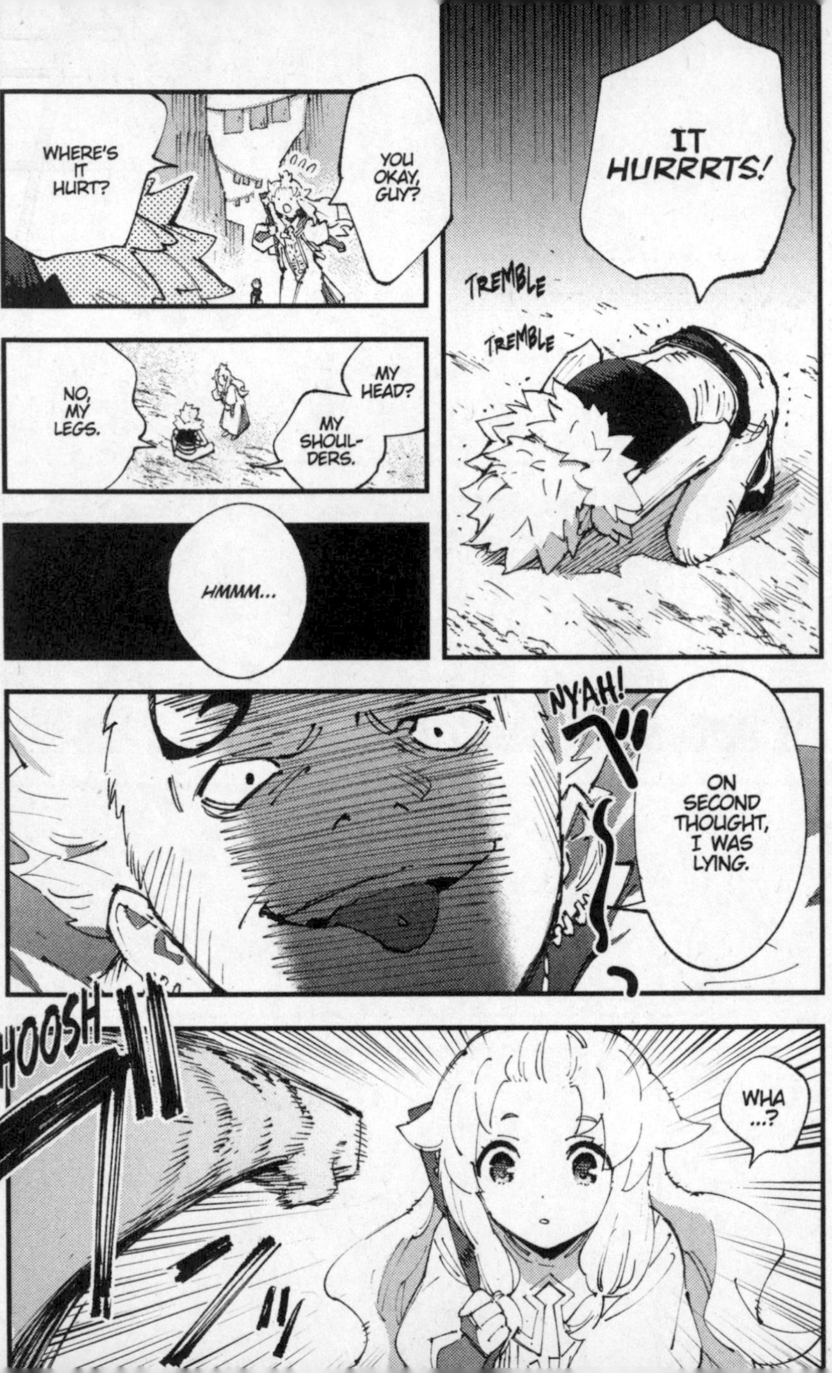
IT HURRRTS!
TREMBLE
TREMBLE
YOU OKAY, GUY?
WHERE'S IT HURT?
MY HEAD?
MY SHOULDERS.
NO, MY LEGS.
HMMM...
NYAH!
ON SECOND THOUGHT, I WAS LYING.
WHA ...?
WHOOSH

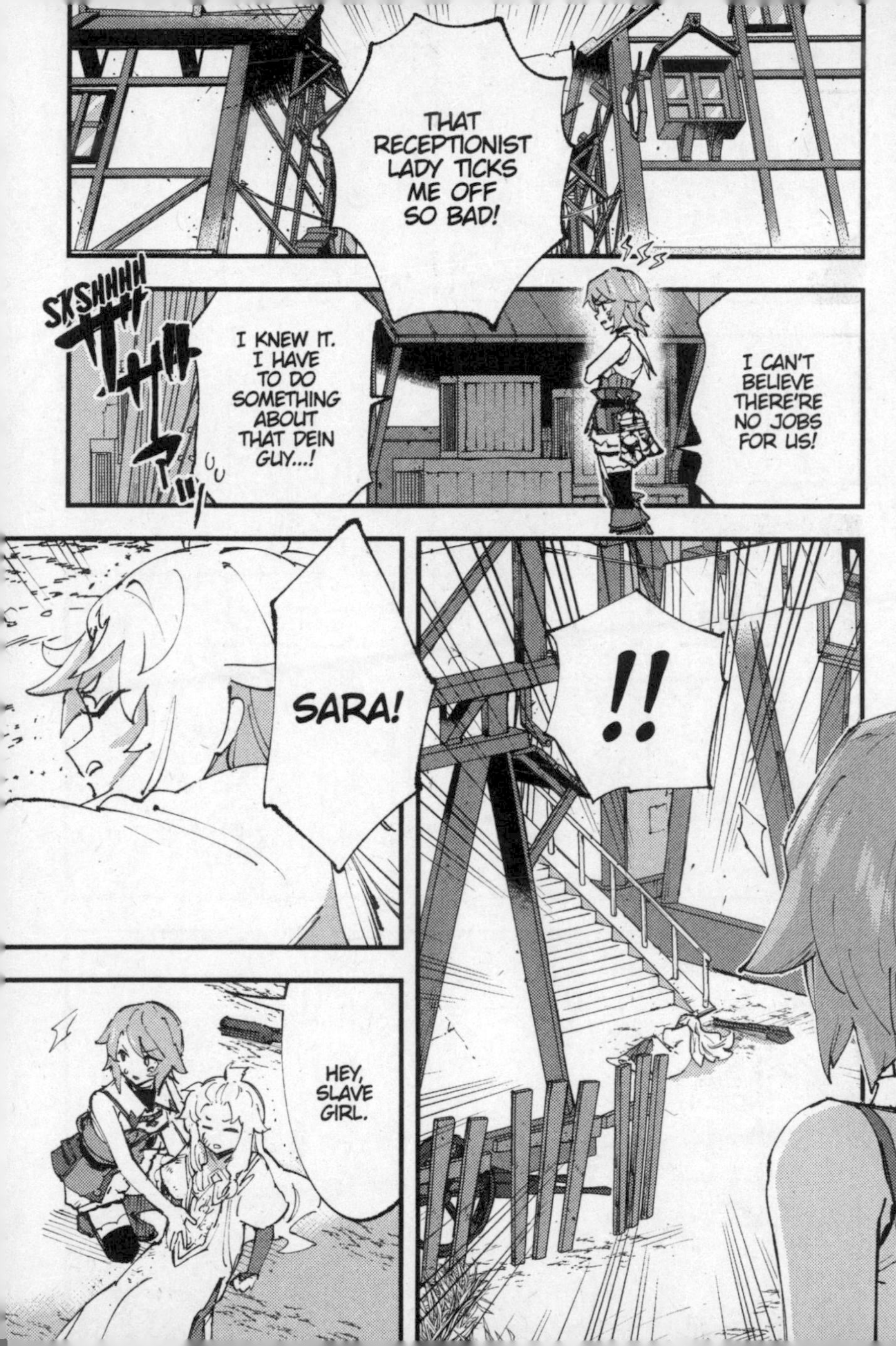
THAT RECEPTIONIST LADY TICKS ME OFF SO BAD!
I CAN'T BELIEVE THERE'RE NO JOBS FOR US!
I KNEW IT. I HAVE TO DO SOMETHING ABOUT THAT DEIN GUY...!
SKSHHHH
!!
SARA!
HEY, SLAVE GIRL.

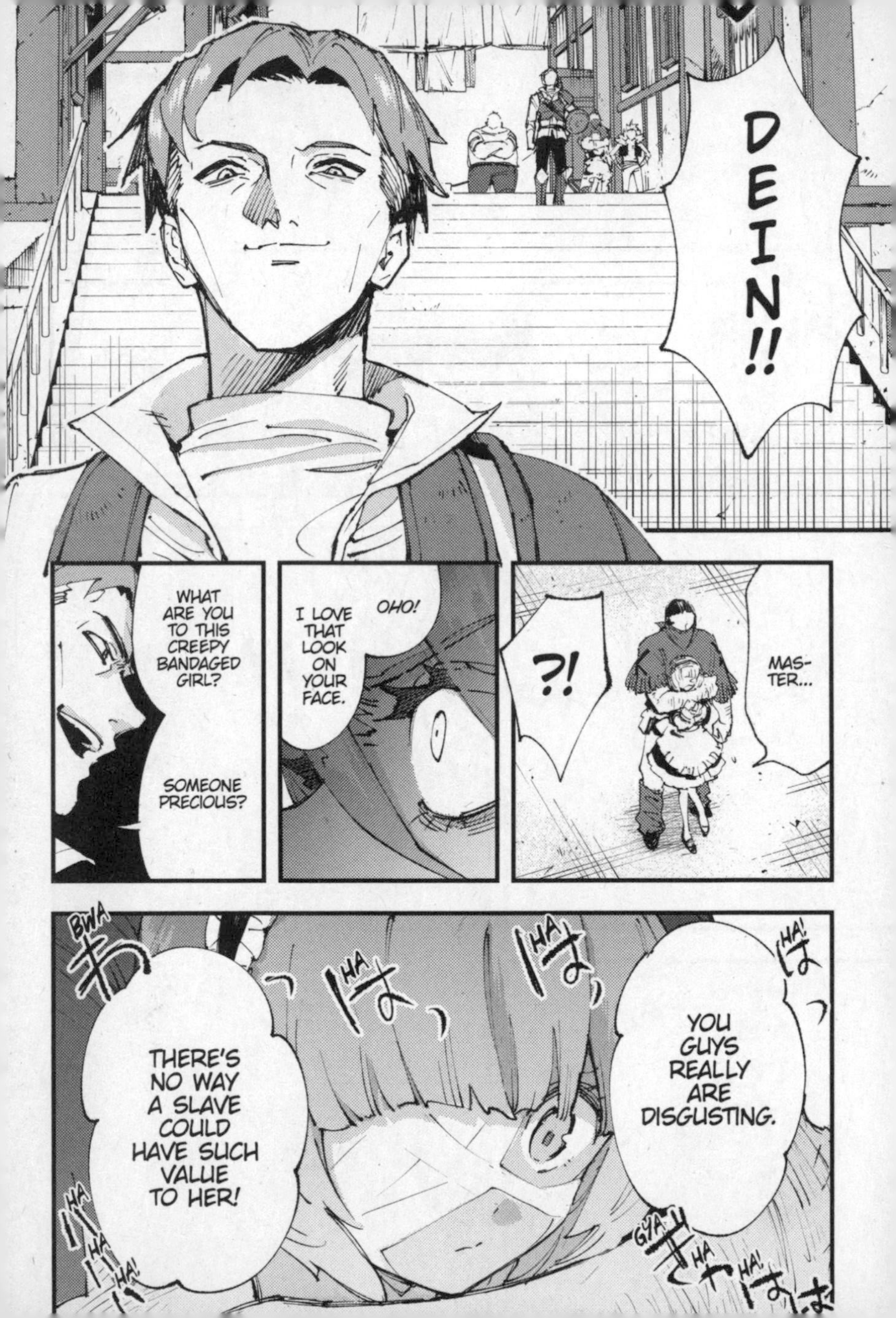
DEIN!!
MAS-TER...
?!
OHO!
I LOVE THAT LOOK ON YOUR FACE.
WHAT ARE YOU TO THIS CREEPY BANDAGED GIRL?
SOMEONE PRECIOUS?
HA!
HA
YOU GUYS REALLY ARE DISGUSTING.
HA
BWA
THERE'S NO WAY A SLAVE COULD HAVE SUCH VALUE TO HER!
GYA HA HA!
HA HA HA!

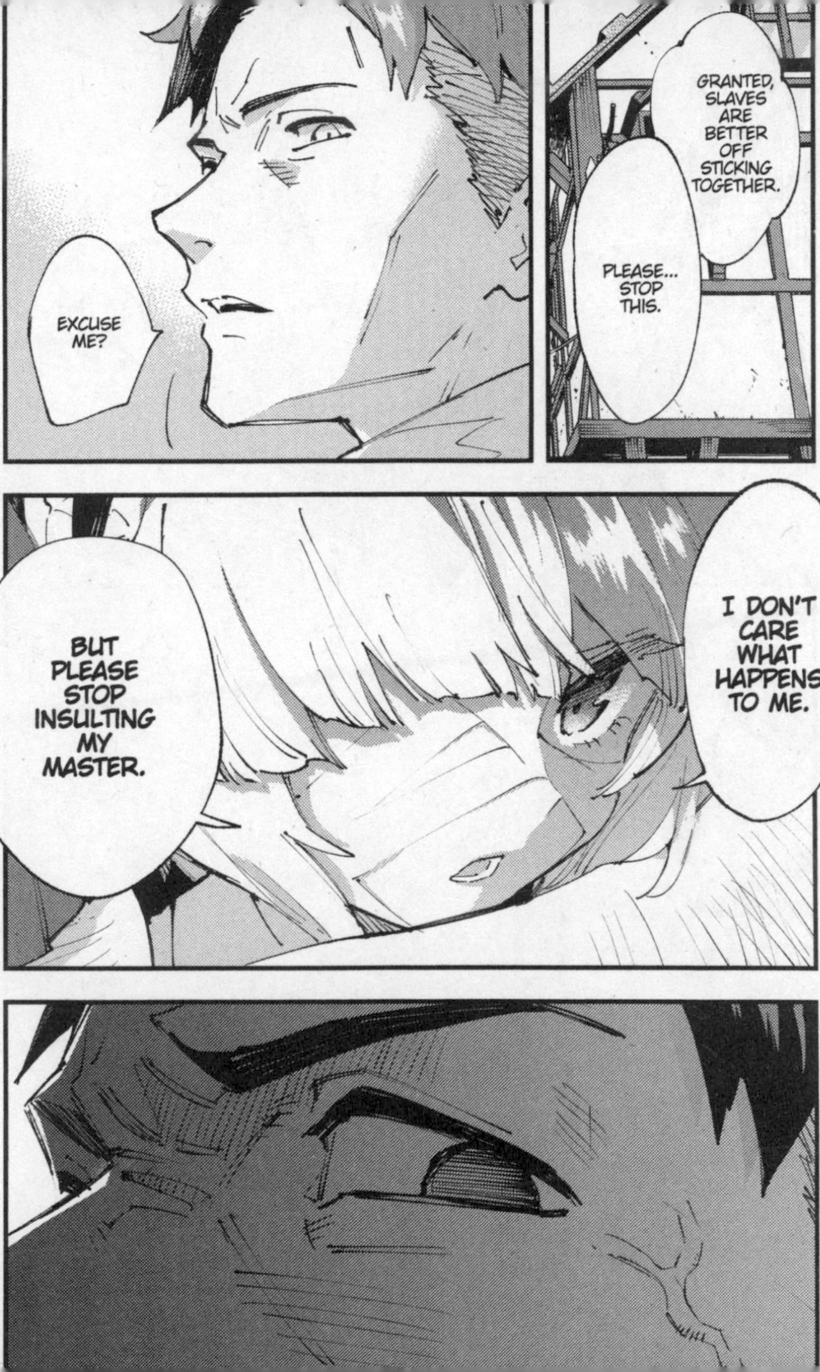
GRANTED, SLAVES ARE BETTER OFF STICKING TOGETHER.
PLEASE... STOP THIS.
EXCUSE ME?
I DON'T CARE WHAT HAPPENS TO ME.
BUT PLEASE STOP INSULTING MY MASTER.

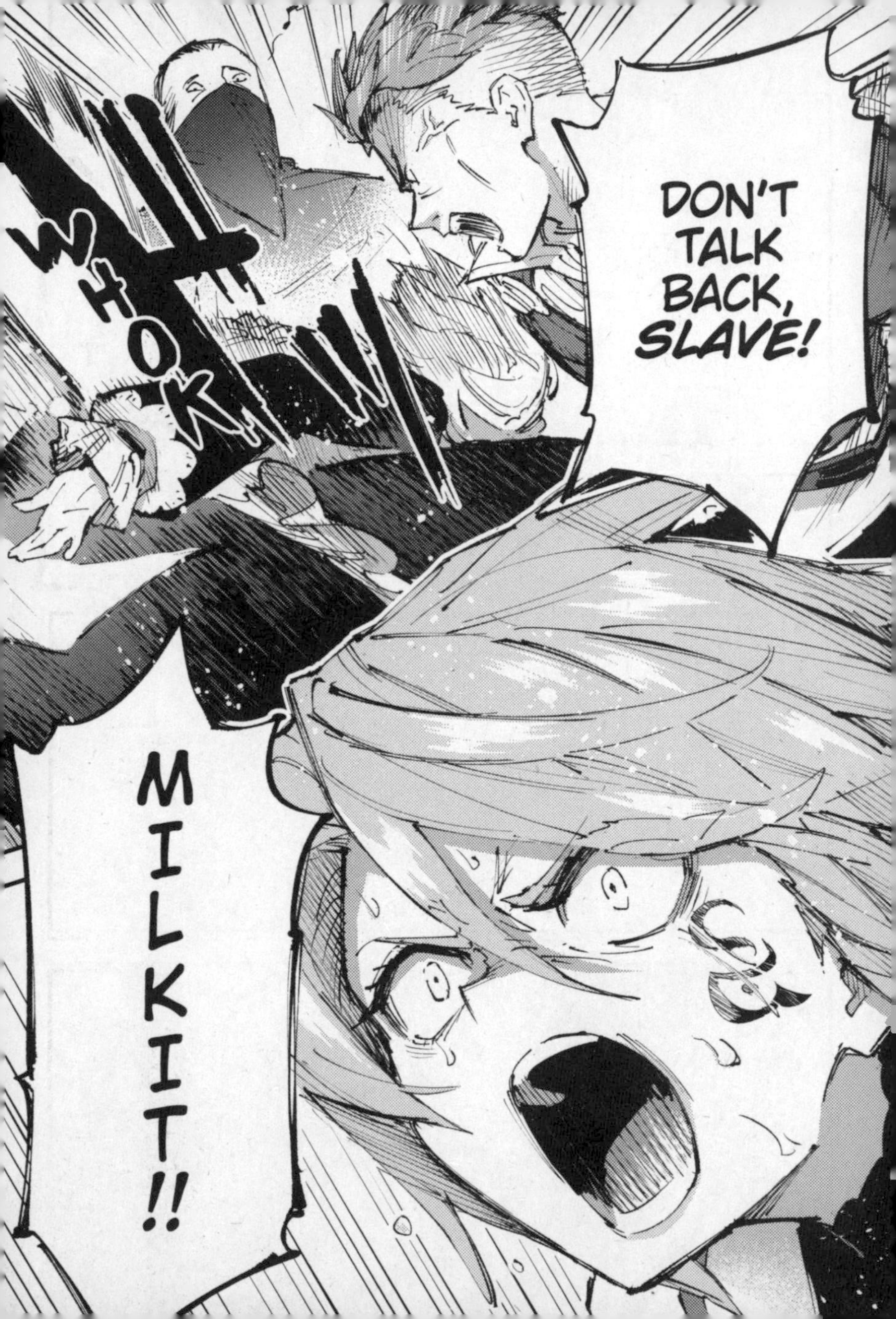
DON'T TALK BACK, *SLAVE!*
WHOK
MILKIT!!

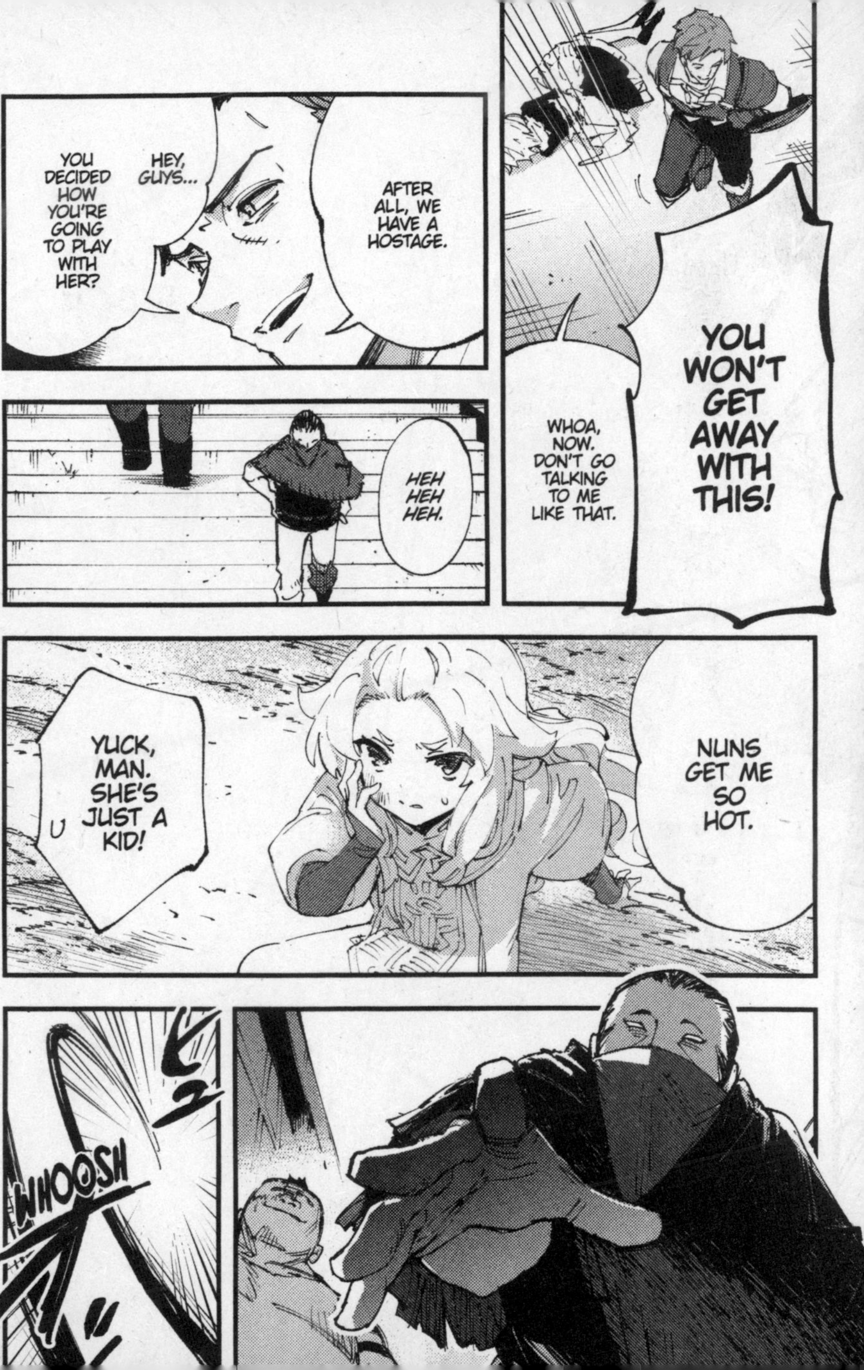
YOU WON'T GET AWAY WITH THIS!
WHOA, NOW. DON'T GO TALKING TO ME LIKE THAT.
AFTER ALL, WE HAVE A HOSTAGE.
HEY, GUYS...
YOU DECIDED HOW YOU'RE GOING TO PLAY WITH HER?
HEH HEH HEH.
NUNS GET ME SO HOT.
YUCK, MAN. SHE'S JUST A KID!
WHOOSH

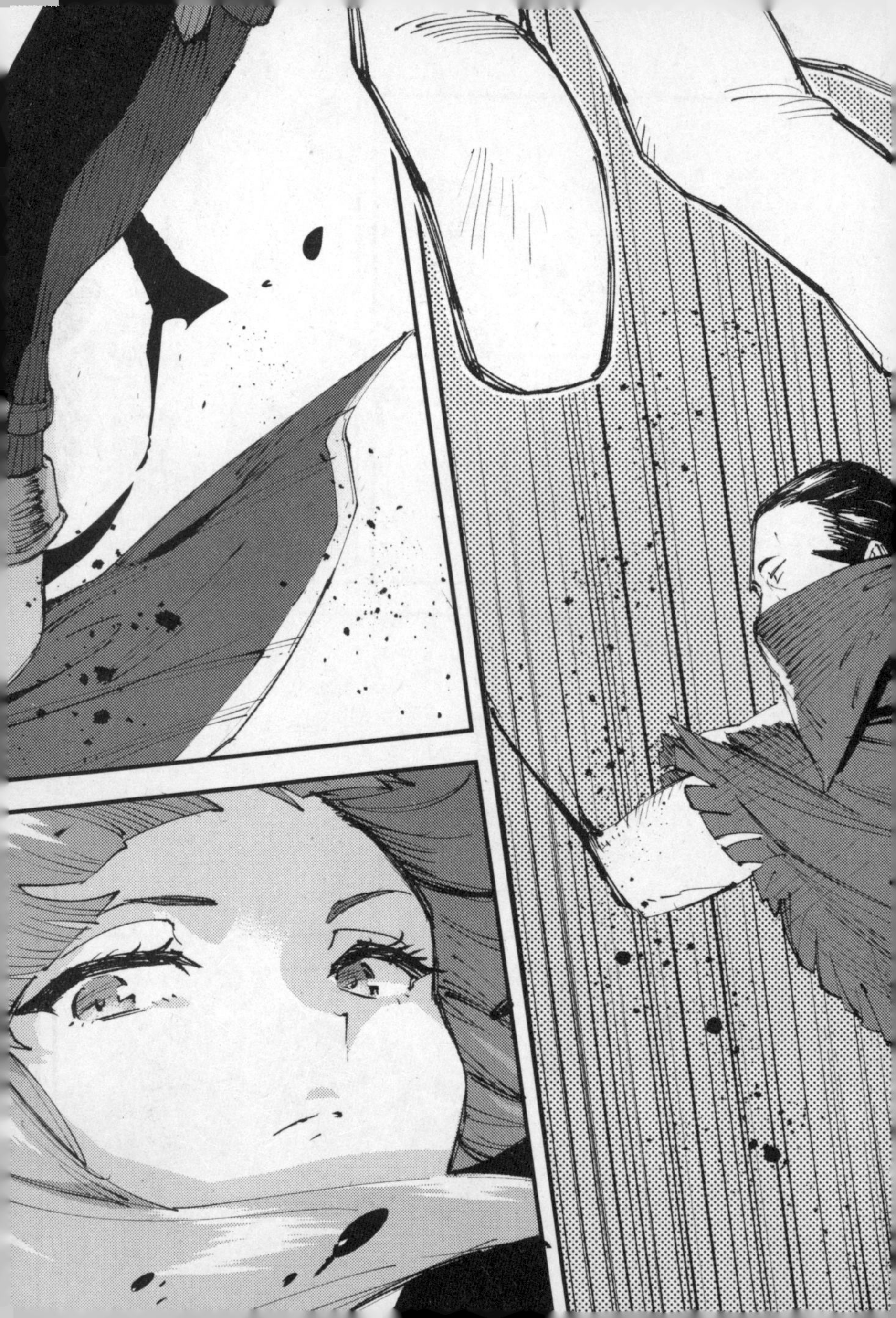

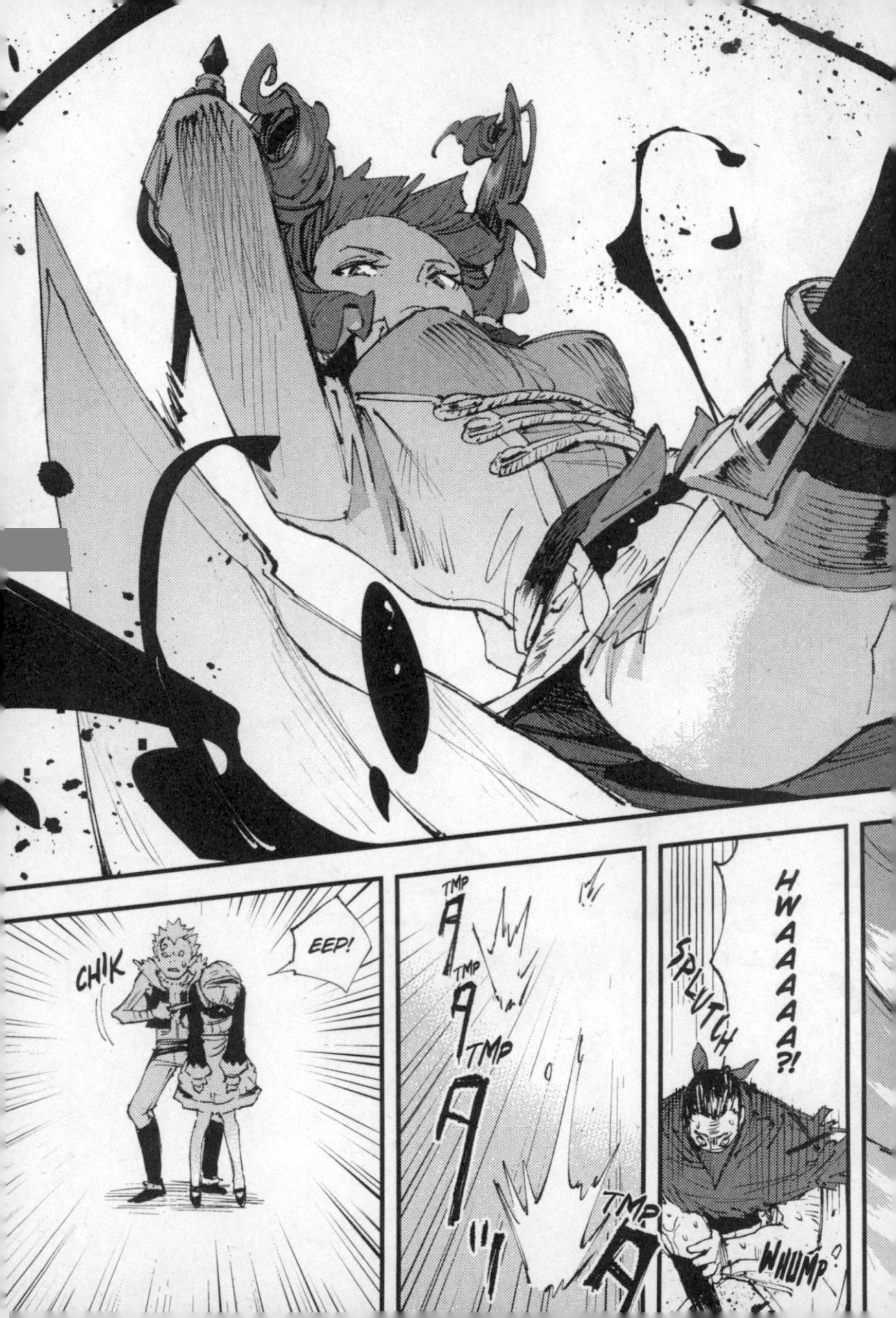
HWAAAAAA?!
SPLUTCH
WHUMP
TMP
TMP
TMP
TMP
EEP!
CHIK

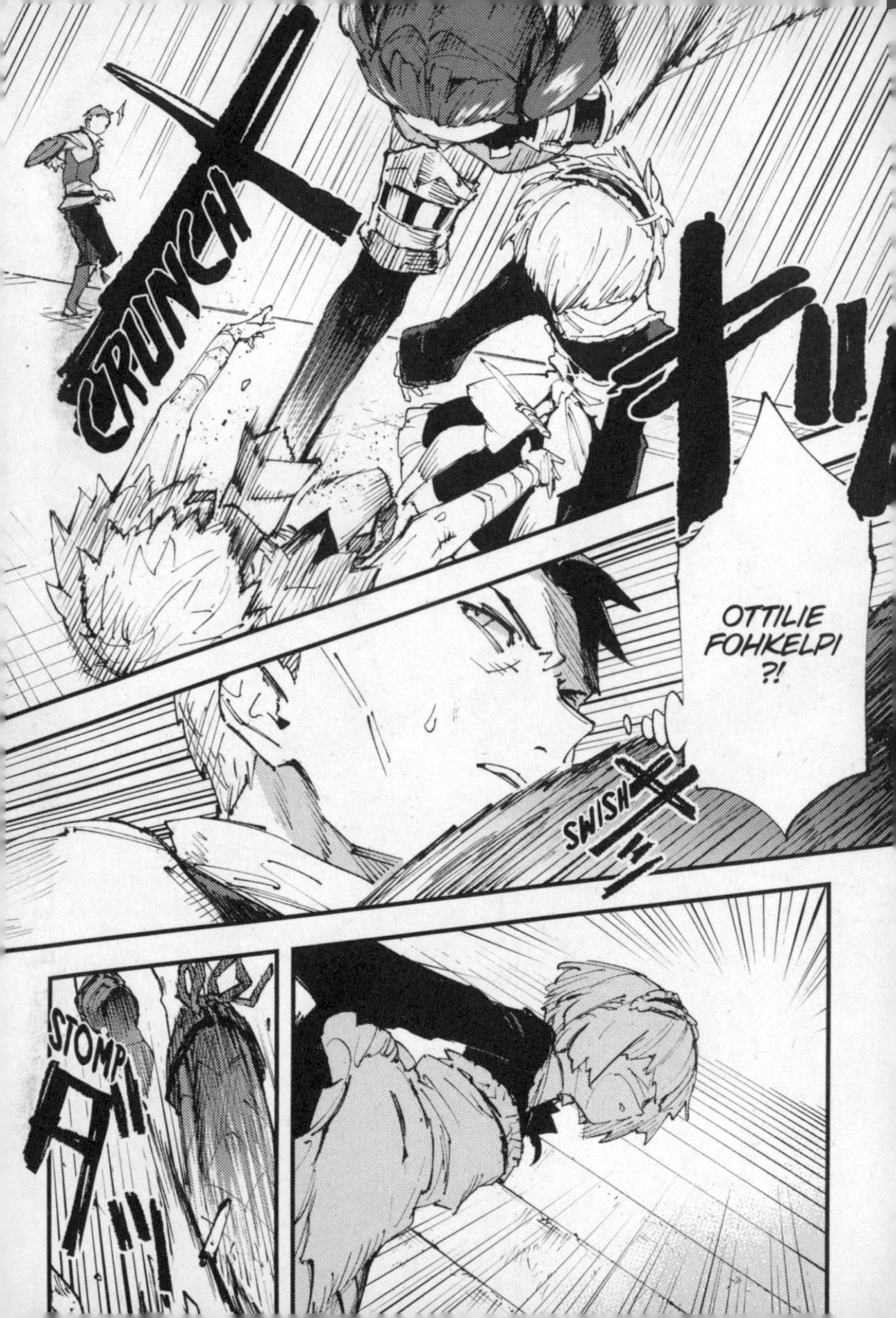
CRUNCH
OTTILIE FOHKELPI ?!
SWISH
STOMP

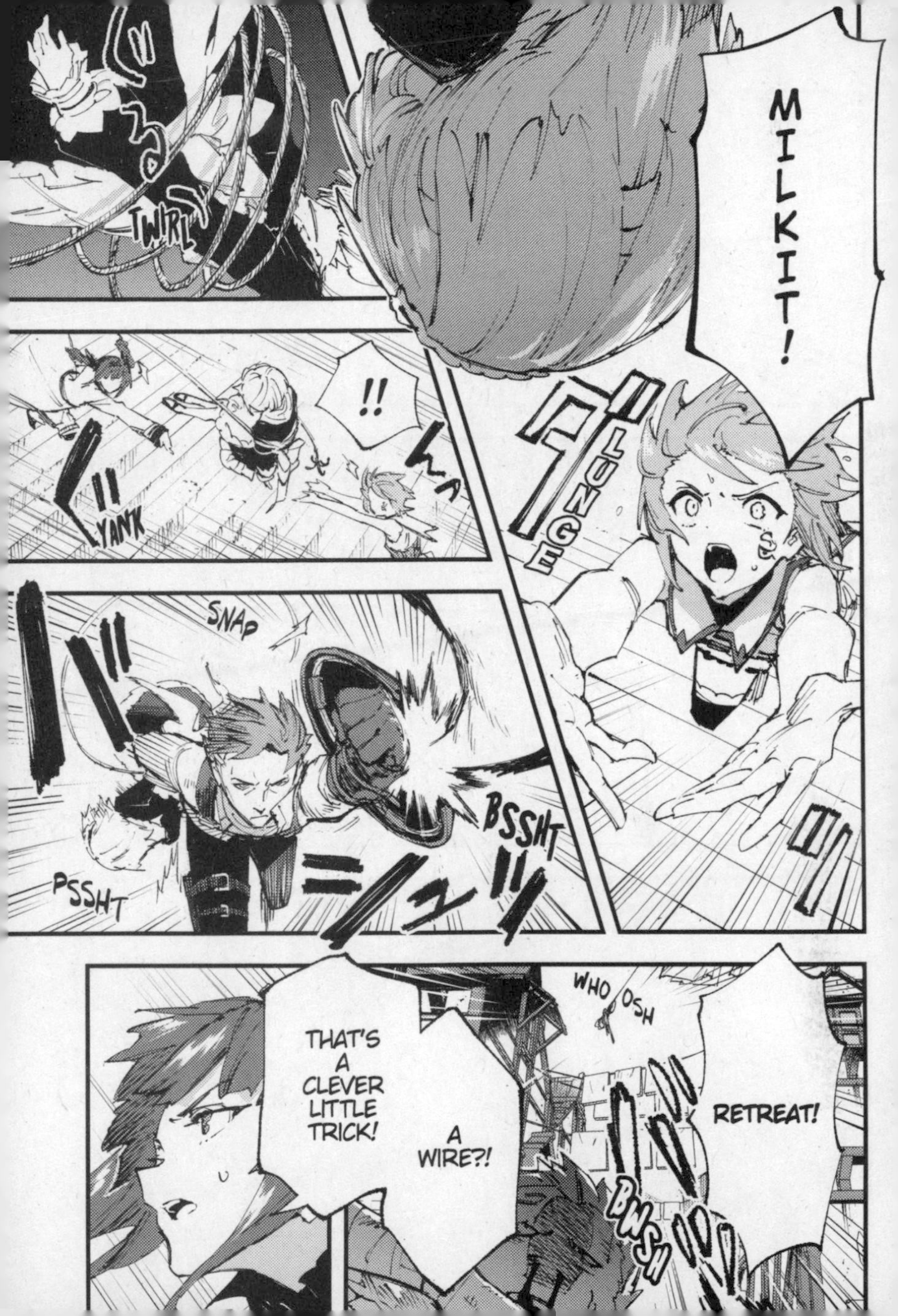

MILKIT!
LUNGE
TWIRL
!!
YANK
SNAP
BSSHT
PSSHT
WHOOSH
RETREAT!
THAT'S A CLEVER LITTLE TRICK!
A WIRE?!
BWSH

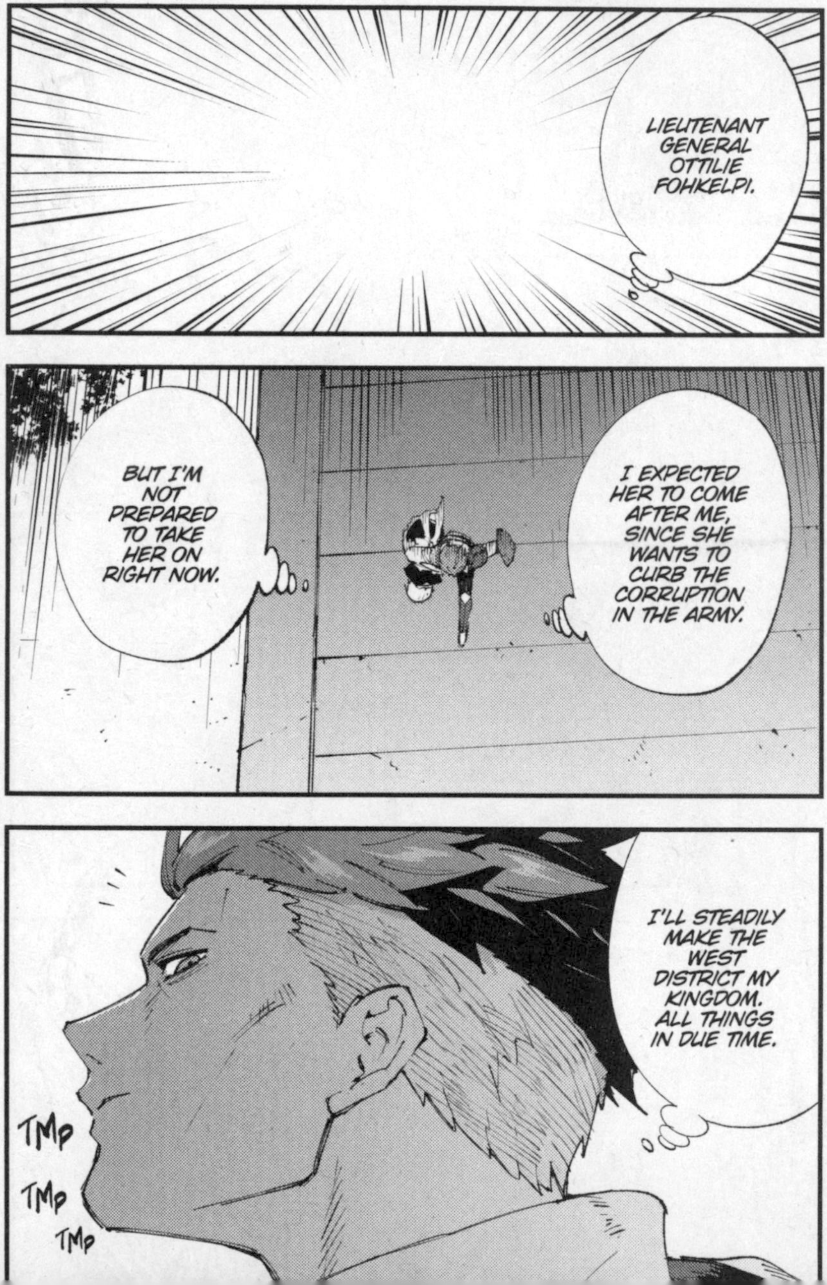
LIEUTENANT GENERAL OTTILIE FOHKELPI.
I EXPECTED HER TO COME AFTER ME, SINCE SHE WANTS TO CURB THE CORRUPTION IN THE ARMY.
BUT I'M NOT PREPARED TO TAKE HER ON RIGHT NOW.
I'LL STEADILY MAKE THE WEST DISTRICT MY KINGDOM. ALL THINGS IN DUE TIME.
TMP
TMP
TMP

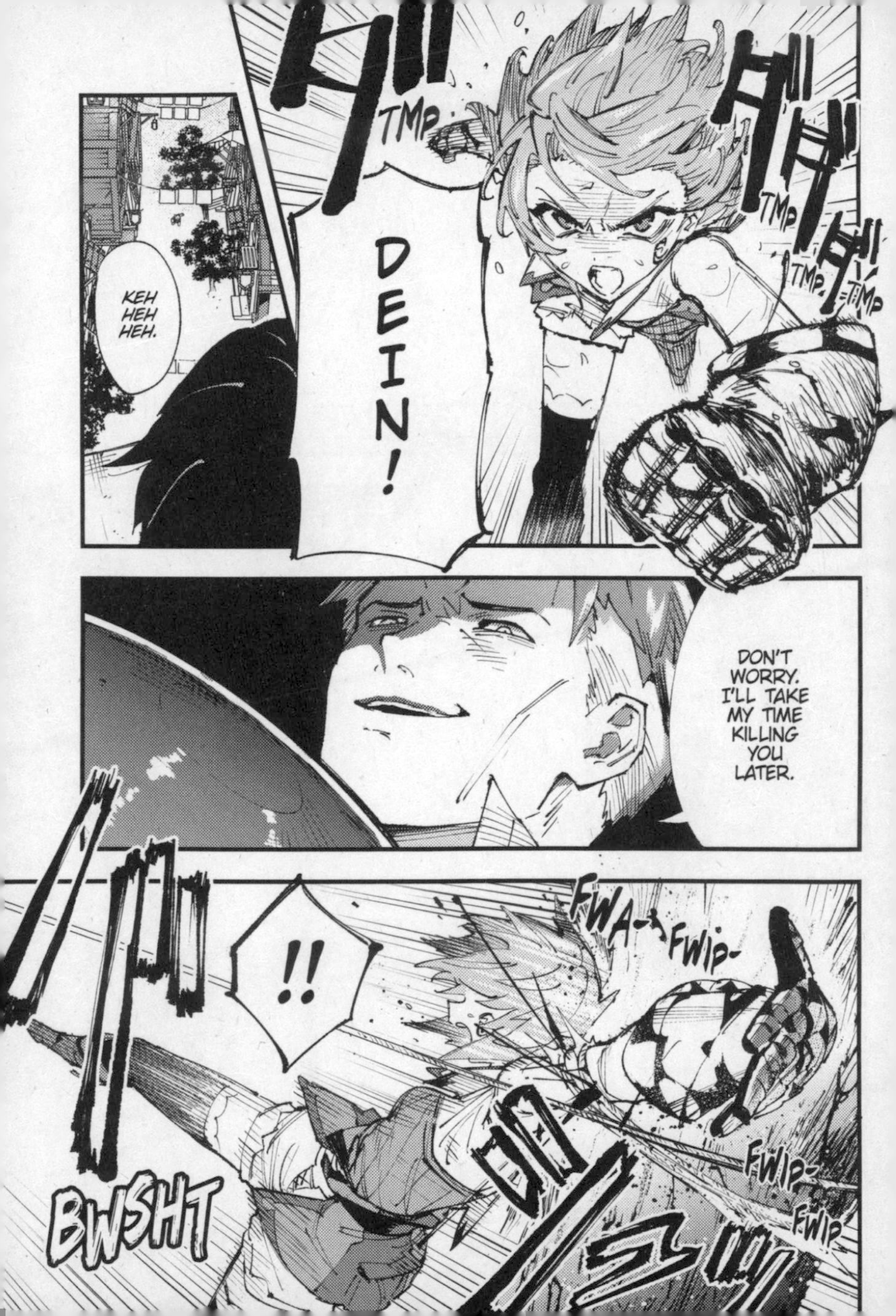
TMP
TMP
TMP
TMP
TMP
DEIN!
KEH HEH HEH.
DON'T WORRY. I'LL TAKE MY TIME KILLING YOU LATER.
!!
FWA-
FWIP-
FWIP-
FWIP-
BWSHT

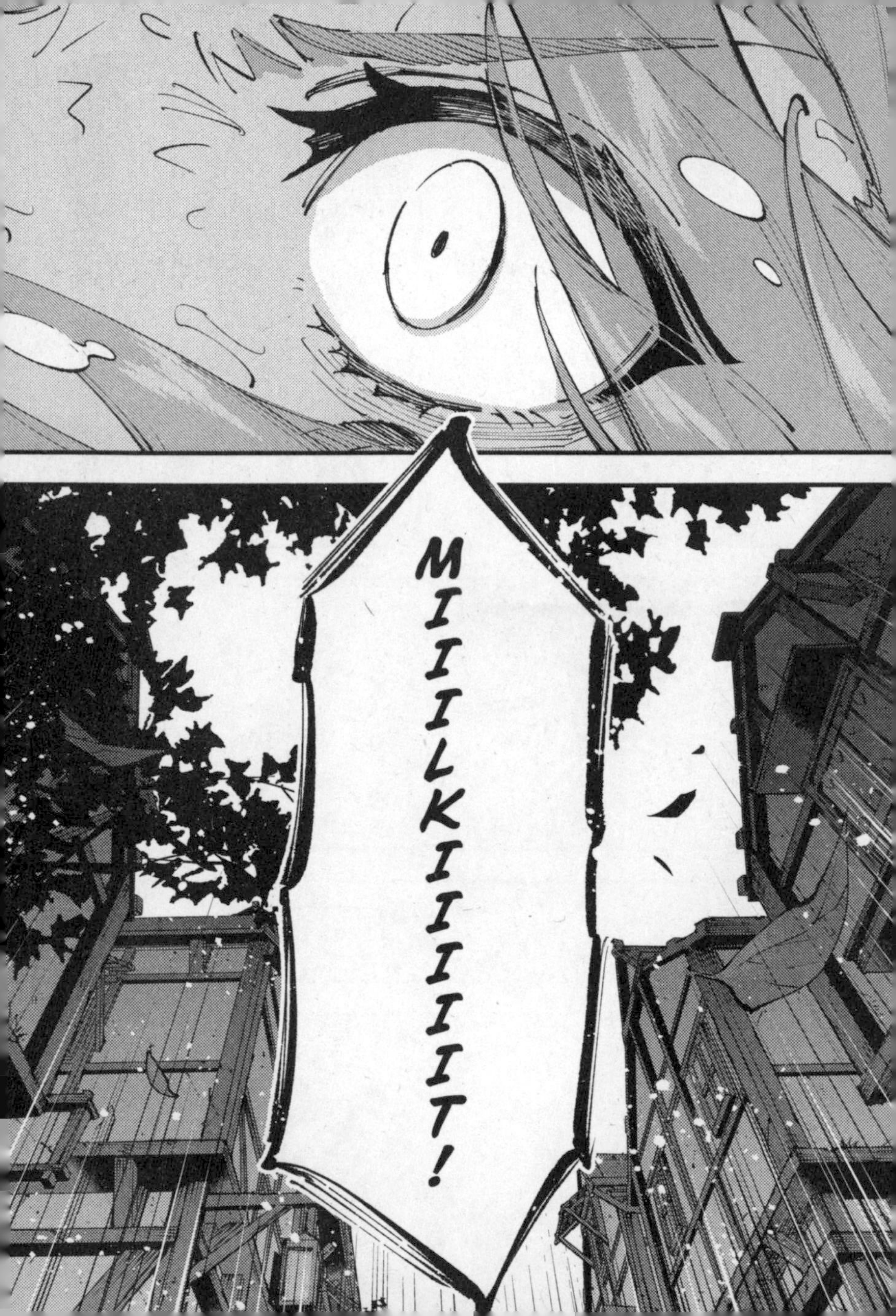
MIIILKIIIIIIIT!

Chapter 13: The Loyal Knight of Blood

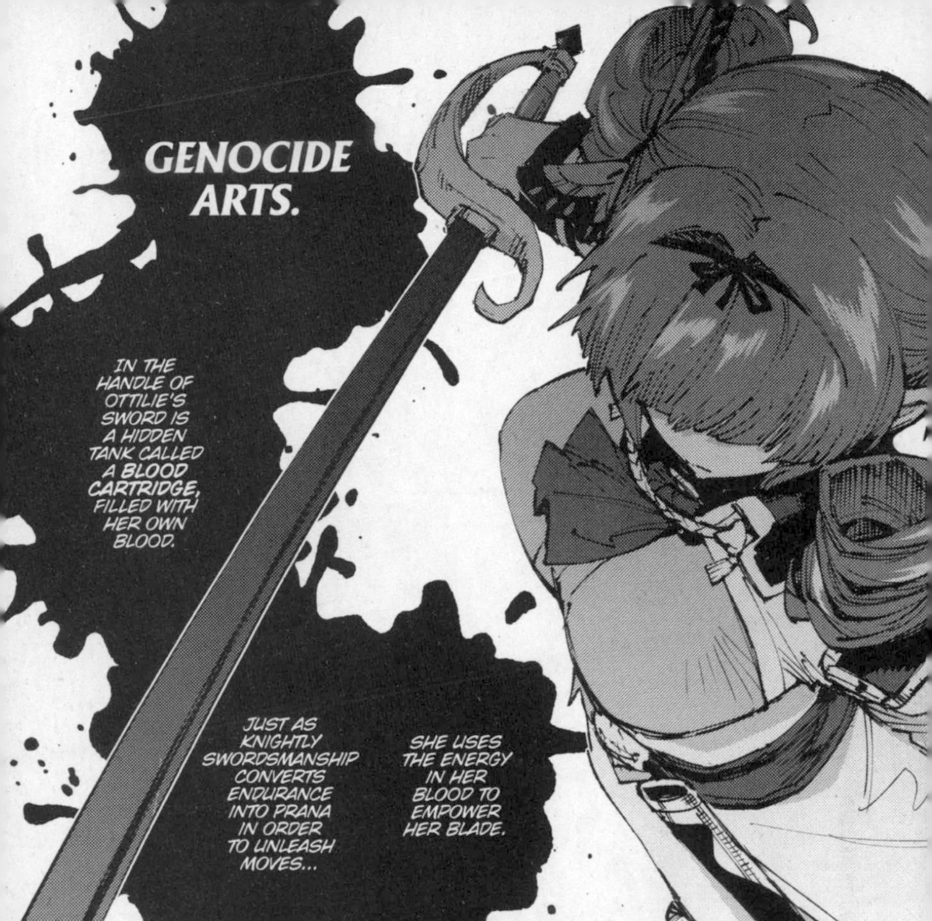
GENOCIDE ARTS.
IN THE HANDLE OF OTTILIE'S SWORD IS A HIDDEN TANK CALLED A **BLOOD CARTRIDGE,** FILLED WITH HER OWN BLOOD.
JUST AS KNIGHTLY SWORDSMANSHIP CONVERTS ENDURANCE INTO PRANA IN ORDER TO UNLEASH MOVES...
SHE USES THE ENERGY IN HER BLOOD TO EMPOWER HER BLADE.

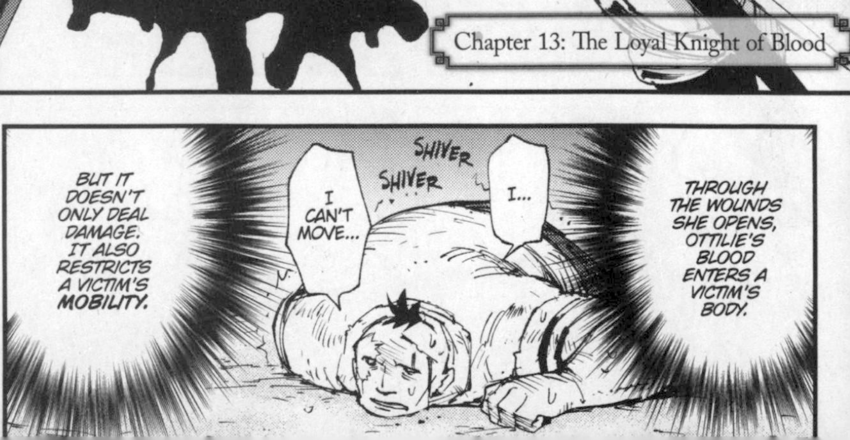
THROUGH THE WOUNDS SHE OPENS, OTTILIE'S BLOOD ENTERS A VICTIM'S BODY.
I...
SHIVER
SHIVER
I CAN'T MOVE...
BUT IT DOESN'T ONLY DEAL DAMAGE. IT ALSO RESTRICTS A VICTIM'S **MOBILITY.**

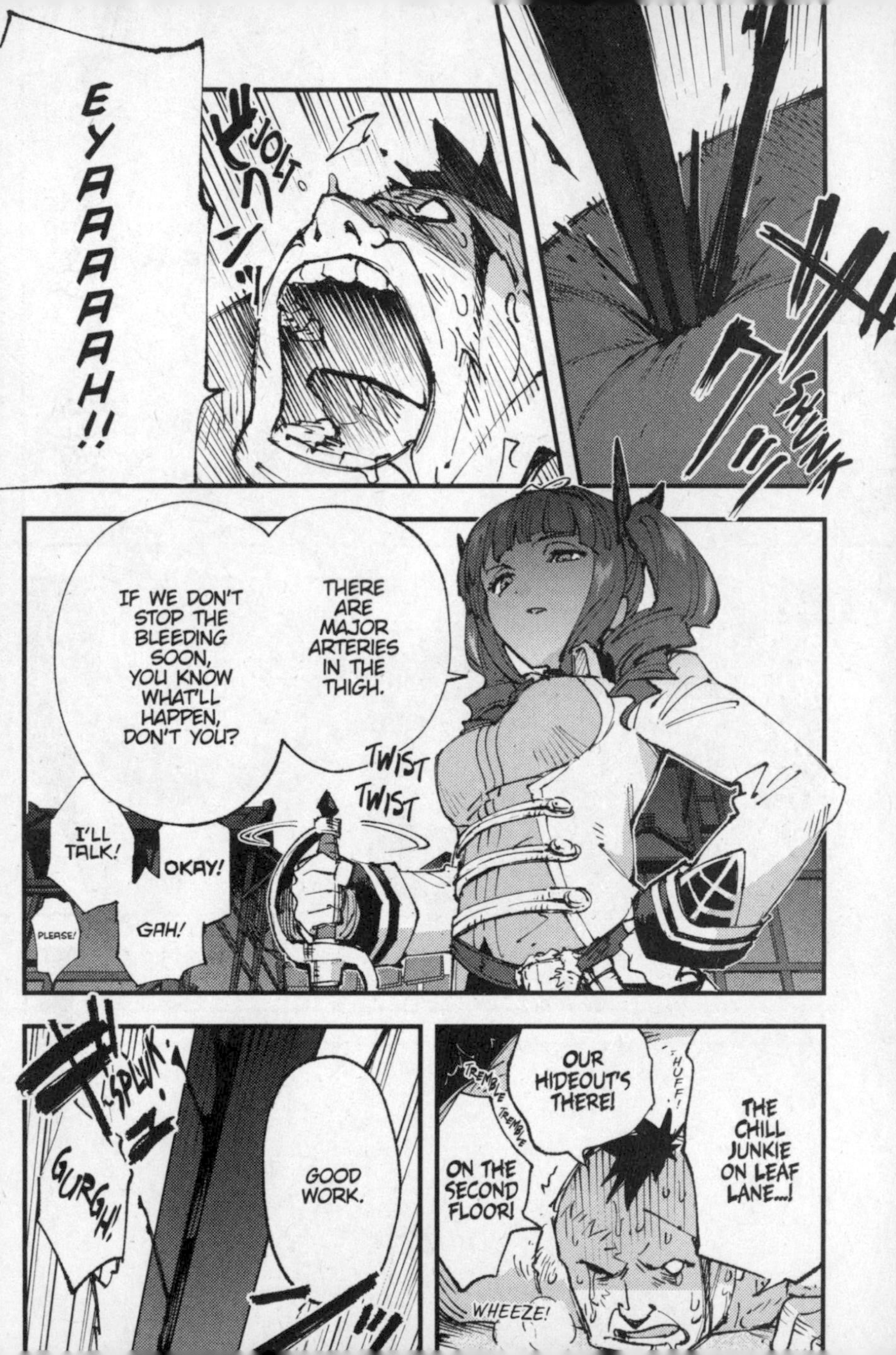
SHUNK
JOLT
EYAAAAAAAH!!
THERE ARE MAJOR ARTERIES IN THE THIGH.
IF WE DON'T STOP THE BLEEDING SOON, YOU KNOW WHAT'LL HAPPEN, DON'T YOU?
TWIST TWIST
OKAY!
I'LL TALK!
GAH!
PLEASE!
THE CHILL JUNKIE ON LEAF LANE...!
HUFF!
OUR HIDEOUT'S THERE!
TREMBLE TREMBLE
ON THE SECOND FLOOR!
WHEEZE!
GOOD WORK.
SPLUK
GURGH!

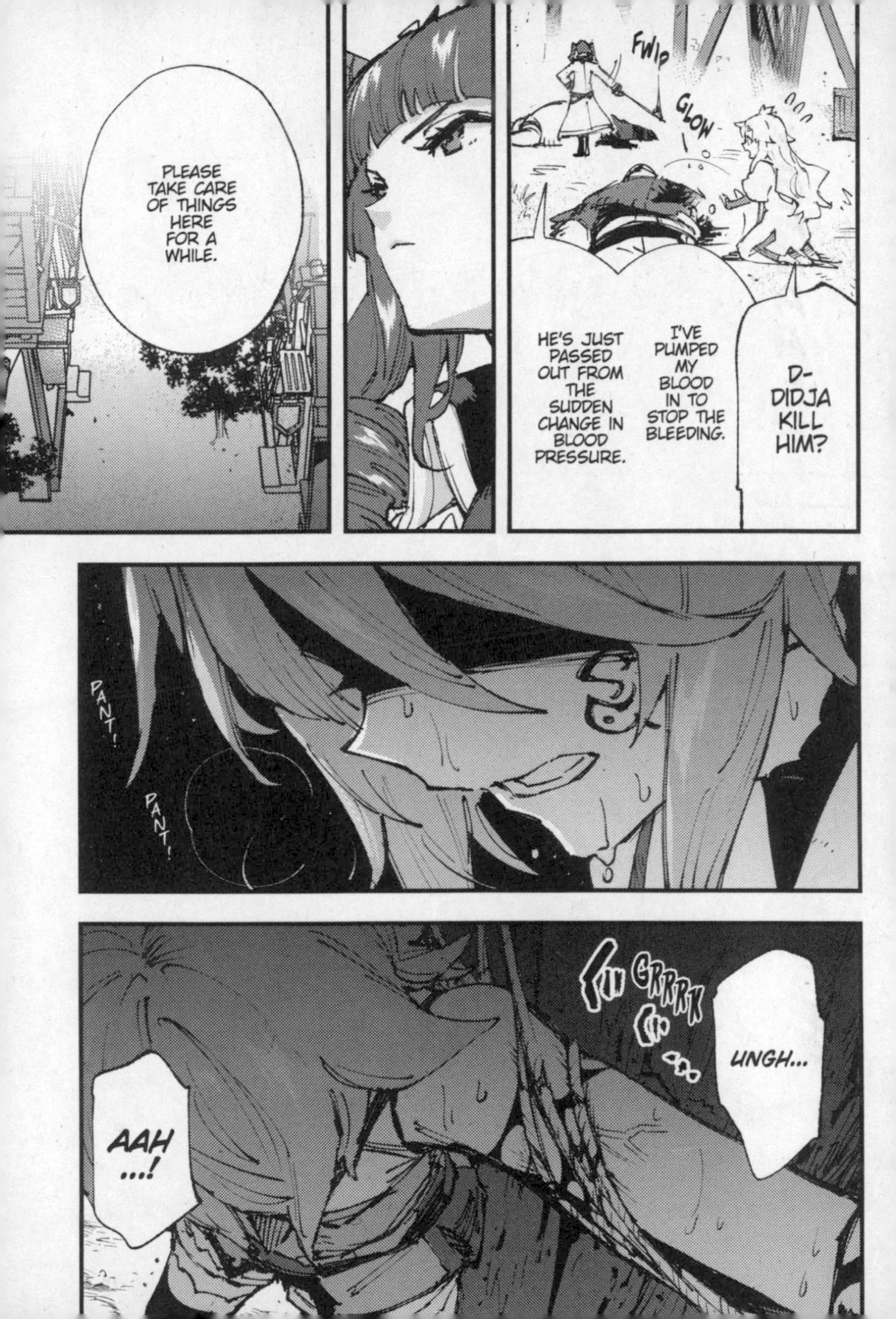
FWIP
GLOW
D-DIDJA KILL HIM?
I'VE PUMPED MY BLOOD IN TO STOP THE BLEEDING.
HE'S JUST PASSED OUT FROM THE SUDDEN CHANGE IN BLOOD PRESSURE.
PLEASE TAKE CARE OF THINGS HERE FOR A WHILE.
PANT!
PANT!
UNGH...
GRRRK
AAH ...!

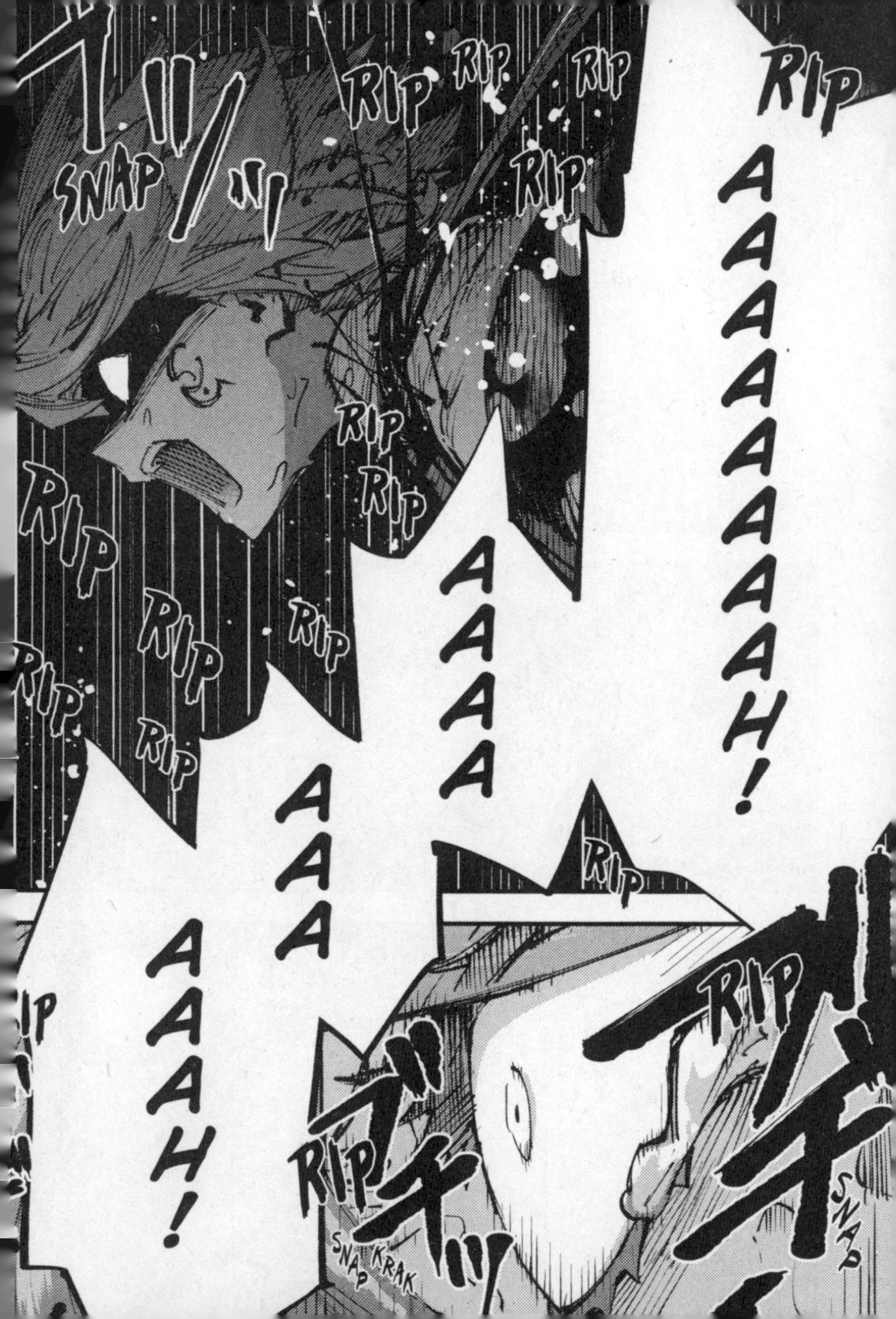
RIP
AAAAAAAAAAAH!
RIP
RIP
RIP
RIP
SNAP
RIP
RIP
RIP
AAAA
AAA
AAAAH!
RIP
RIP
RIP
RIP
RIP
RIP
RIP
SNAP
RIP
SNAP
KRAK

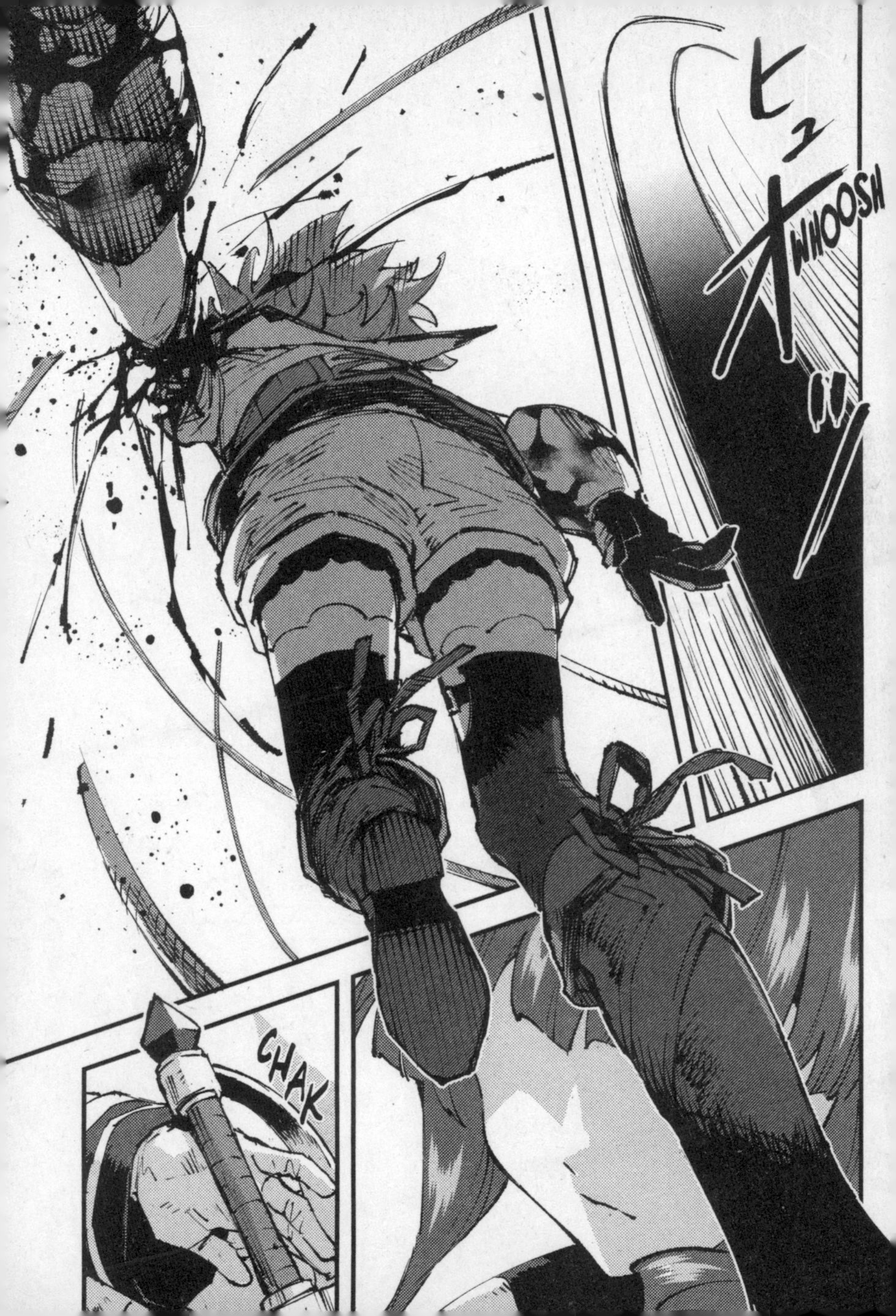
ヒュオ
WHOOSH
CHAK

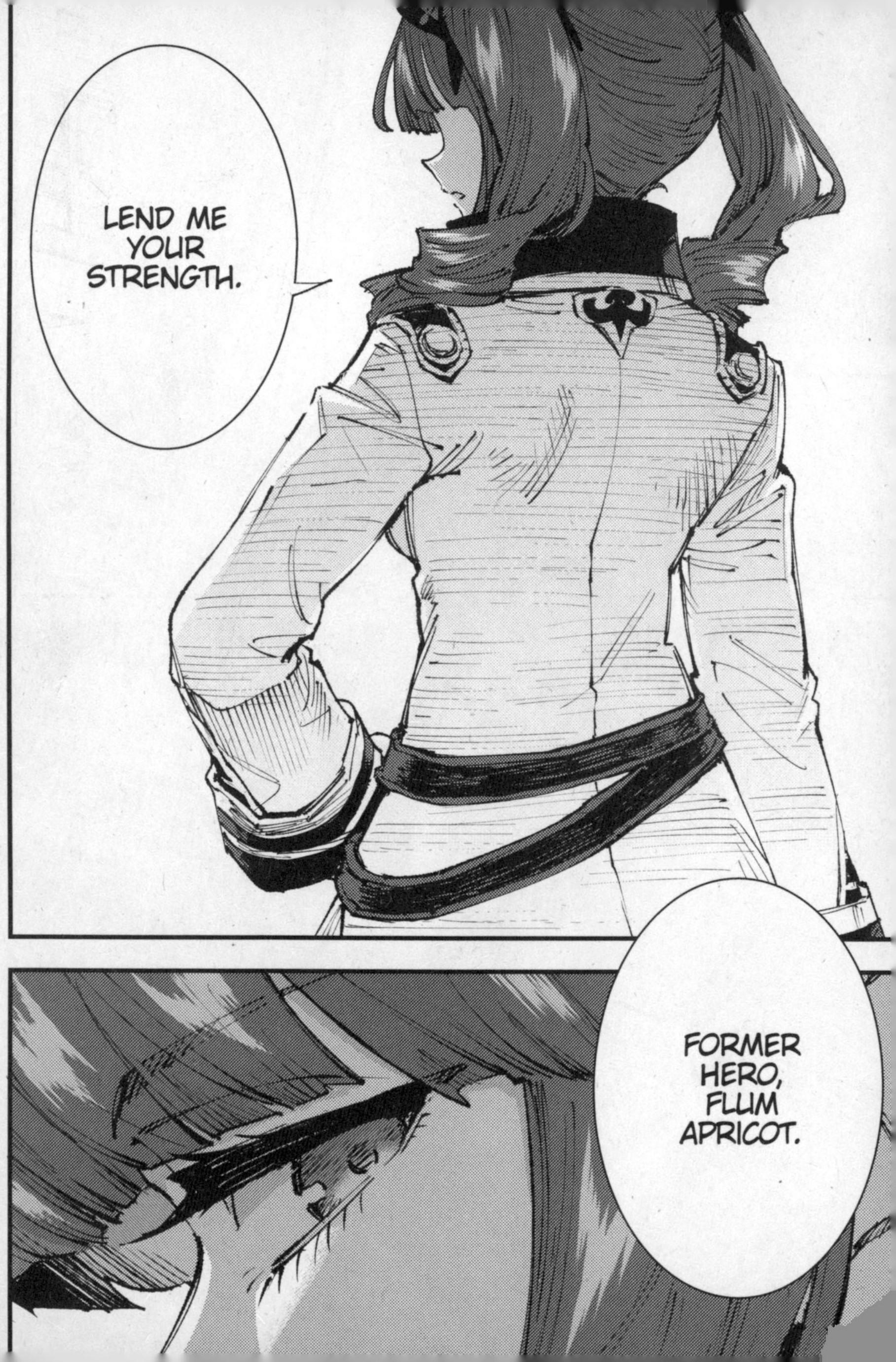
LEND ME YOUR STRENGTH.
FORMER HERO, FLUM APRICOT.

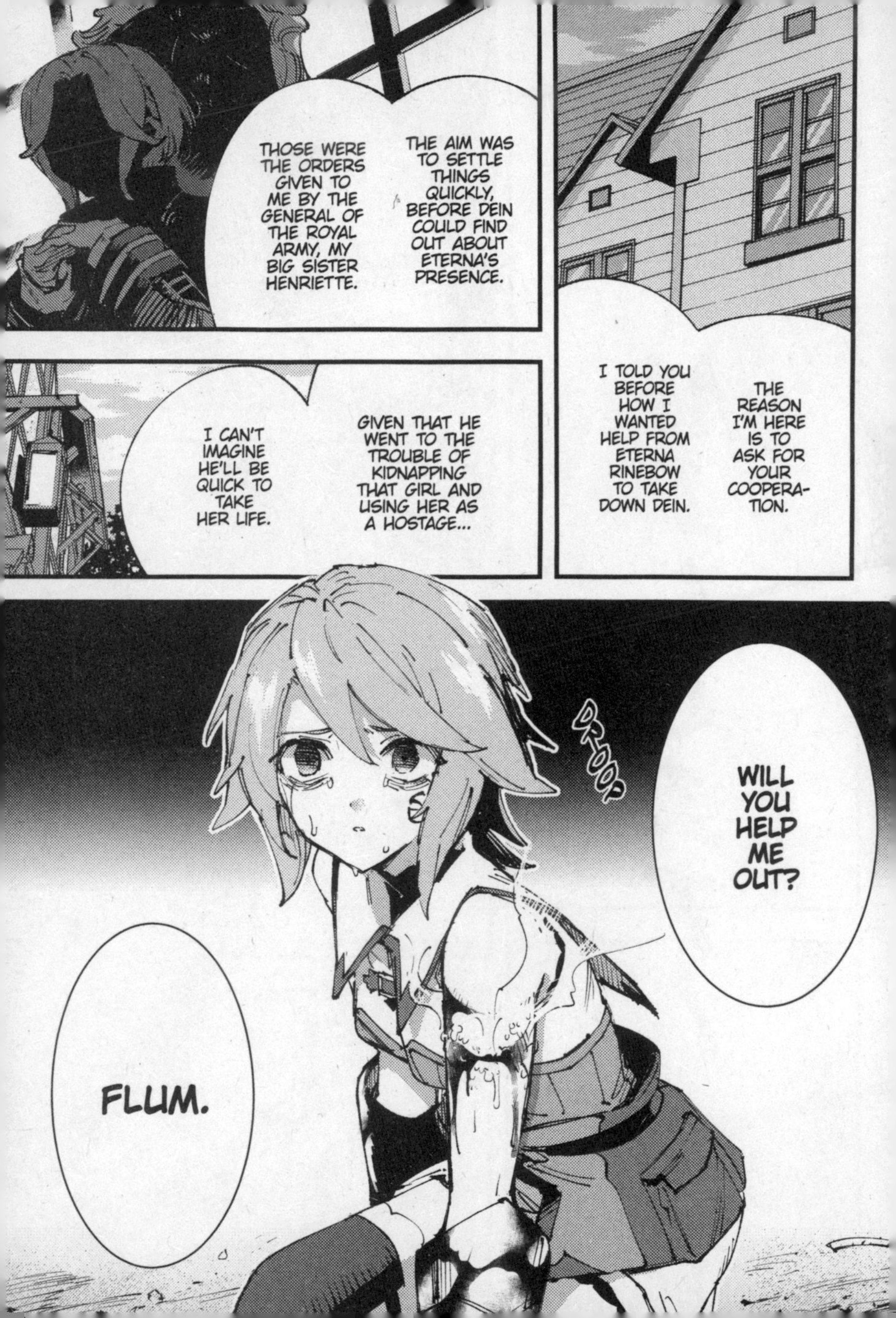
THE REASON I'M HERE IS TO ASK FOR YOUR COOPERATION.
I TOLD YOU BEFORE HOW I WANTED HELP FROM ETERNA RINEBOW TO TAKE DOWN DEIN.
THE AIM WAS TO SETTLE THINGS QUICKLY, BEFORE DEIN COULD FIND OUT ABOUT ETERNA'S PRESENCE.
THOSE WERE THE ORDERS GIVEN TO ME BY THE GENERAL OF THE ROYAL ARMY, MY BIG SISTER HENRIETTE.
GIVEN THAT HE WENT TO THE TROUBLE OF KIDNAPPING THAT GIRL AND USING HER AS A HOSTAGE...
I CAN'T IMAGINE HE'LL BE QUICK TO TAKE HER LIFE.
DROOP
WILL YOU HELP ME OUT?
FLUM.

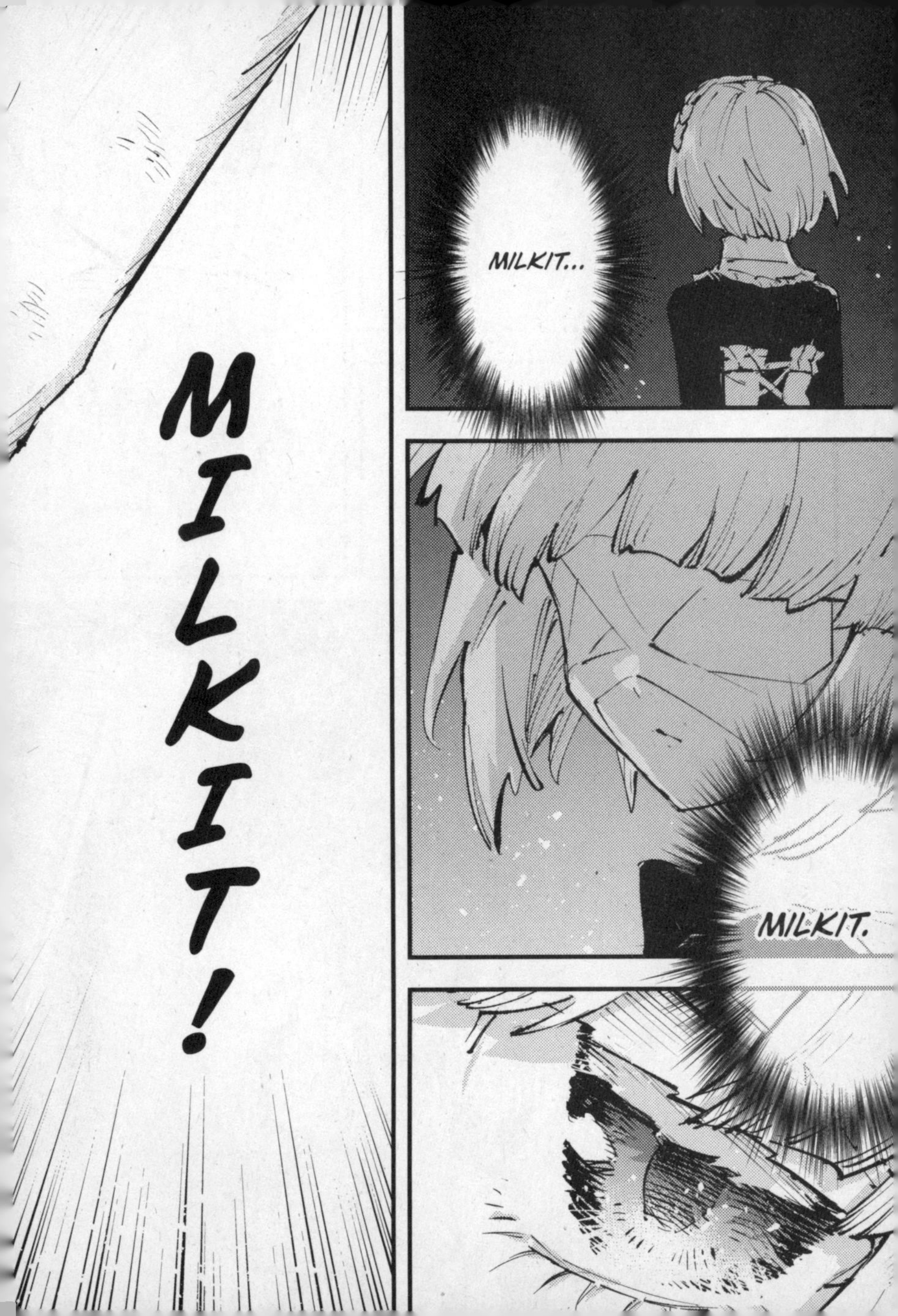
MILKIT...
MILKIT.
MILKIT!

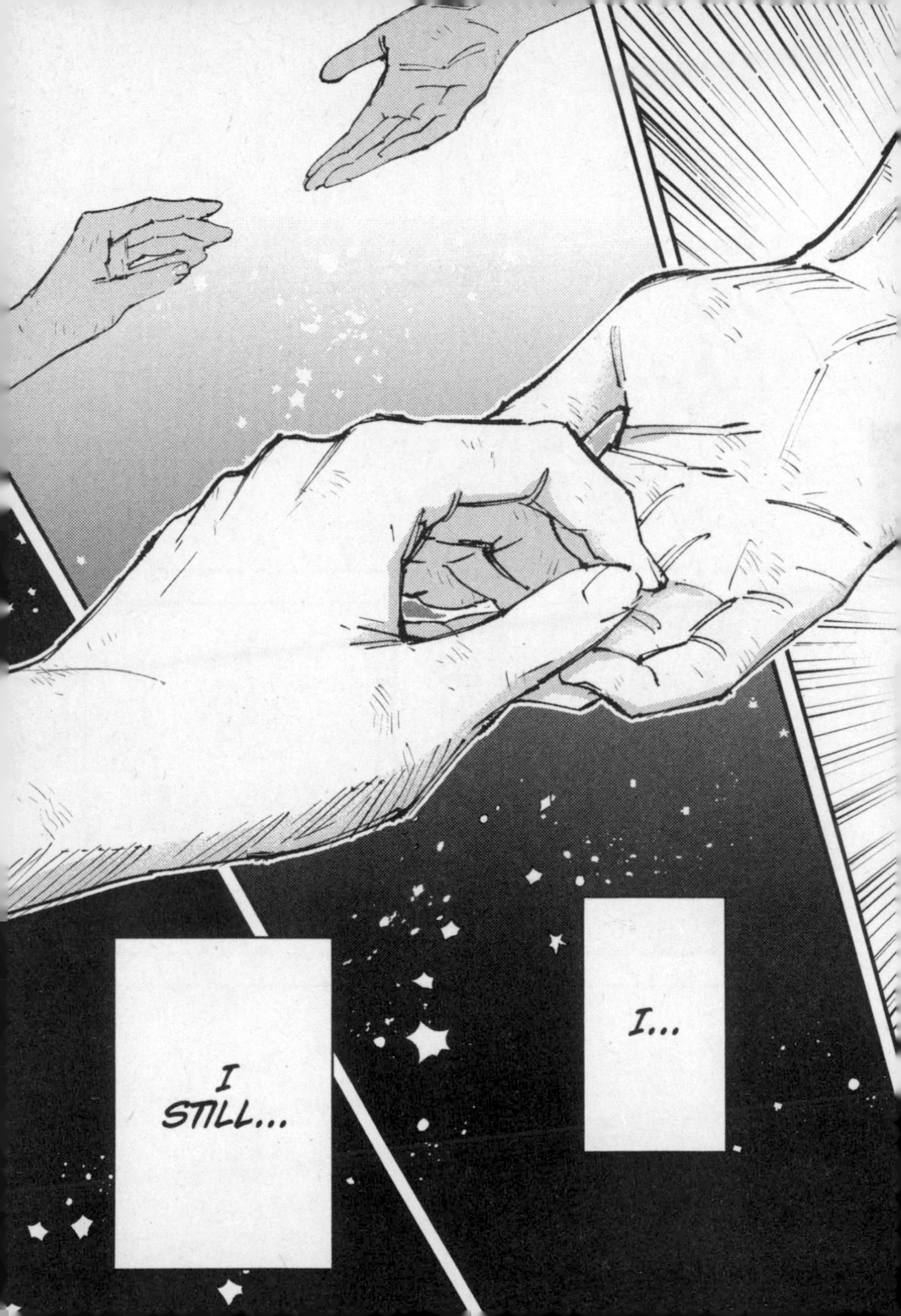
I...
I STILL...

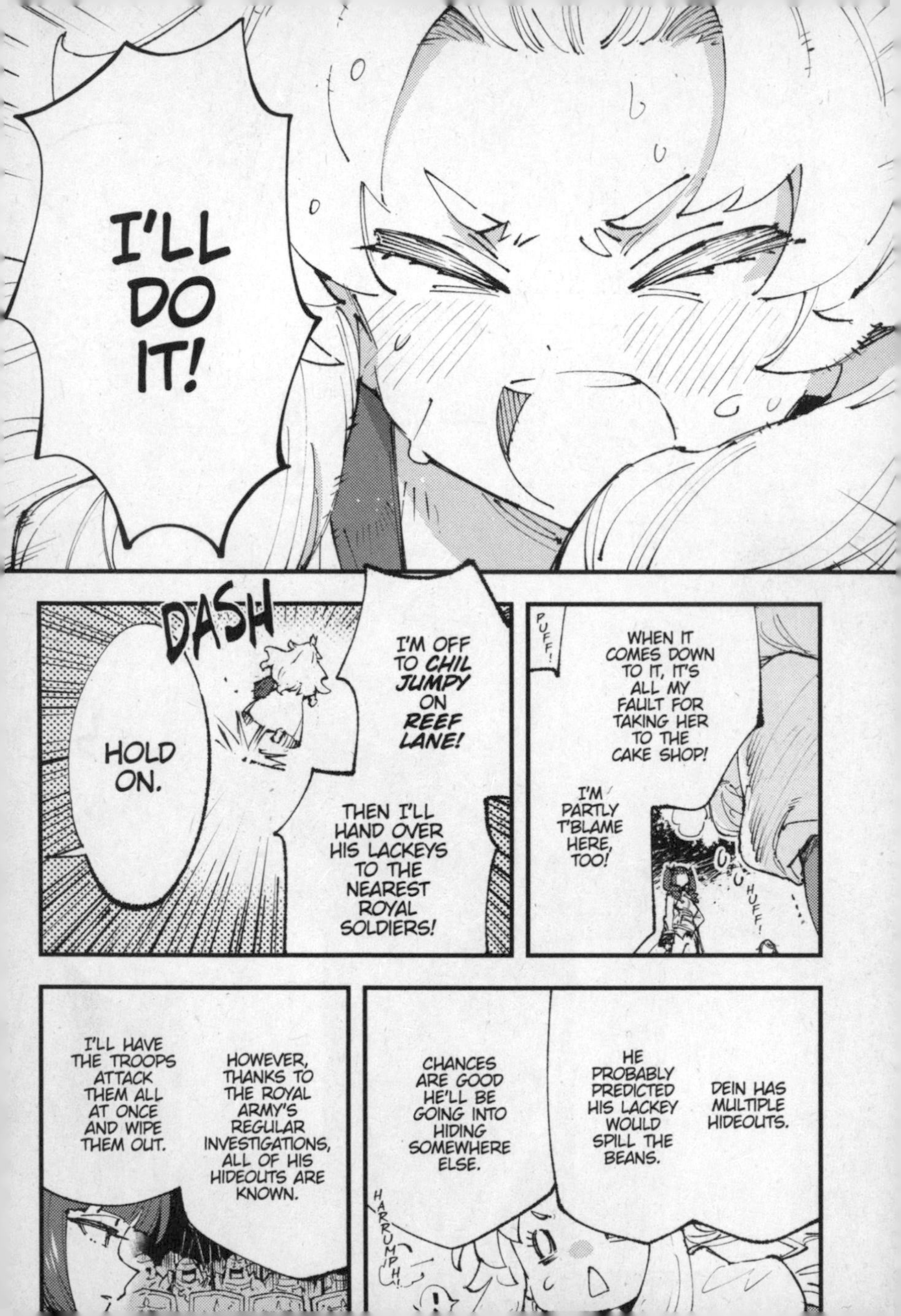
I'LL DO IT!
PUFF!
WHEN IT COMES DOWN TO IT, IT'S ALL MY FAULT FOR TAKING HER TO THE CAKE SHOP!
I'M PARTLY T'BLAME HERE, TOO!
HUFF!
I'M OFF TO CHIL JUMPY ON REEF LANE!
THEN I'LL HAND OVER HIS LACKEYS TO THE NEAREST ROYAL SOLDIERS!
DASH
HOLD ON.
DEIN HAS MULTIPLE HIDEOUTS.
HE PROBABLY PREDICTED HIS LACKEY WOULD SPILL THE BEANS.
CHANCES ARE GOOD HE'LL BE GOING INTO HIDING SOMEWHERE ELSE.
HARRUMPH!
HOWEVER, THANKS TO THE ROYAL ARMY'S REGULAR INVESTIGATIONS, ALL OF HIS HIDEOUTS ARE KNOWN.
I'LL HAVE THE TROOPS ATTACK THEM ALL AT ONCE AND WIPE THEM OUT.

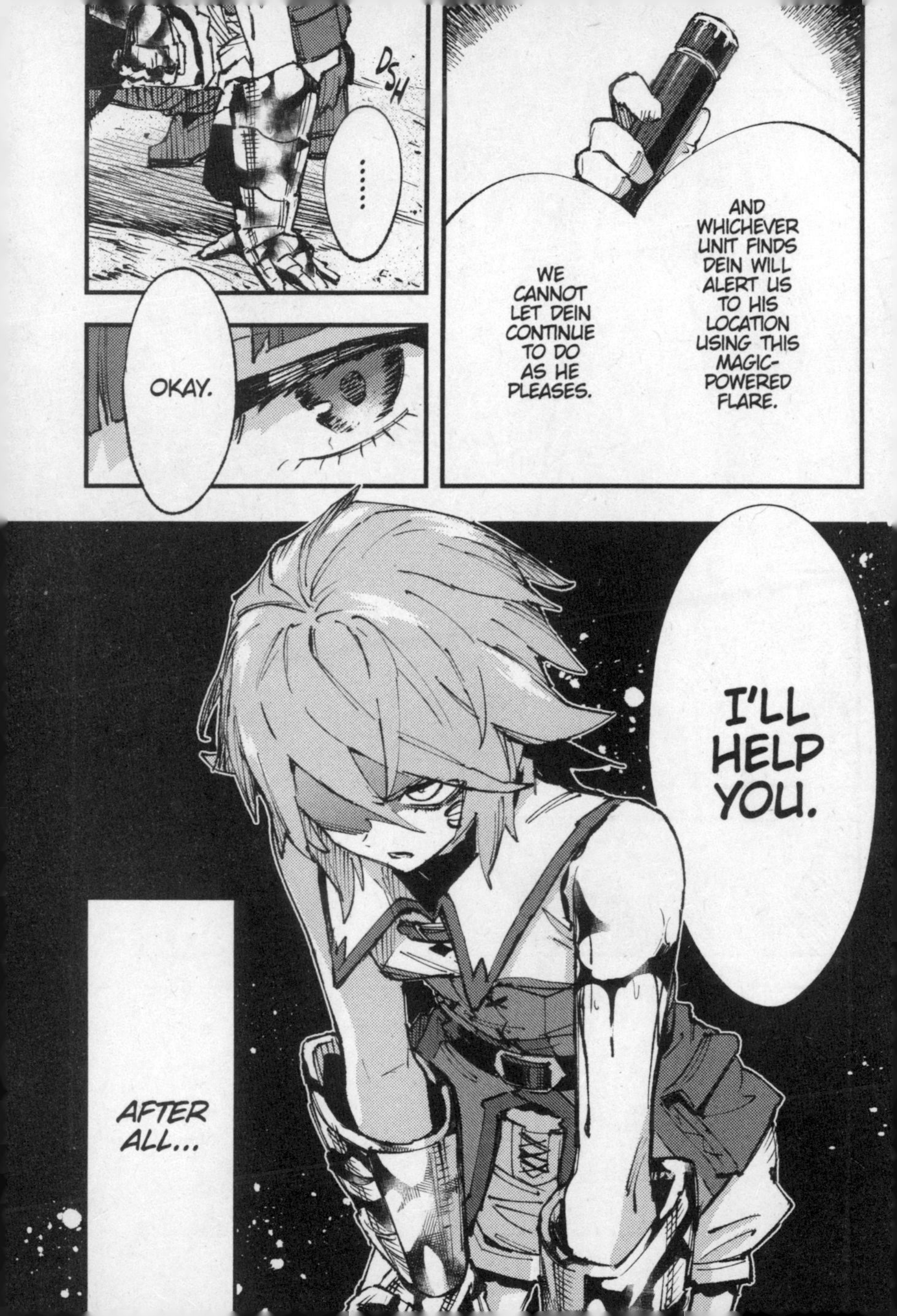
AND WHICHEVER UNIT FINDS DEIN WILL ALERT US TO HIS LOCATION USING THIS MAGIC-POWERED FLARE.
WE CANNOT LET DEIN CONTINUE TO DO AS HE PLEASES.
DSH
......
OKAY.
I'LL HELP YOU.
AFTER ALL...

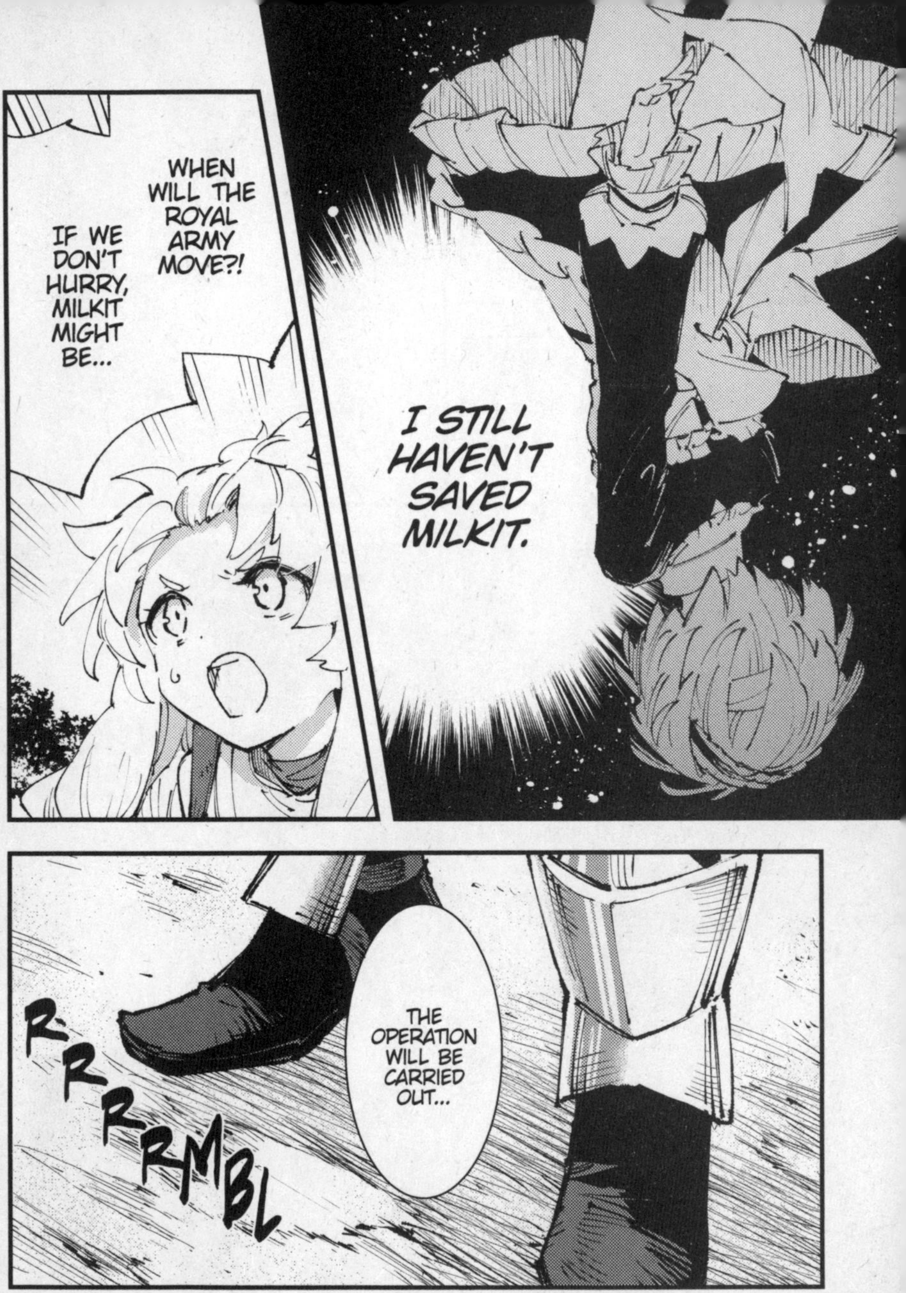
I STILL HAVEN'T SAVED MILKIT.
WHEN WILL THE ROYAL ARMY MOVE?!
IF WE DON'T HURRY, MILKIT MIGHT BE...
THE OPERATION WILL BE CARRIED OUT...
R-RRRRMBL

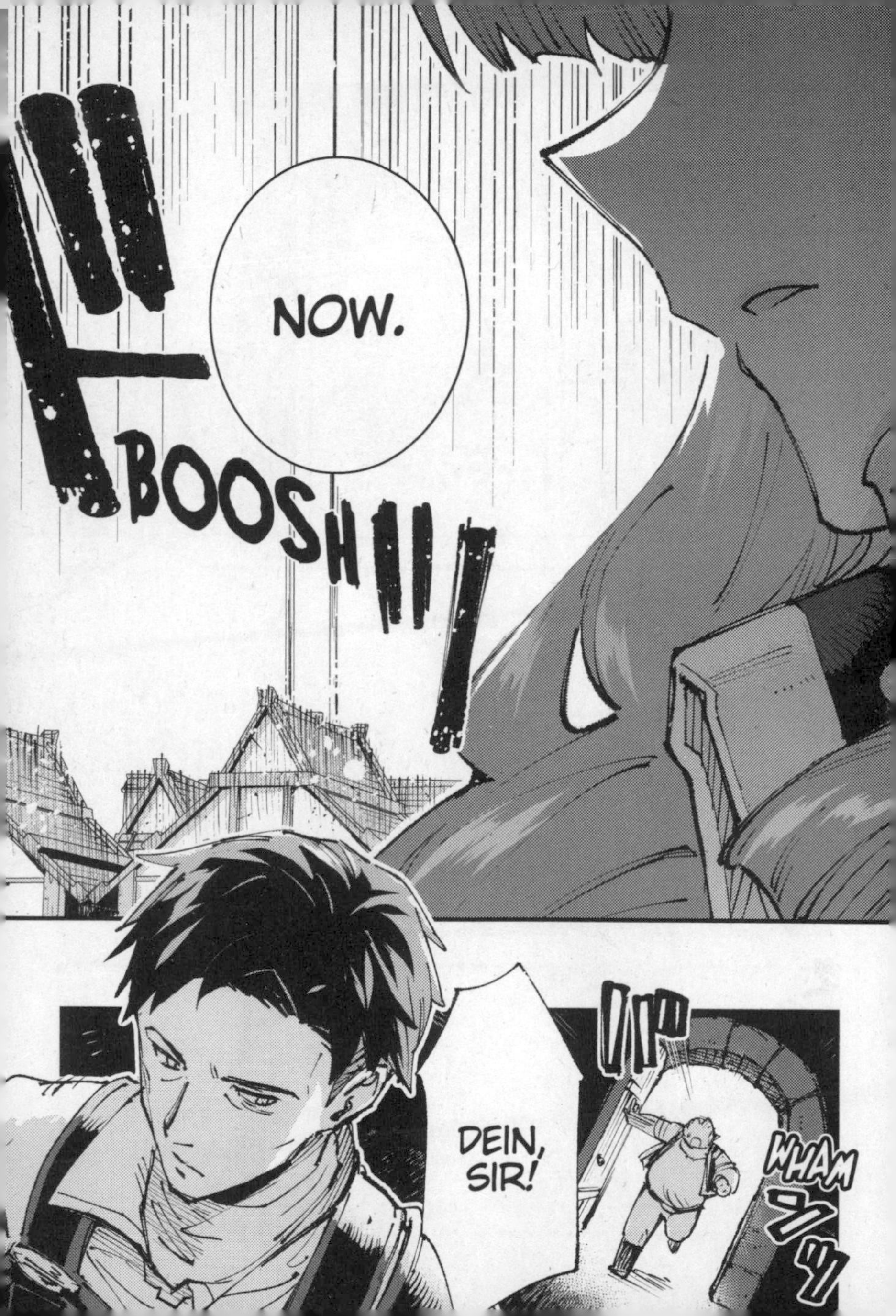
NOW.
BOOSH
DEIN, SIR!
WHAM

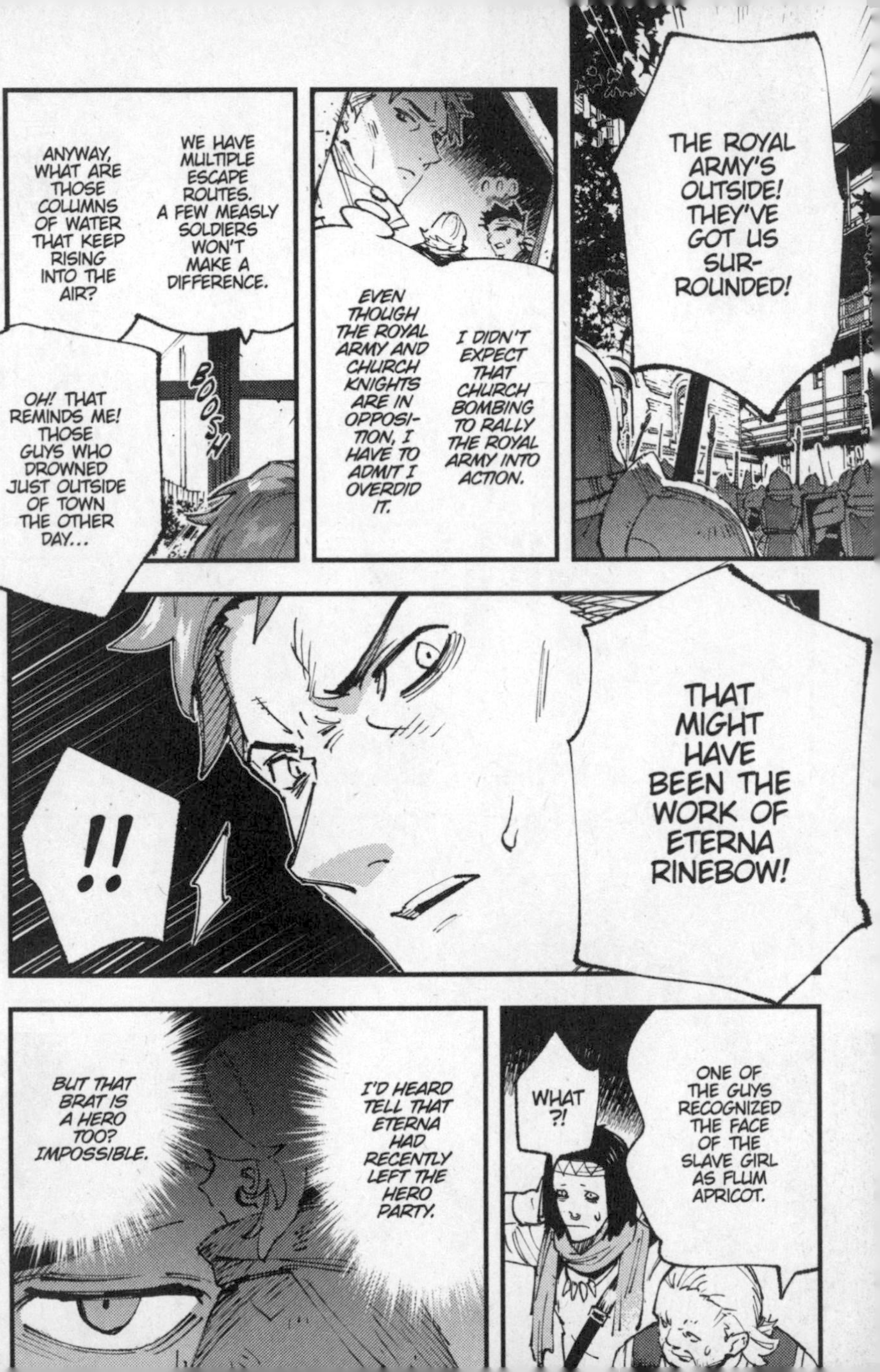
THE ROYAL ARMY'S OUTSIDE! THEY'VE GOT US SUR-ROUNDED!
I DIDN'T EXPECT THAT CHURCH BOMBING TO RALLY THE ROYAL ARMY INTO ACTION.
EVEN THOUGH THE ROYAL ARMY AND CHURCH KNIGHTS ARE IN OPPOSI-TION, I HAVE TO ADMIT I OVERDID IT.
WE HAVE MULTIPLE ESCAPE ROUTES. A FEW MEASLY SOLDIERS WON'T MAKE A DIFFERENCE.
ANYWAY, WHAT ARE THOSE COLUMNS OF WATER THAT KEEP RISING INTO THE AIR?
BOOSH
OH! THAT REMINDS ME! THOSE GUYS WHO DROWNED JUST OUTSIDE OF TOWN THE OTHER DAY...
THAT MIGHT HAVE BEEN THE WORK OF ETERNA RINEBOW!
!!
ONE OF THE GUYS RECOGNIZED THE FACE OF THE SLAVE GIRL AS FLUM APRICOT.
WHAT?!
I'D HEARD TELL THAT ETERNA HAD RECENTLY LEFT THE HERO PARTY.
BUT THAT BRAT IS A HERO TOO? IMPOSSIBLE.

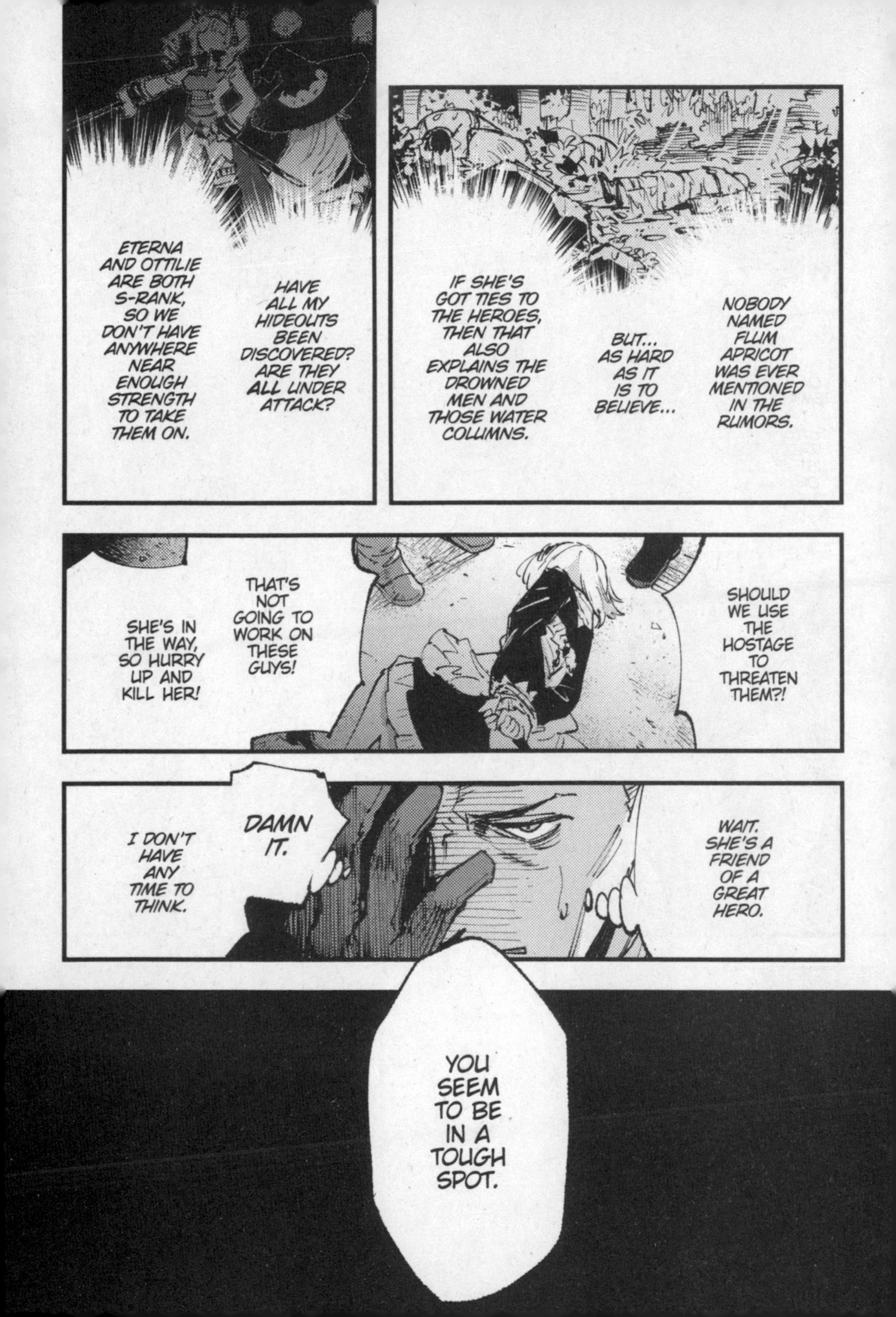
NOBODY NAMED FLUM APRICOT WAS EVER MENTIONED IN THE RUMORS.
BUT... AS HARD AS IT IS TO BELIEVE...
IF SHE'S GOT TIES TO THE HEROES, THEN THAT ALSO EXPLAINS THE DROWNED MEN AND THOSE WATER COLUMNS.
HAVE ALL MY HIDEOUTS BEEN DISCOVERED? ARE THEY ALL UNDER ATTACK?
ETERNA AND OTTILIE ARE BOTH S-RANK, SO WE DON'T HAVE ANYWHERE NEAR ENOUGH STRENGTH TO TAKE THEM ON.
SHOULD WE USE THE HOSTAGE TO THREATEN THEM?!
THAT'S NOT GOING TO WORK ON THESE GUYS!
SHE'S IN THE WAY, SO HURRY UP AND KILL HER!
WAIT. SHE'S A FRIEND OF A GREAT HERO.
DAMN IT.
I DON'T HAVE ANY TIME TO THINK.
YOU SEEM TO BE IN A TOUGH SPOT.

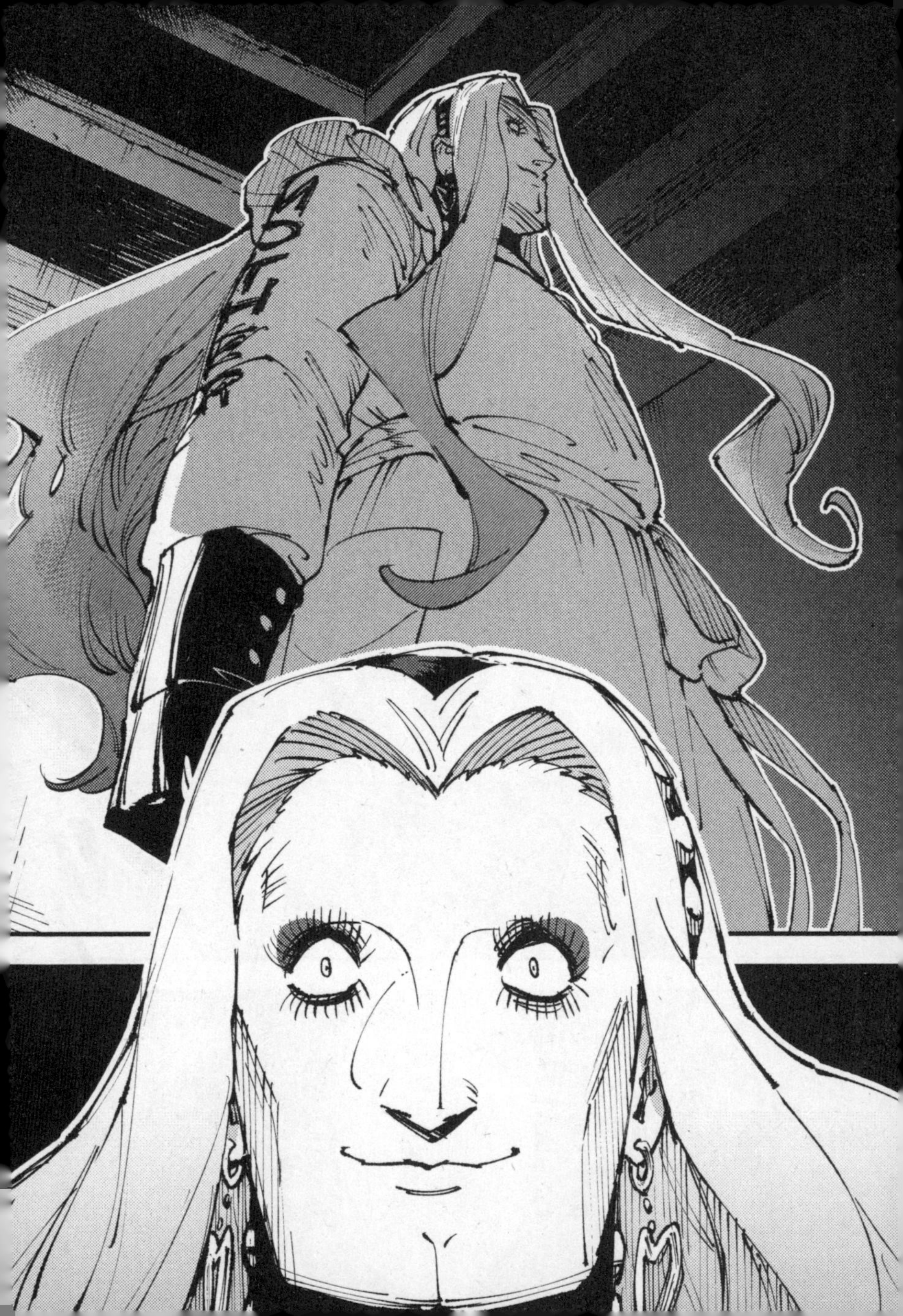

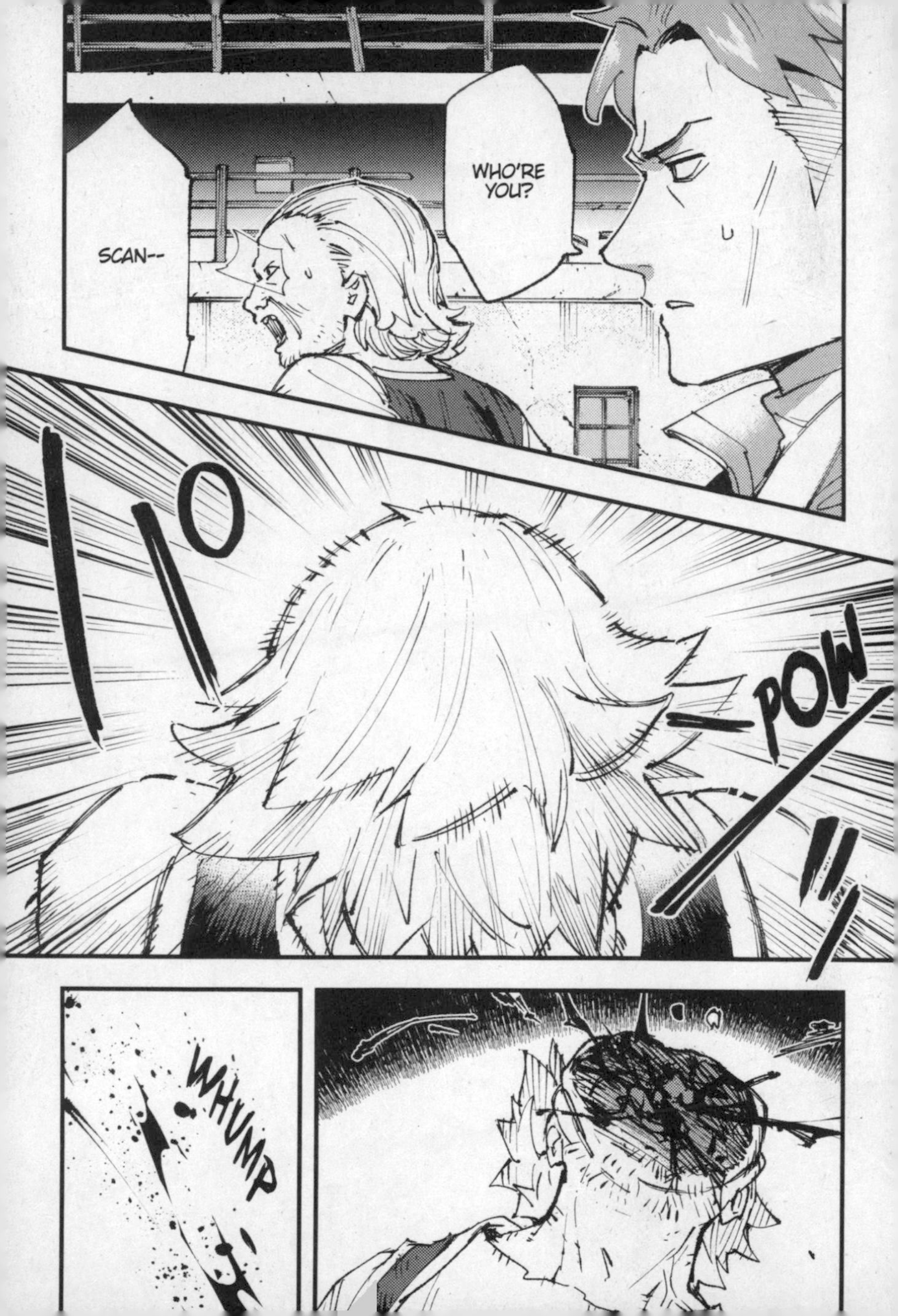
WHO'RE YOU?
SCAN--
POW
WHUMP

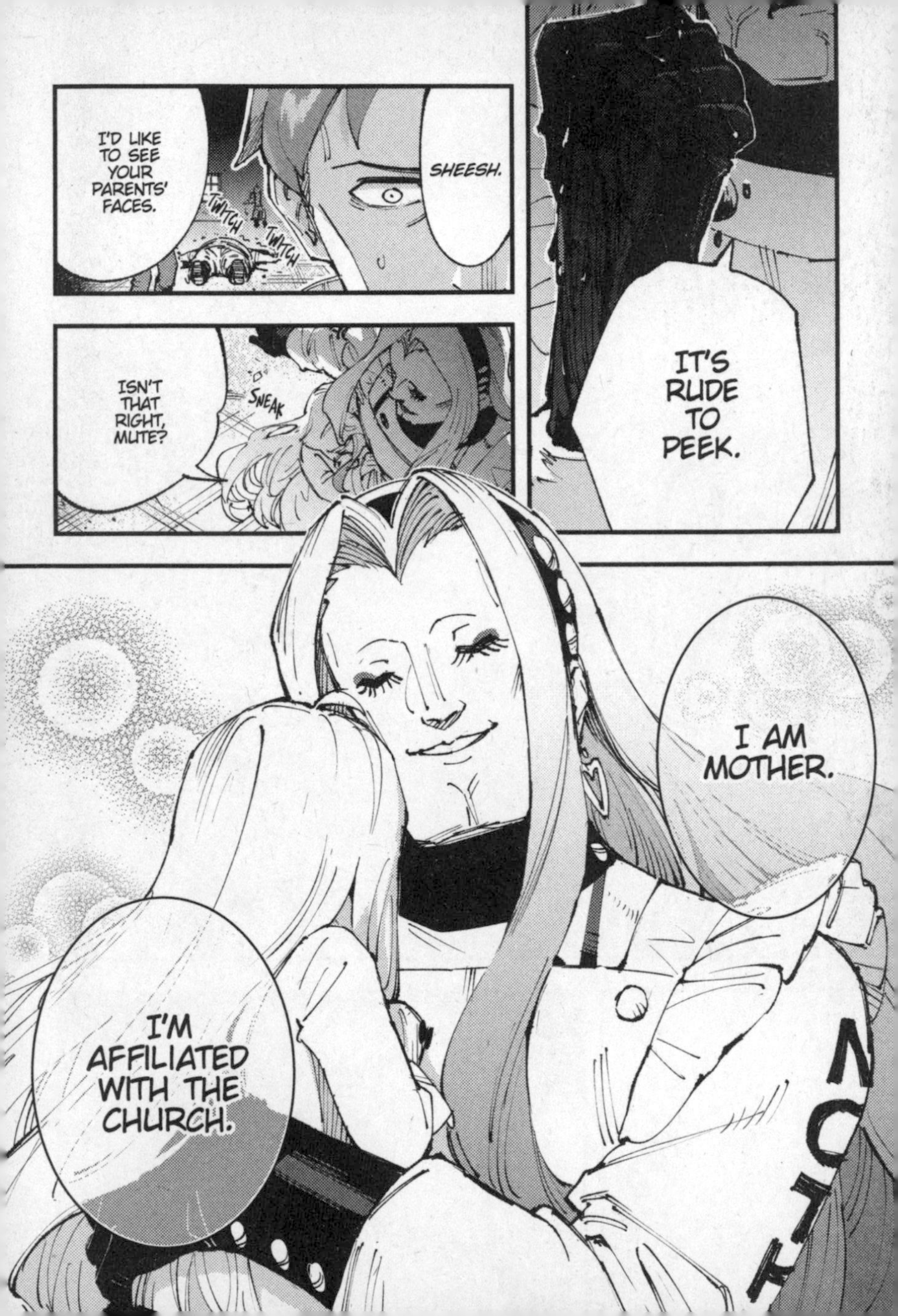
IT'S RUDE TO PEEK.
SHEESH.
TWITCH TWITCH
I'D LIKE TO SEE YOUR PARENTS' FACES.
SNEAK
ISN'T THAT RIGHT, MUTE?
I AM MOTHER.
I'M AFFILIATED WITH THE CHURCH.

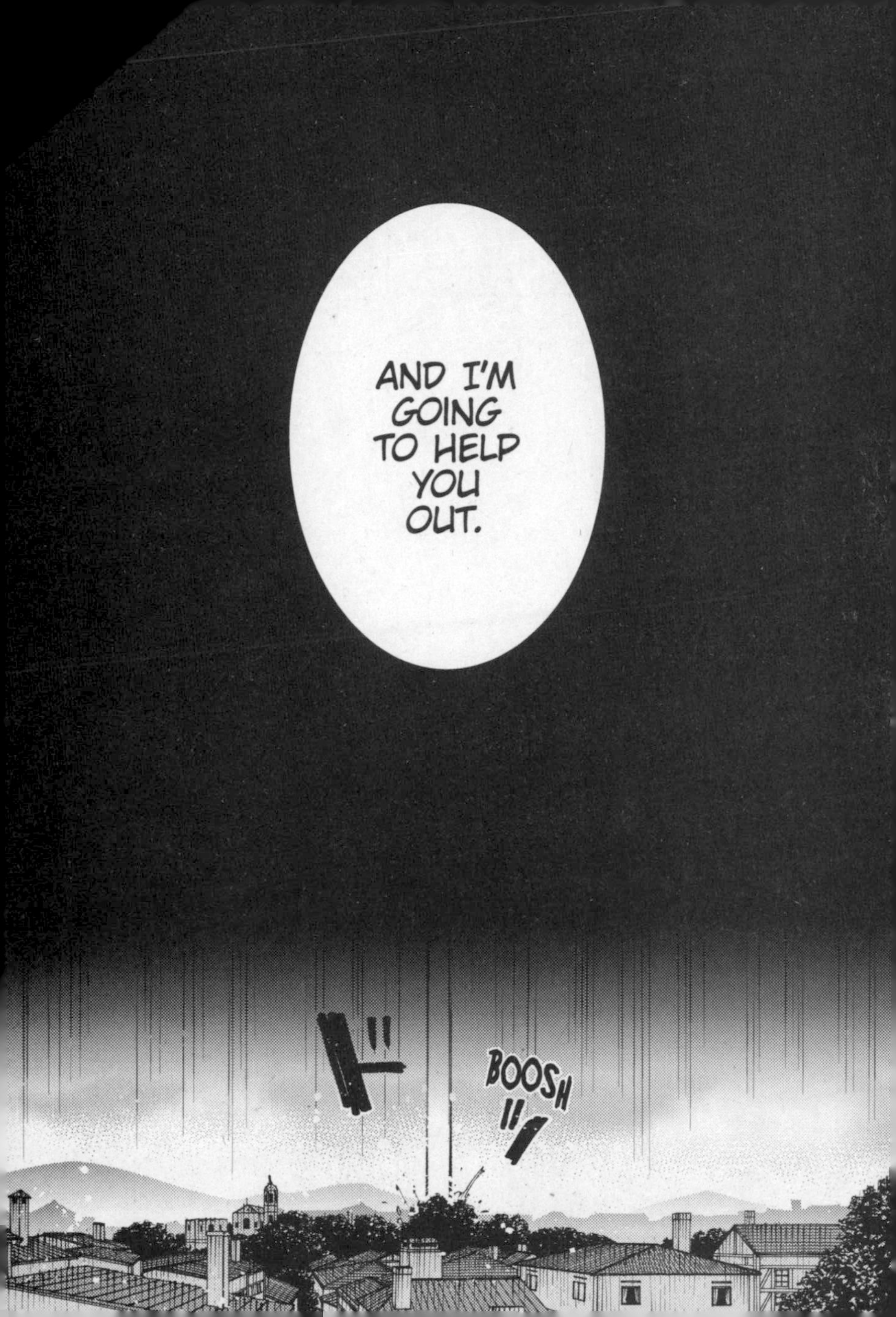
AND I'M GOING TO HELP YOU OUT.
BOOSH

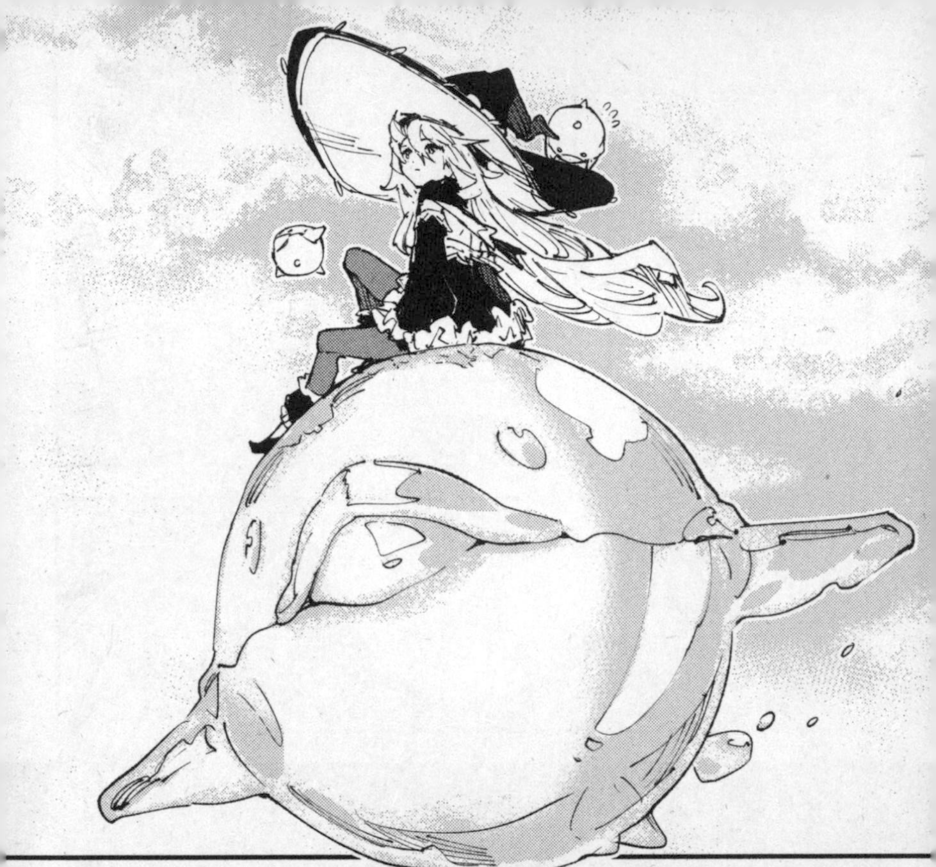

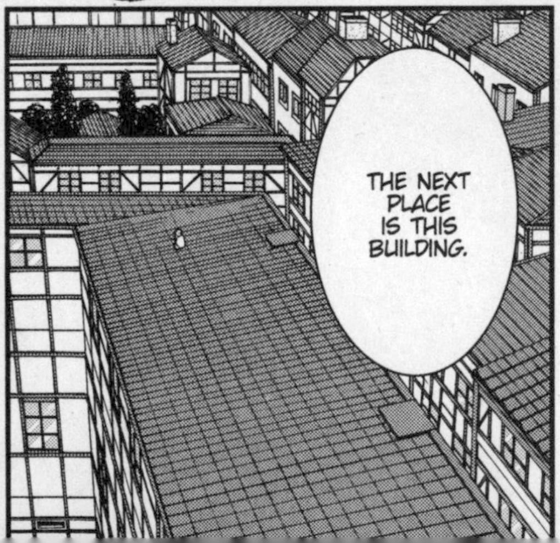
THE NEXT PLACE IS THIS BUILDING.

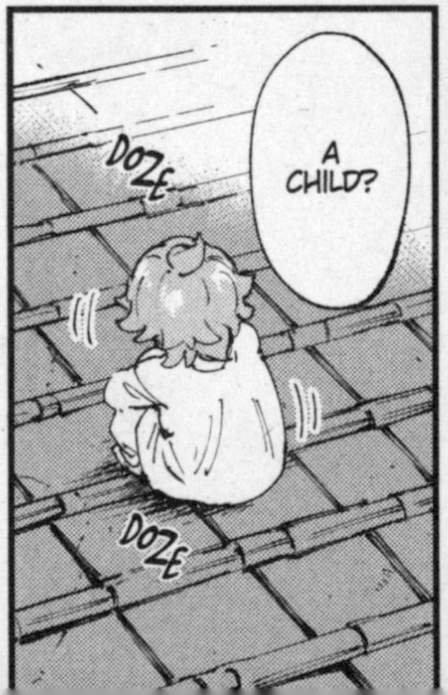
A CHILD?
DOZE
DOZE

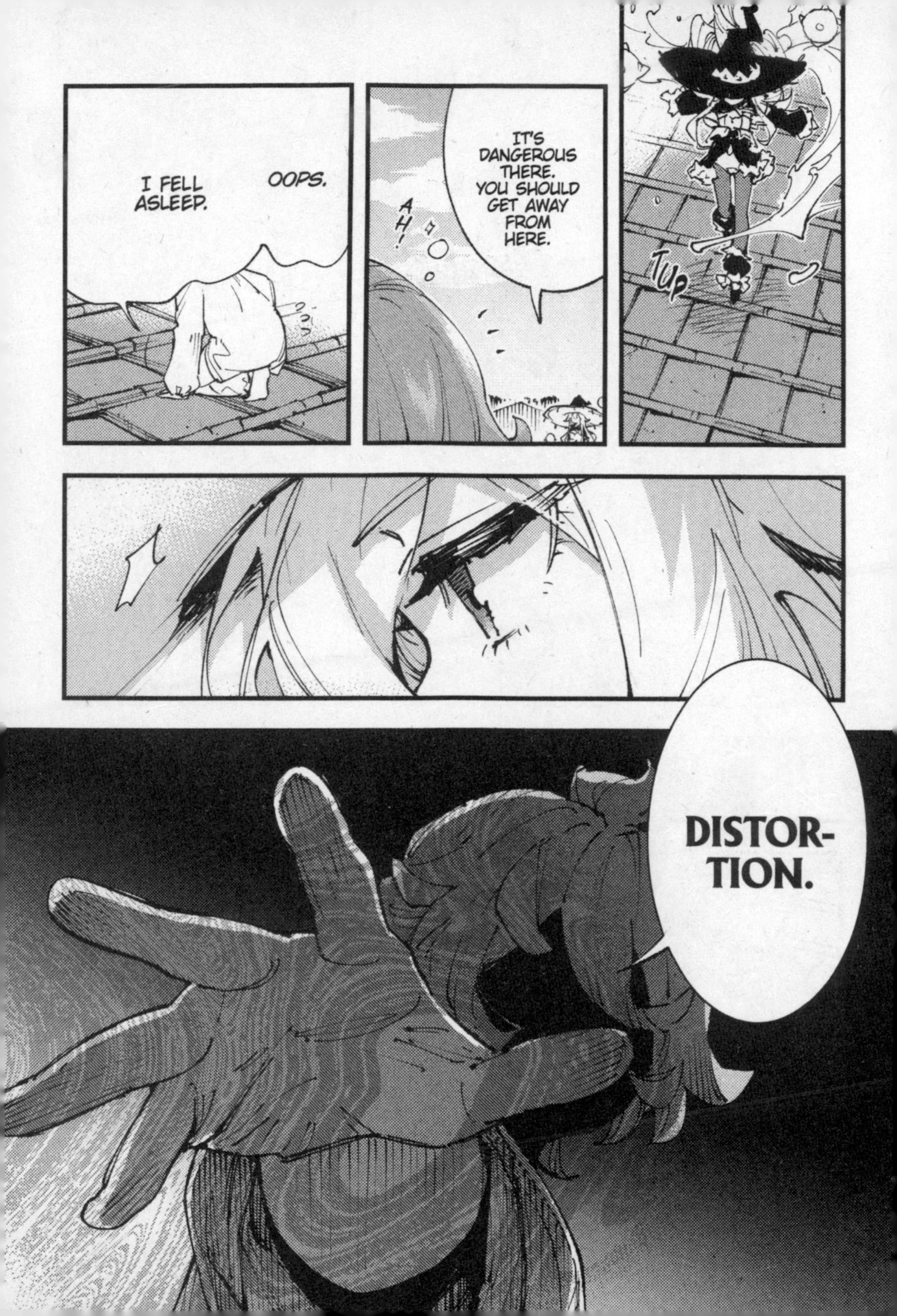
TUP
IT'S DANGEROUS THERE. YOU SHOULD GET AWAY FROM HERE.
AH!
OOPS.
I FELL ASLEEP.
DISTOR-TION.

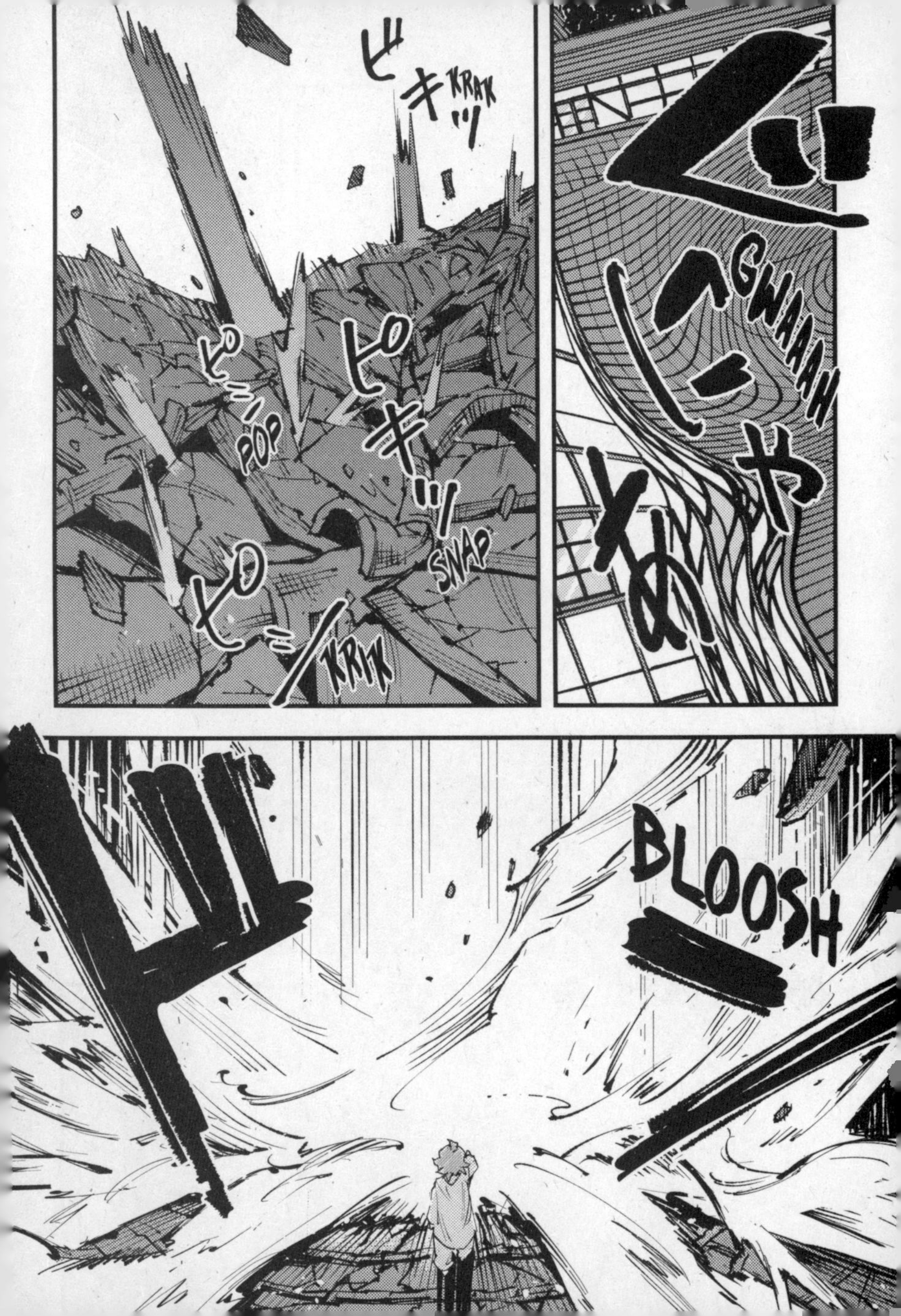
GWAAAAH
KRAK
POP
SNAP
KRIK
BLOOSH

THE SPACE AROUND ME WARPED?

FLAKE FLUTTER

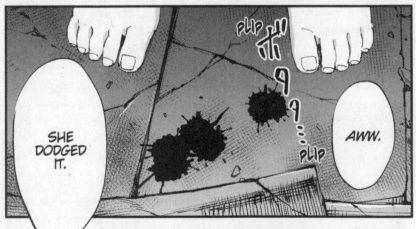

SHE DODGED IT.

PLIP

AWW.

...PLIP

!

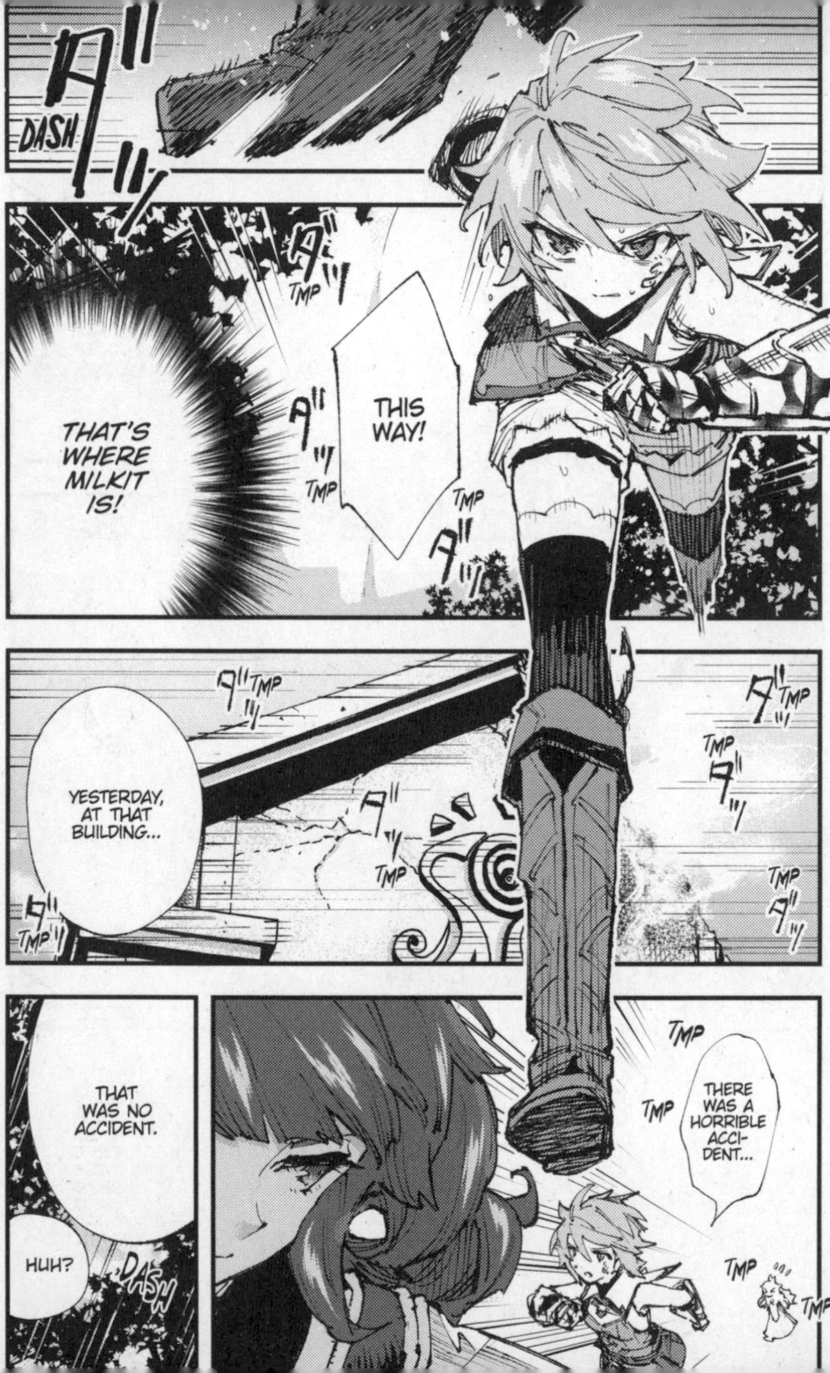
DASH
TMP
THIS WAY!
TMP
TMP
THAT'S WHERE MILKIT IS!
TMP
TMP
TMP
TMP
YESTERDAY, AT THAT BUILDING...
TMP
TMP
TMP
THERE WAS A HORRIBLE ACCI-DENT...
TMP
TMP
TMP
THAT WAS NO ACCIDENT.
HUH?
DASH

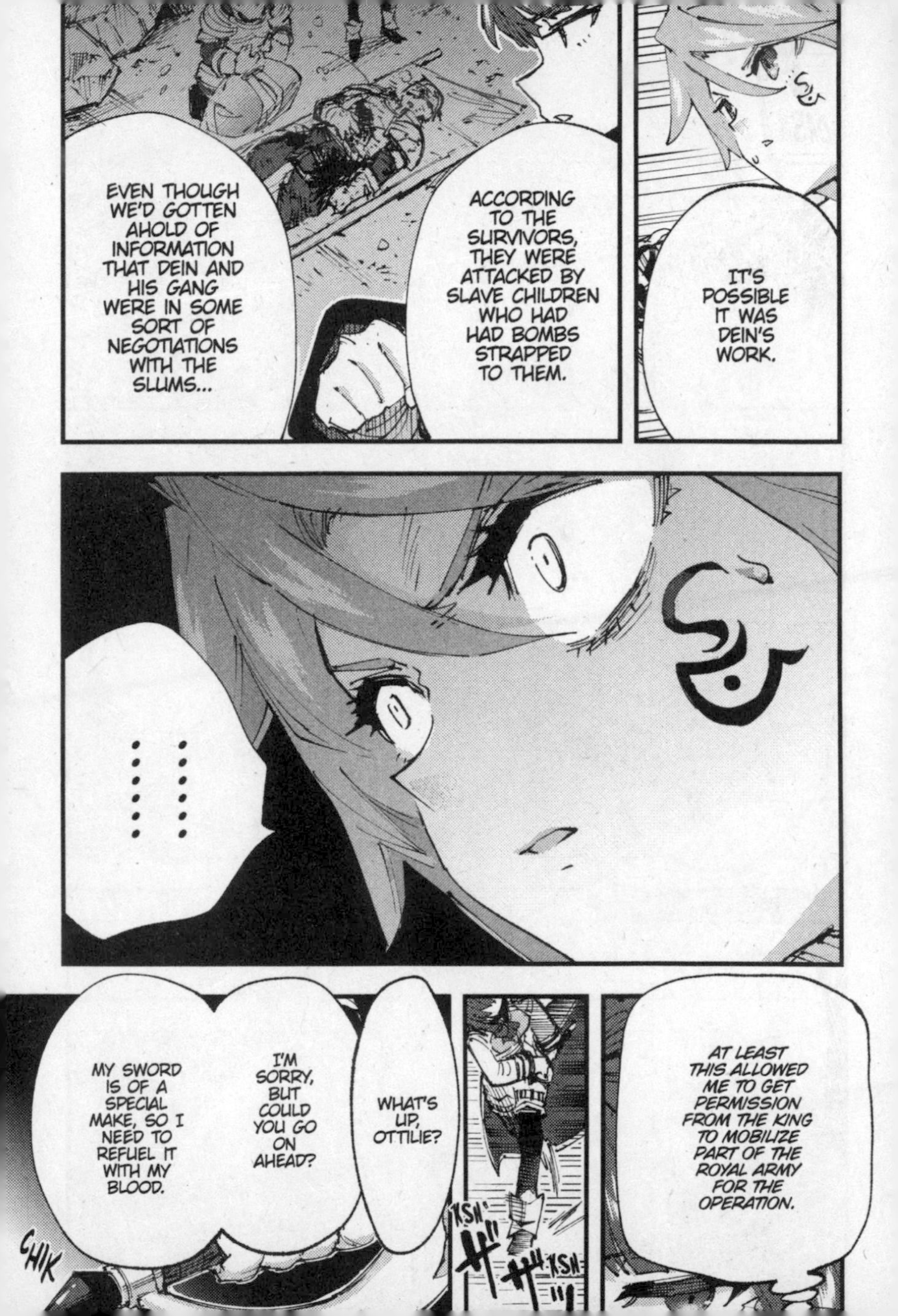
IT'S POSSIBLE IT WAS DEIN'S WORK.
ACCORDING TO THE SURVIVORS, THEY WERE ATTACKED BY SLAVE CHILDREN WHO HAD HAD BOMBS STRAPPED TO THEM.
EVEN THOUGH WE'D GOTTEN AHOLD OF INFORMATION THAT DEIN AND HIS GANG WERE IN SOME SORT OF NEGOTIATIONS WITH THE SLUMS...
......
AT LEAST THIS ALLOWED ME TO GET PERMISSION FROM THE KING TO MOBILIZE PART OF THE ROYAL ARMY FOR THE OPERATION.
KSH
KSH
WHAT'S UP, OTTILIE?
I'M SORRY, BUT COULD YOU GO ON AHEAD?
MY SWORD IS OF A SPECIAL MAKE, SO I NEED TO REFUEL IT WITH MY BLOOD.
CHIK

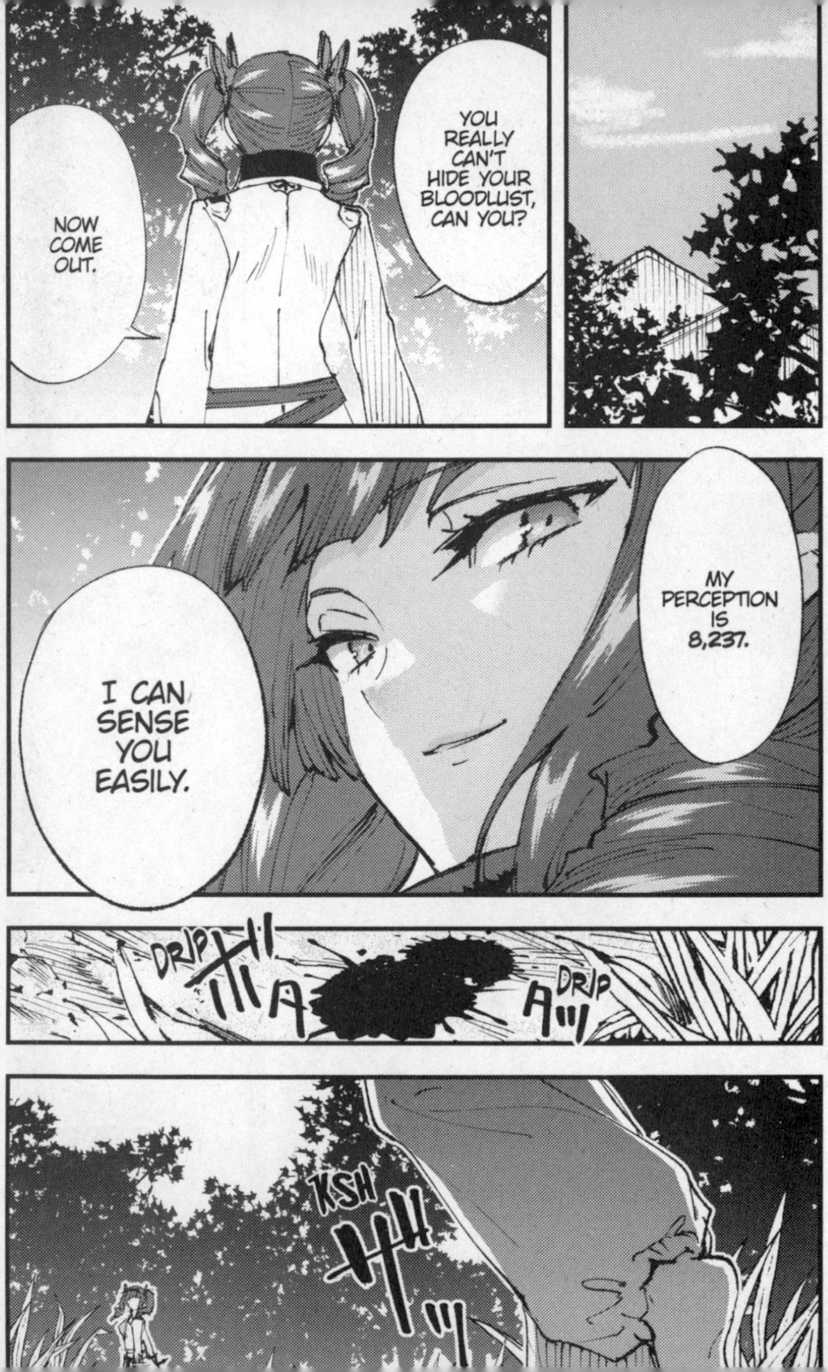
YOU REALLY CAN'T HIDE YOUR BLOODLUST, CAN YOU?
NOW COME OUT.
MY PERCEPTION IS 8,237.
I CAN SENSE YOU EASILY.
DRIP
DRIP
KSH

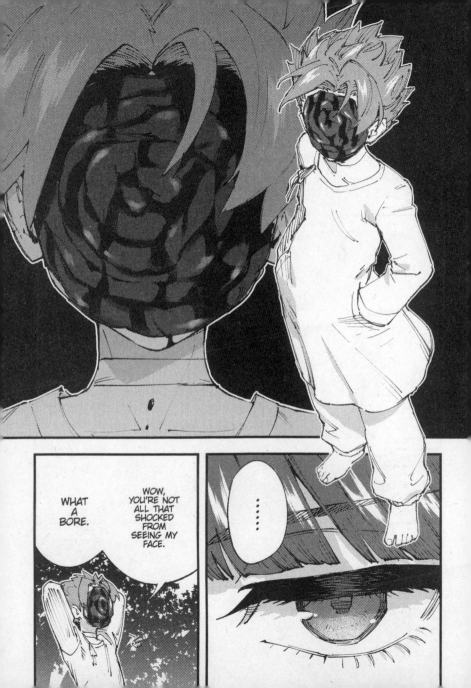

WHAT A BORE.

WOW, YOU'RE NOT ALL THAT SHOCKED FROM SEEING MY FACE.

. . . . .

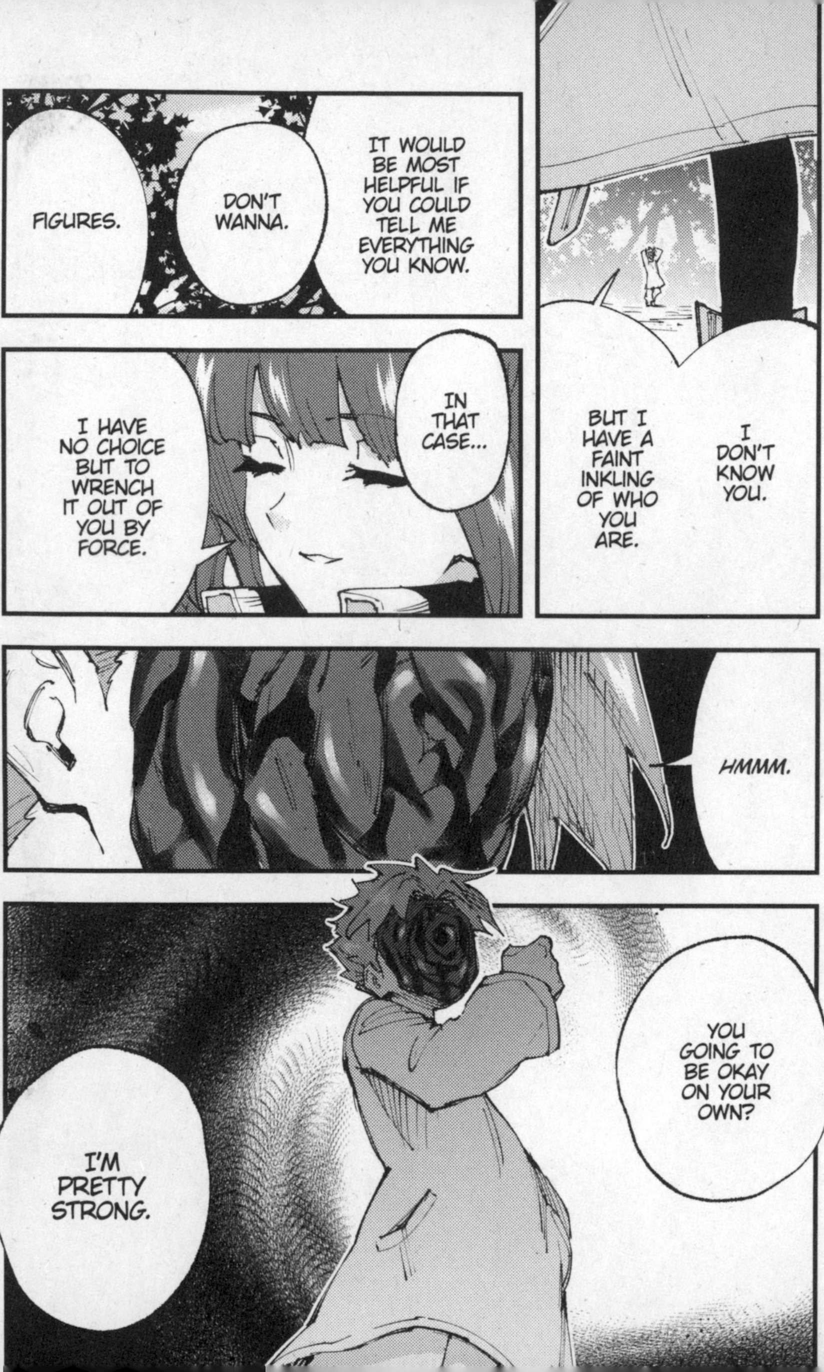
I DON'T KNOW YOU.
BUT I HAVE A FAINT INKLING OF WHO YOU ARE.
IT WOULD BE MOST HELPFUL IF YOU COULD TELL ME EVERYTHING YOU KNOW.
DON'T WANNA.
FIGURES.
IN THAT CASE...
I HAVE NO CHOICE BUT TO WRENCH IT OUT OF YOU BY FORCE.
HMMM.
YOU GOING TO BE OKAY ON YOUR OWN?
I'M PRETTY STRONG.

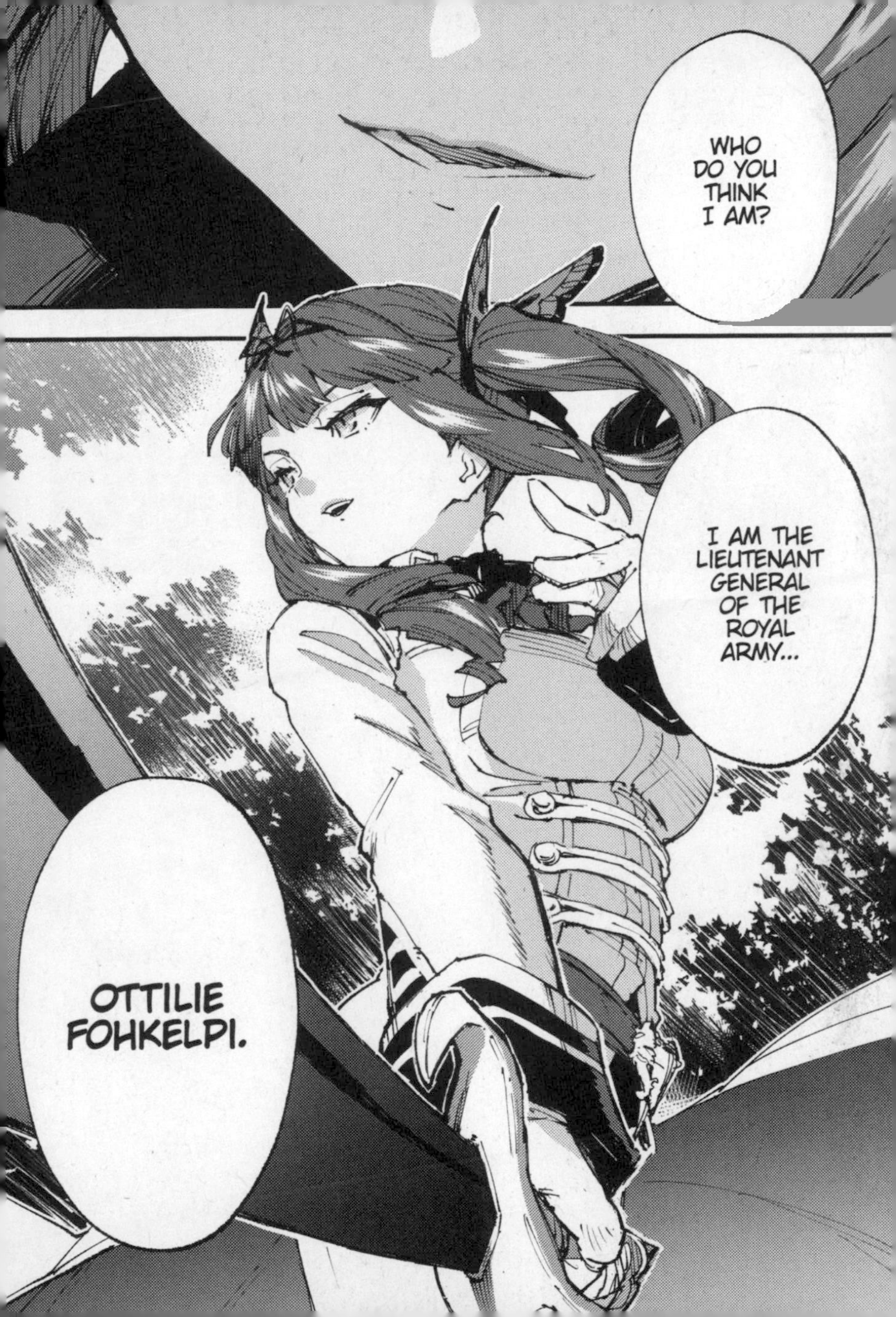
WHO DO YOU THINK I AM?
I AM THE LIEUTENANT GENERAL OF THE ROYAL ARMY...
OTTILIE FOHKELPI.

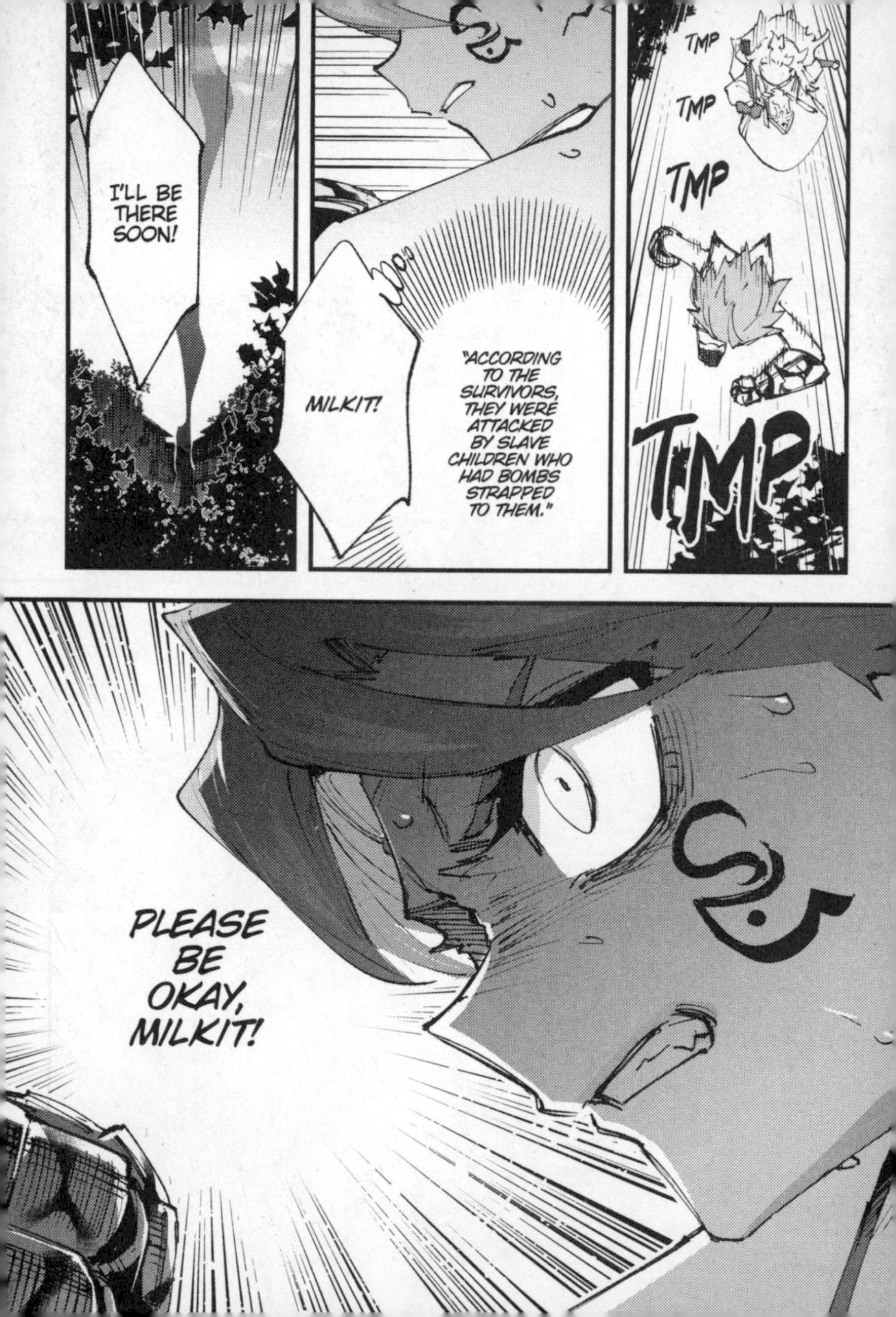
TMP
TMP
TMP
TMP
"ACCORDING TO THE SURVIVORS, THEY WERE ATTACKED BY SLAVE CHILDREN WHO HAD BOMBS STRAPPED TO THEM."
MILKIT!
I'LL BE THERE SOON!
PLEASE BE OKAY, MILKIT!

Chapter 14: If It Costs Me My Life

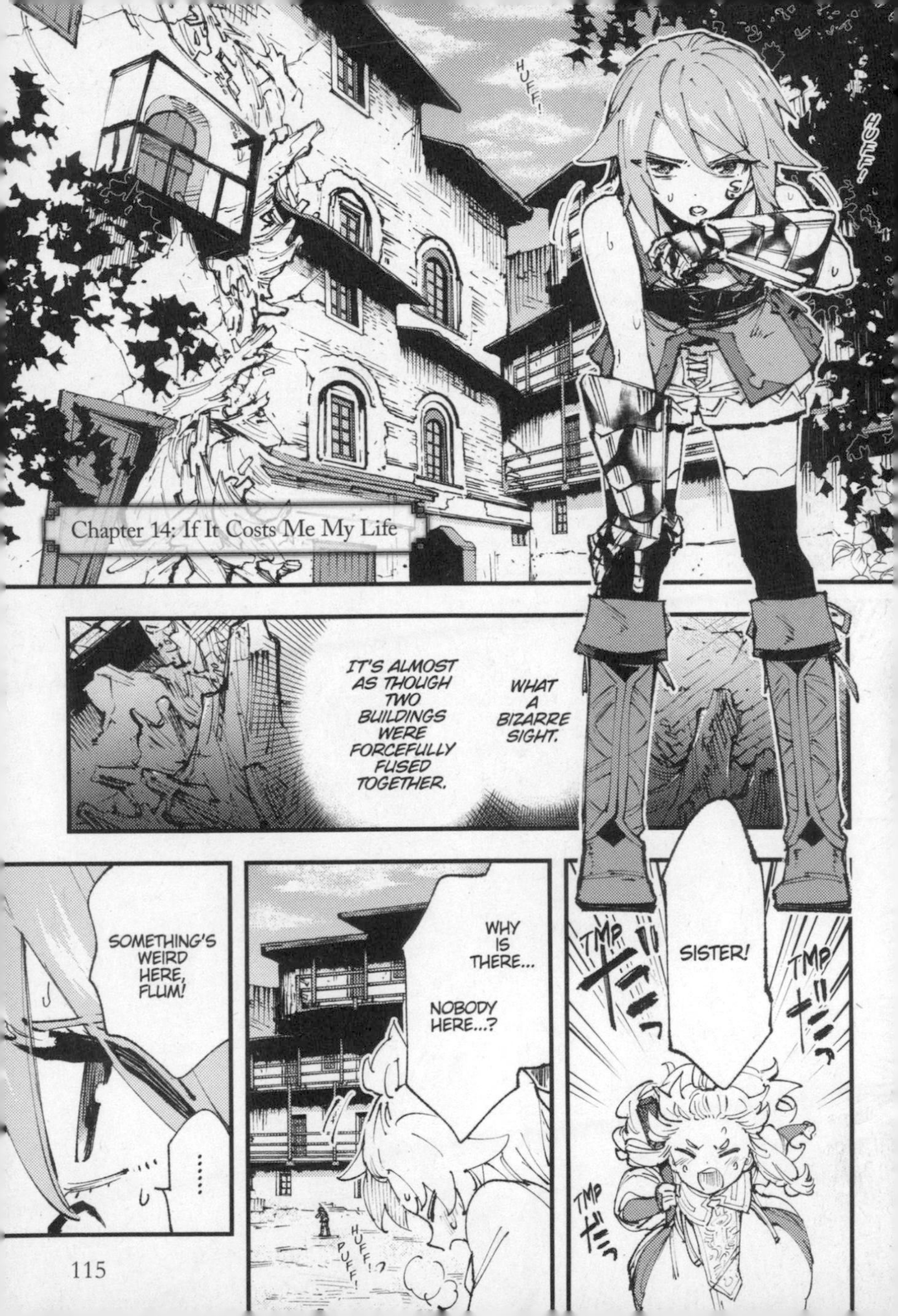
HUFF!
HUFF!
WHAT A BIZARRE SIGHT.
IT'S ALMOST AS THOUGH TWO BUILDINGS WERE FORCEFULLY FUSED TOGETHER.
TMP
SISTER!
TMP
TMP
WHY IS THERE...
NOBODY HERE...?
HUFF!
PUFF!
SOMETHING'S WEIRD HERE, FLUM!
......

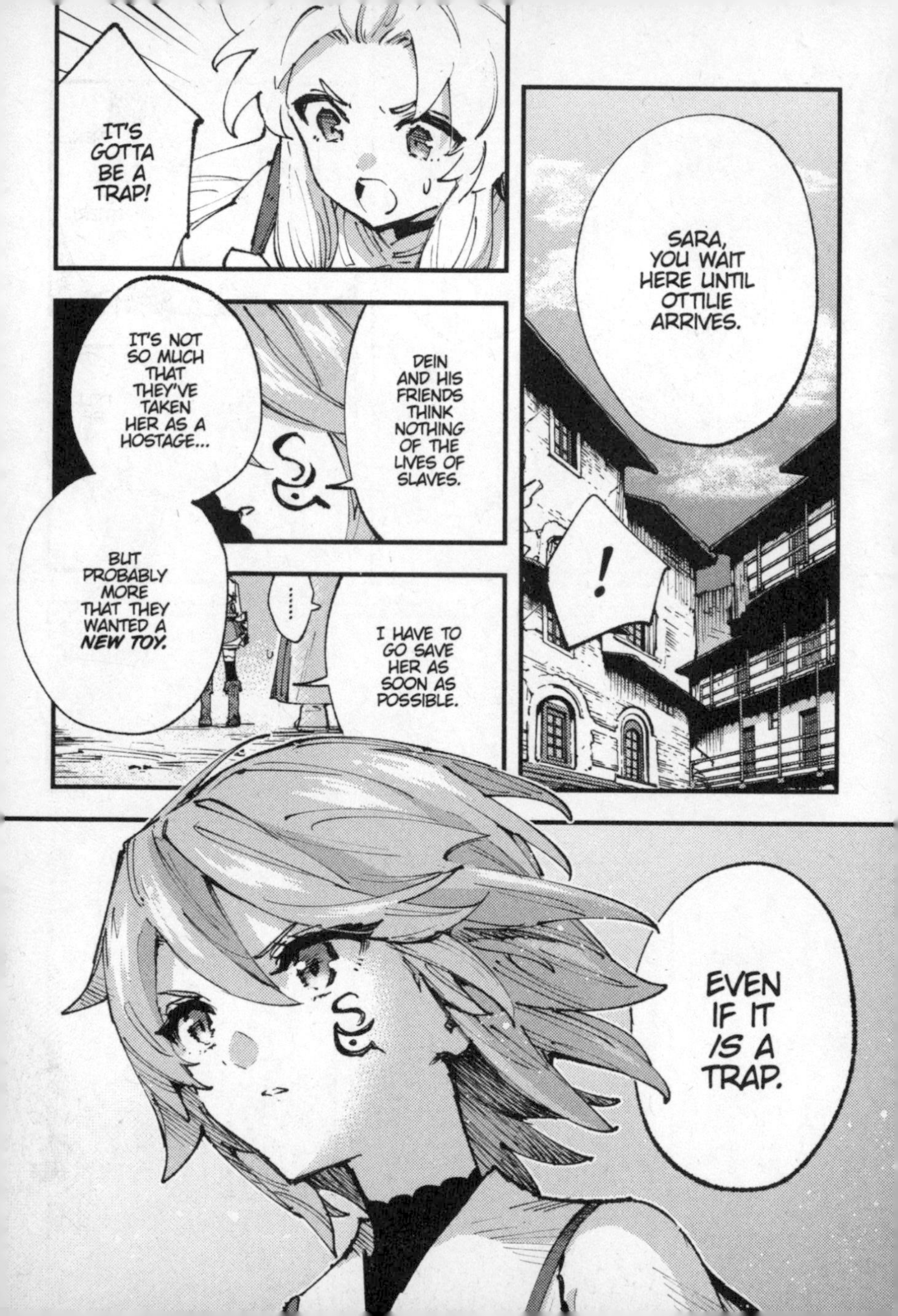
SARA, YOU WAIT HERE UNTIL OTTILIE ARRIVES.
!
IT'S GOTTA BE A TRAP!
DEIN AND HIS FRIENDS THINK NOTHING OF THE LIVES OF SLAVES.
IT'S NOT SO MUCH THAT THEY'VE TAKEN HER AS A HOSTAGE...
BUT PROBABLY MORE THAT THEY WANTED A *NEW TOY.*
......
I HAVE TO GO SAVE HER AS SOON AS POSSIBLE.
EVEN IF IT *IS* A TRAP.

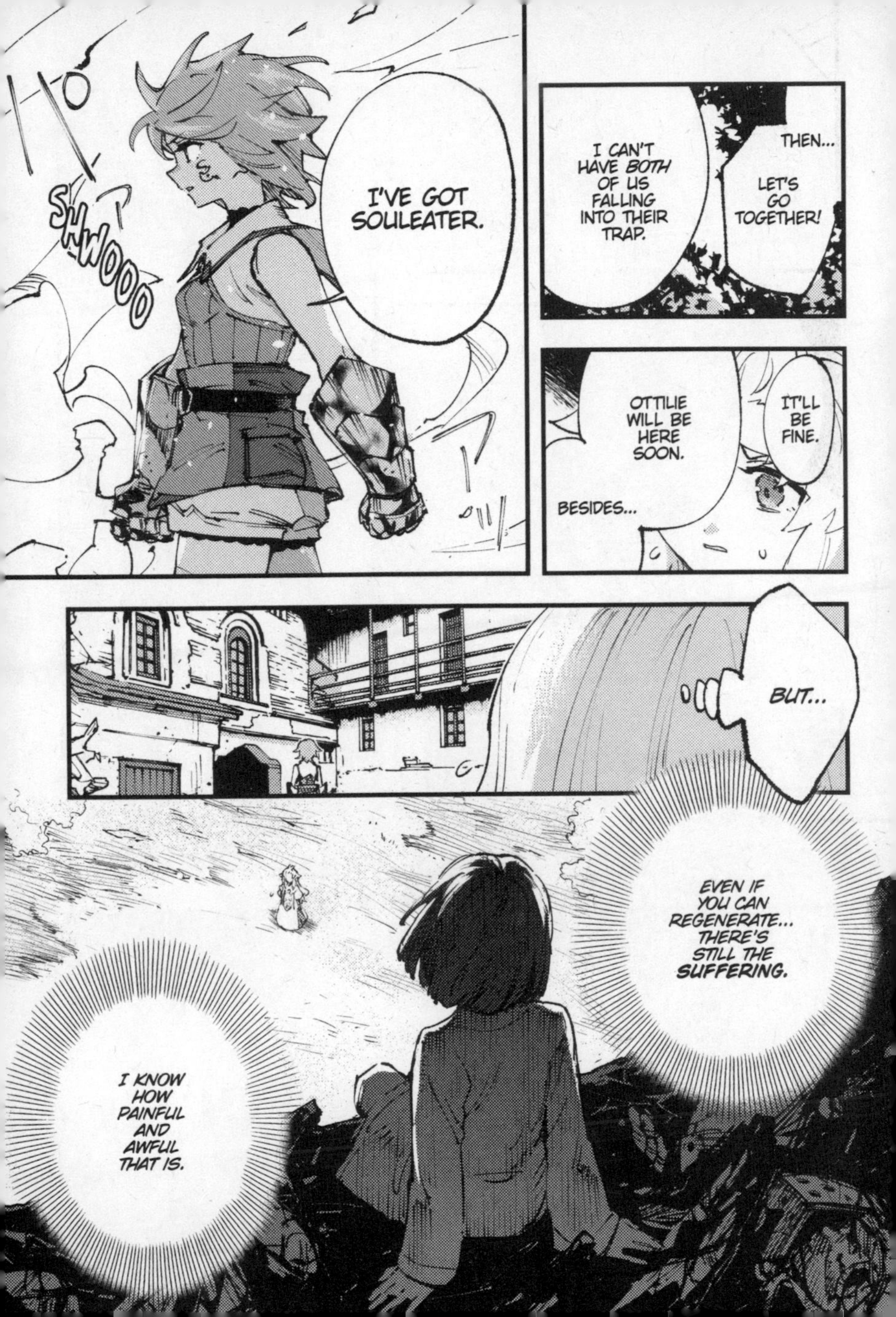
THEN...
LET'S GO TOGETHER!
I CAN'T HAVE *BOTH* OF US FALLING INTO THEIR TRAP.
IT'LL BE FINE.
OTTILIE WILL BE HERE SOON.
BESIDES...
I'VE GOT SOULEATER.
SHWOOO
BUT...
EVEN IF YOU CAN REGENERATE... THERE'S STILL THE SUFFERING.
I KNOW HOW PAINFUL AND AWFUL THAT IS.

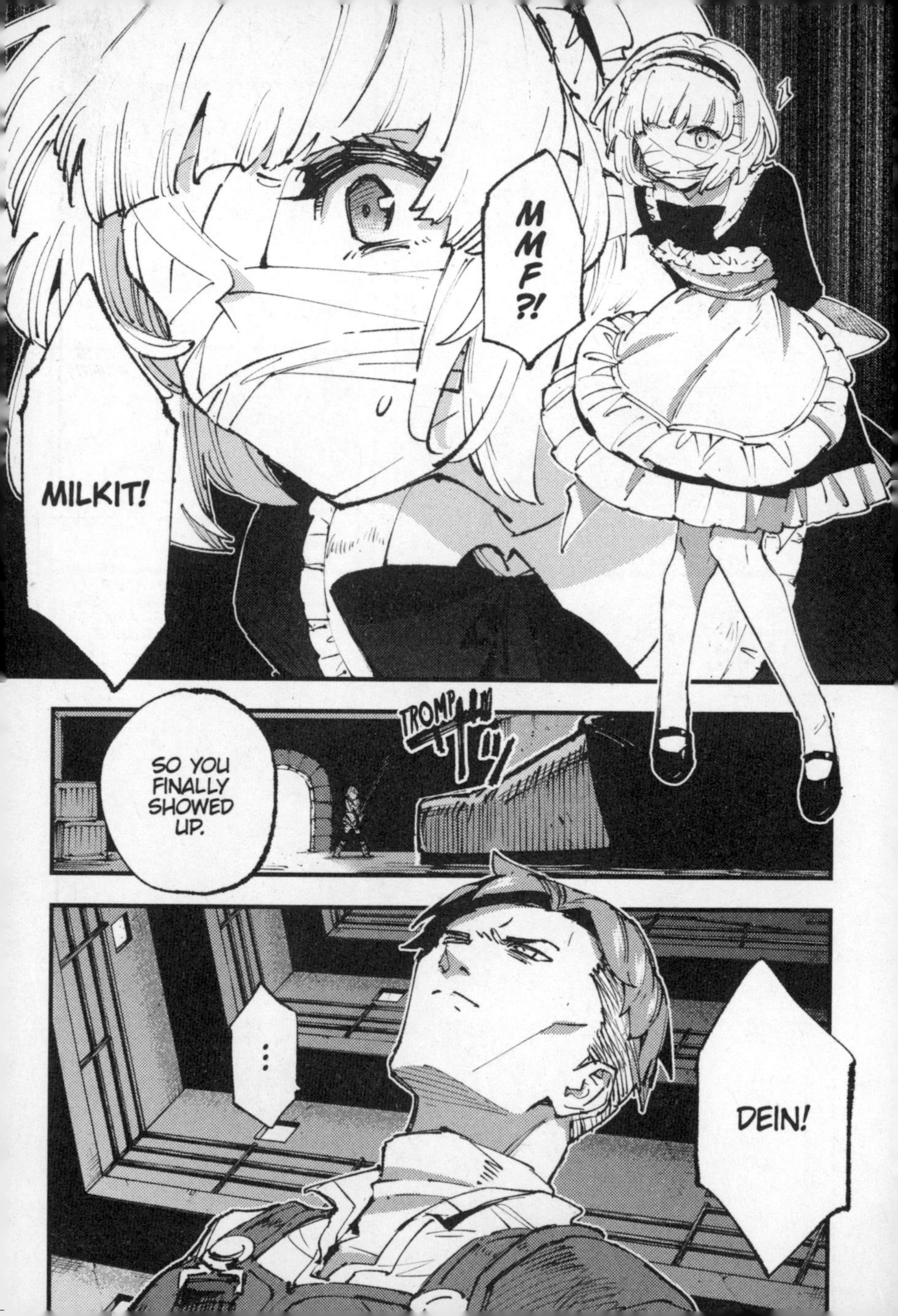
MMF?!
MILKIT!
TROMP
SO YOU FINALLY SHOWED UP.
DEIN!
...

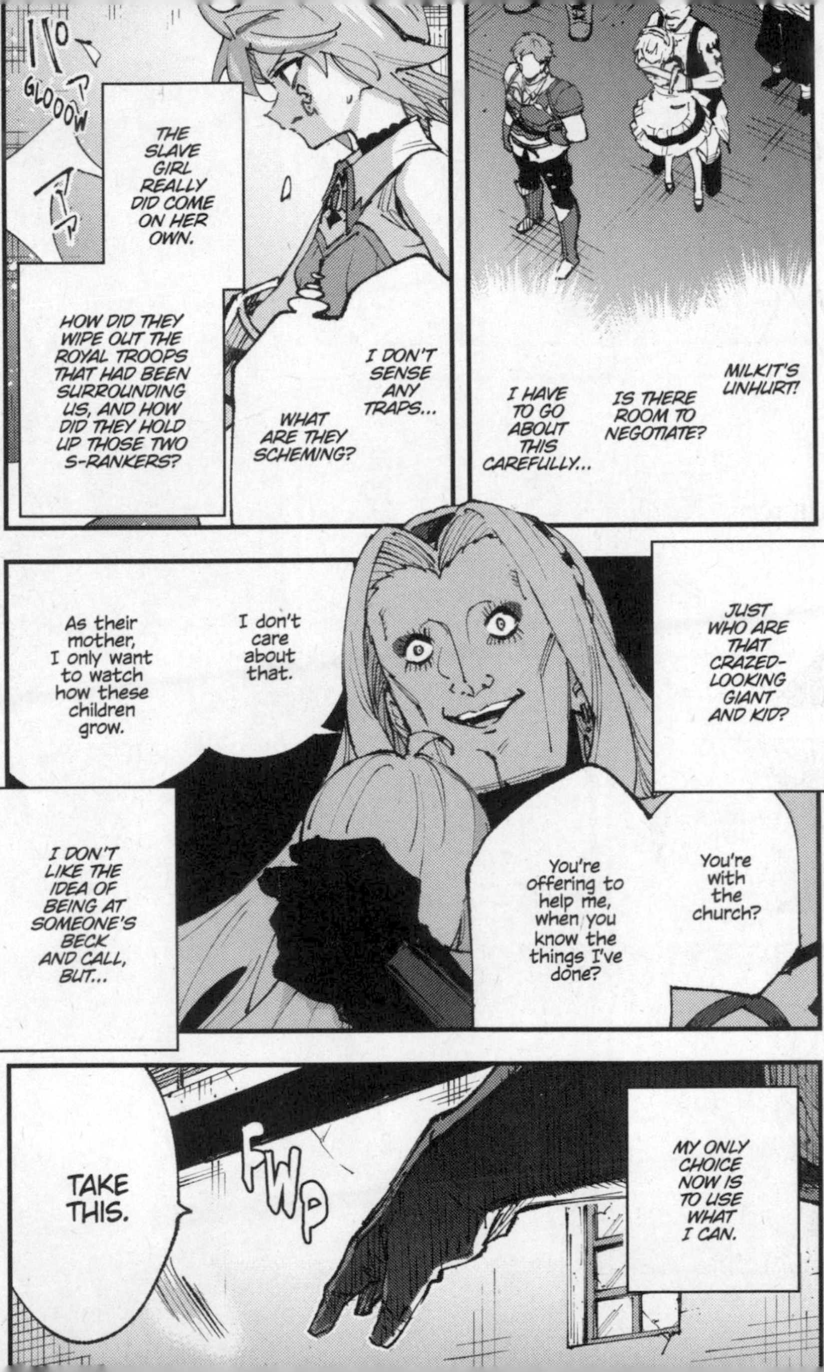
MILKIT'S UNHURT!
IS THERE ROOM TO NEGOTIATE?
I HAVE TO GO ABOUT THIS CAREFULLY...
GLOOOW
THE SLAVE GIRL REALLY DID COME ON HER OWN.
I DON'T SENSE ANY TRAPS...
WHAT ARE THEY SCHEMING?
HOW DID THEY WIPE OUT THE ROYAL TROOPS THAT HAD BEEN SURROUNDING US, AND HOW DID THEY HOLD UP THOSE TWO S-RANKERS?
JUST WHO ARE THAT CRAZED-LOOKING GIANT AND KID?
You're with the church?
You're offering to help me, when you know the things I've done?
I don't care about that.
As their mother, I only want to watch how these children grow.
I DON'T LIKE THE IDEA OF BEING AT SOMEONE'S BECK AND CALL, BUT...
MY ONLY CHOICE NOW IS TO USE WHAT I CAN.
FWP
TAKE THIS.

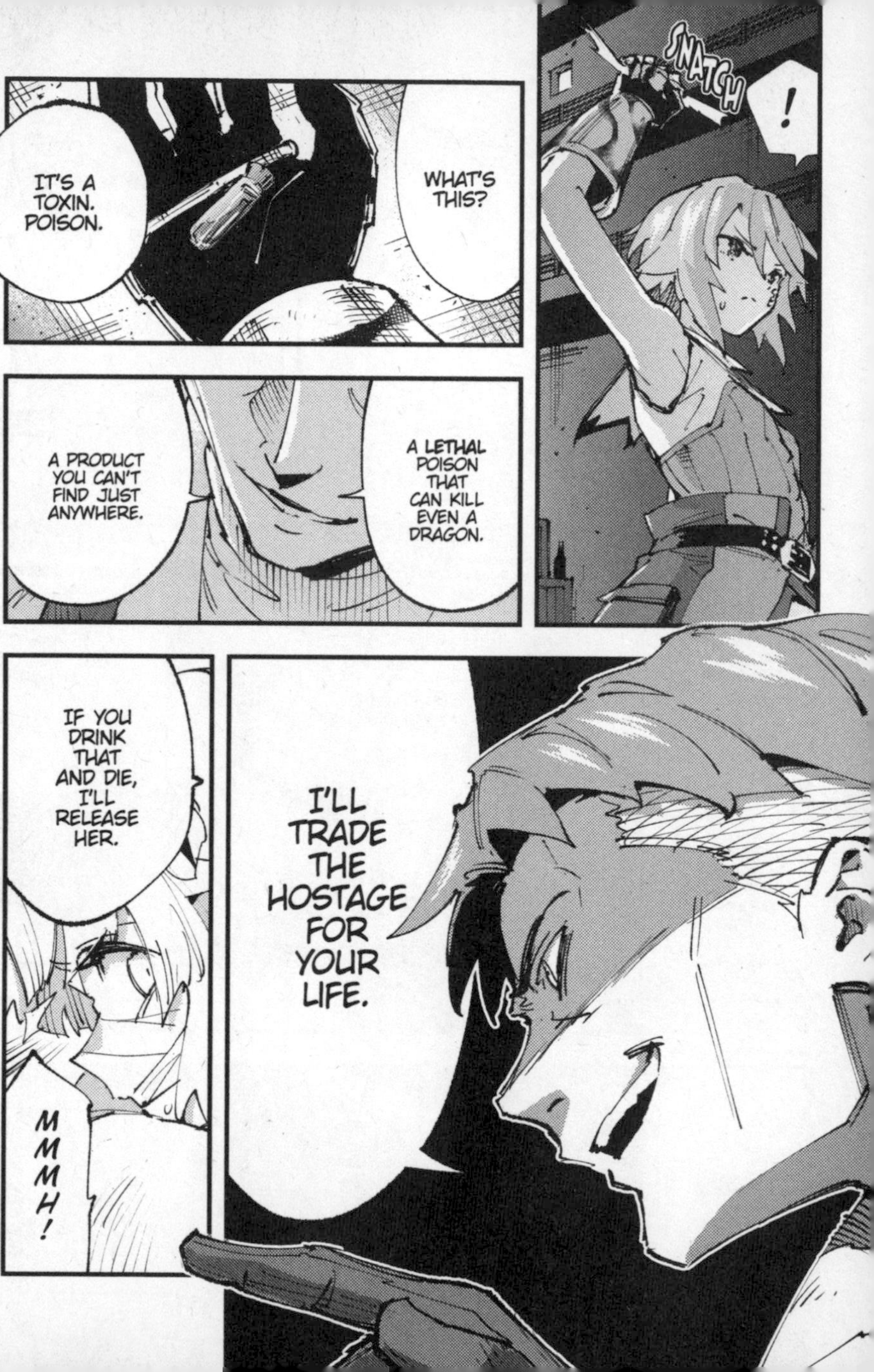
SNATCH
!
WHAT'S THIS?
IT'S A TOXIN. POISON.
A LETHAL POISON THAT CAN KILL EVEN A DRAGON.
A PRODUCT YOU CAN'T FIND JUST ANYWHERE.
I'LL TRADE THE HOSTAGE FOR YOUR LIFE.
IF YOU DRINK THAT AND DIE, I'LL RELEASE HER.
MMMMH!

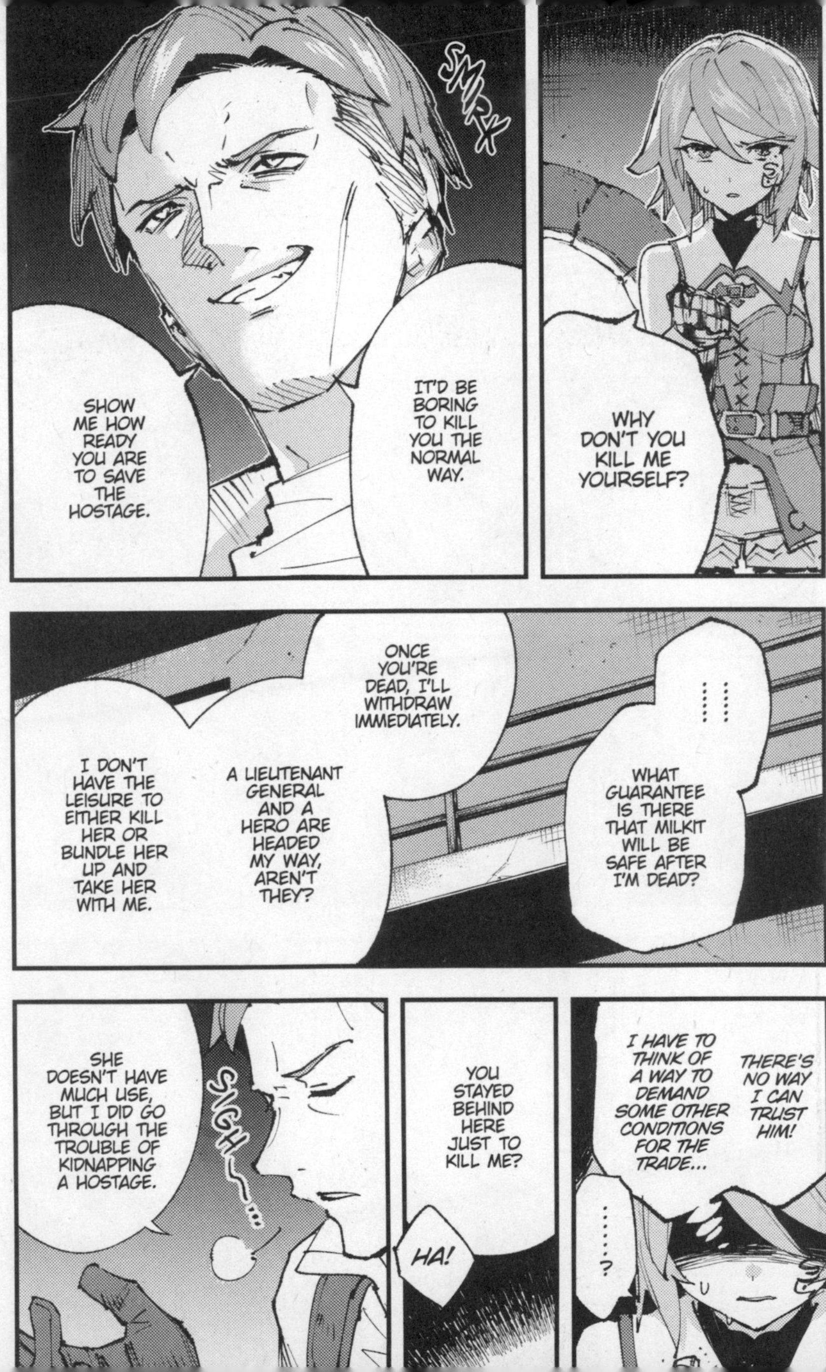
WHY DON'T YOU KILL ME YOURSELF?
SMIRK
IT'D BE BORING TO KILL YOU THE NORMAL WAY.
SHOW ME HOW READY YOU ARE TO SAVE THE HOSTAGE.
......
WHAT GUARANTEE IS THERE THAT MILKIT WILL BE SAFE AFTER I'M DEAD?
ONCE YOU'RE DEAD, I'LL WITHDRAW IMMEDIATELY.
A LIEUTENANT GENERAL AND A HERO ARE HEADED MY WAY, AREN'T THEY?
I DON'T HAVE THE LEISURE TO EITHER KILL HER OR BUNDLE HER UP AND TAKE HER WITH ME.
THERE'S NO WAY I CAN TRUST HIM!
I HAVE TO THINK OF A WAY TO DEMAND SOME OTHER CONDITIONS FOR THE TRADE...
......?
YOU STAYED BEHIND HERE JUST TO KILL ME?
HA!
SIGH~~...
SHE DOESN'T HAVE MUCH USE, BUT I DID GO THROUGH THE TROUBLE OF KIDNAPPING A HOSTAGE.

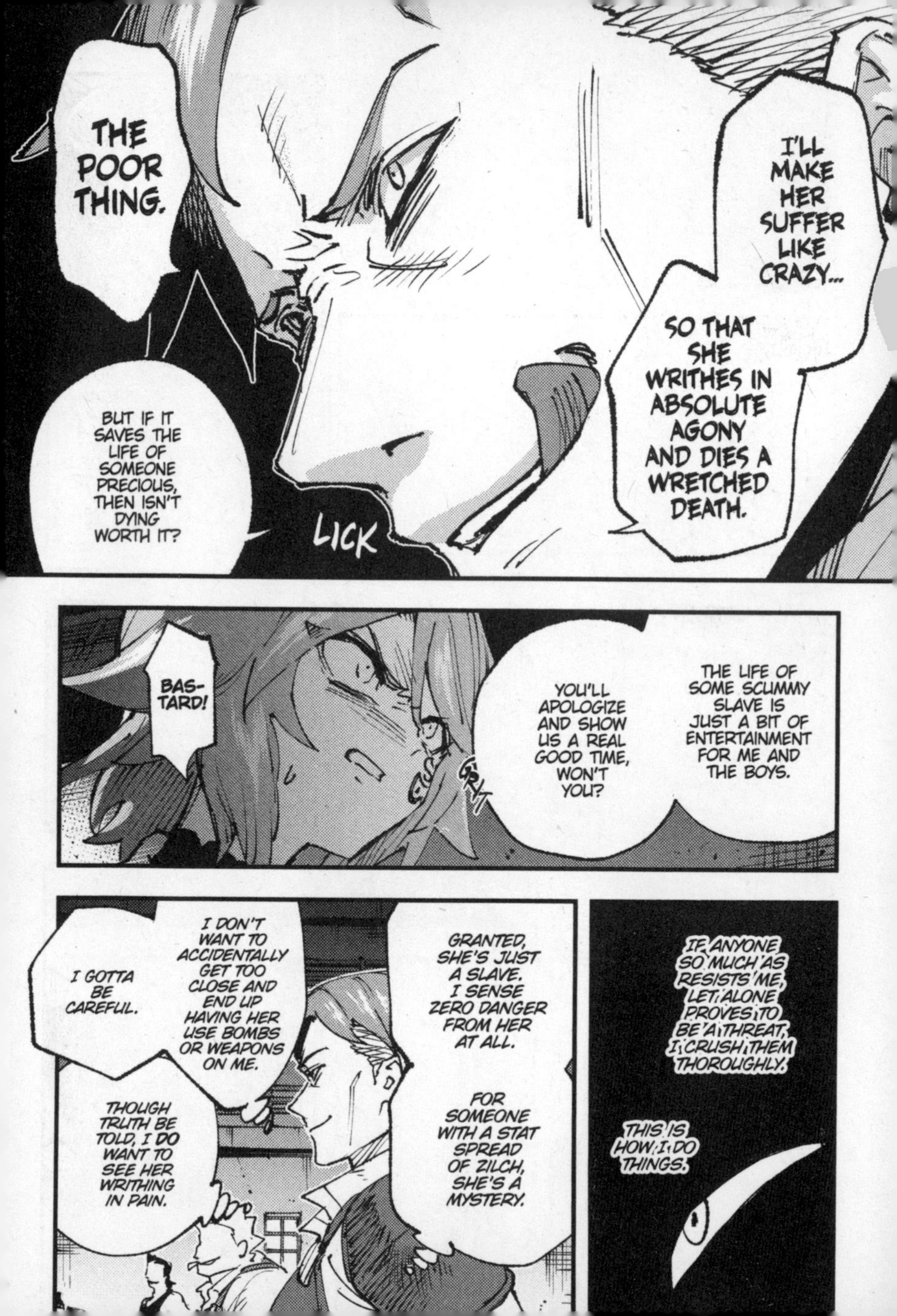
I'LL MAKE HER SUFFER LIKE CRAZY...
SO THAT SHE WRITHES IN ABSOLUTE AGONY AND DIES A WRETCHED DEATH.
THE POOR THING.
BUT IF IT SAVES THE LIFE OF SOMEONE PRECIOUS, THEN ISN'T DYING WORTH IT?
LICK
THE LIFE OF SOME SCUMMY SLAVE IS JUST A BIT OF ENTERTAINMENT FOR ME AND THE BOYS.
YOU'LL APOLOGIZE AND SHOW US A REAL GOOD TIME, WON'T YOU?
BAS-TARD!
IF ANYONE SO MUCH AS RESISTS ME, LET ALONE PROVES TO BE A THREAT, I CRUSH THEM THOROUGHLY.
THIS IS HOW I DO THINGS.
GRANTED, SHE'S JUST A SLAVE. I SENSE ZERO DANGER FROM HER AT ALL.
FOR SOMEONE WITH A STAT SPREAD OF ZILCH, SHE'S A MYSTERY.
I GOTTA BE CAREFUL.
I DON'T WANT TO ACCIDENTALLY GET TOO CLOSE AND END UP HAVING HER USE BOMBS OR WEAPONS ON ME.
THOUGH TRUTH BE TOLD, I DO WANT TO SEE HER WRITHING IN PAIN.

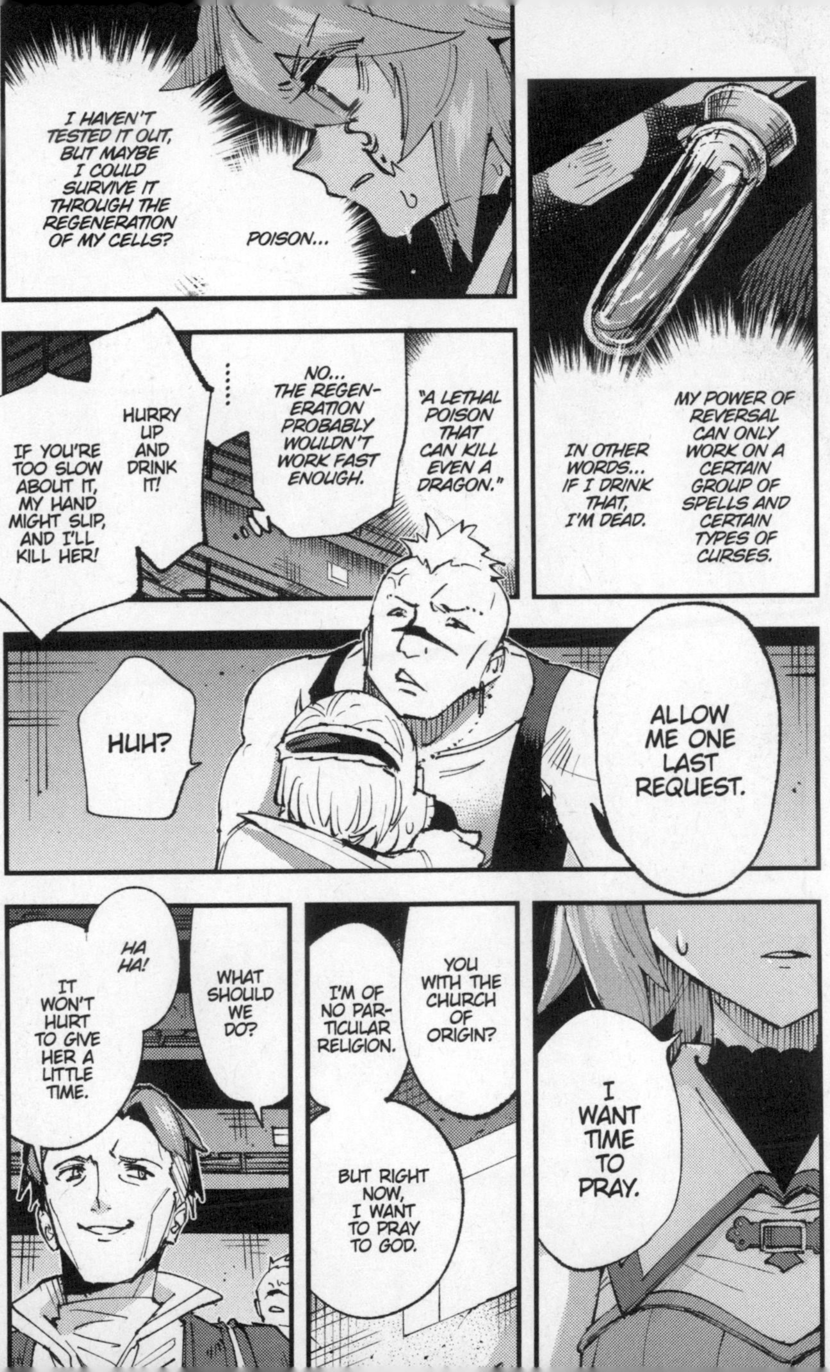
MY POWER OF REVERSAL CAN ONLY WORK ON A CERTAIN GROUP OF SPELLS AND CERTAIN TYPES OF CURSES.
IN OTHER WORDS... IF I DRINK THAT, I'M DEAD.
POISON...
I HAVEN'T TESTED IT OUT, BUT MAYBE I COULD SURVIVE IT THROUGH THE REGENERATION OF MY CELLS?
"A LETHAL POISON THAT CAN KILL EVEN A DRAGON."
NO... THE REGENERATION PROBABLY WOULDN'T WORK FAST ENOUGH.
......
HURRY UP AND DRINK IT!
IF YOU'RE TOO SLOW ABOUT IT, MY HAND MIGHT SLIP, AND I'LL KILL HER!
ALLOW ME ONE LAST REQUEST.
HUH?
I WANT TIME TO PRAY.
YOU WITH THE CHURCH OF ORIGIN?
I'M OF NO PARTICULAR RELIGION.
BUT RIGHT NOW, I WANT TO PRAY TO GOD.
WHAT SHOULD WE DO?
HA HA!
IT WON'T HURT TO GIVE HER A LITTLE TIME.

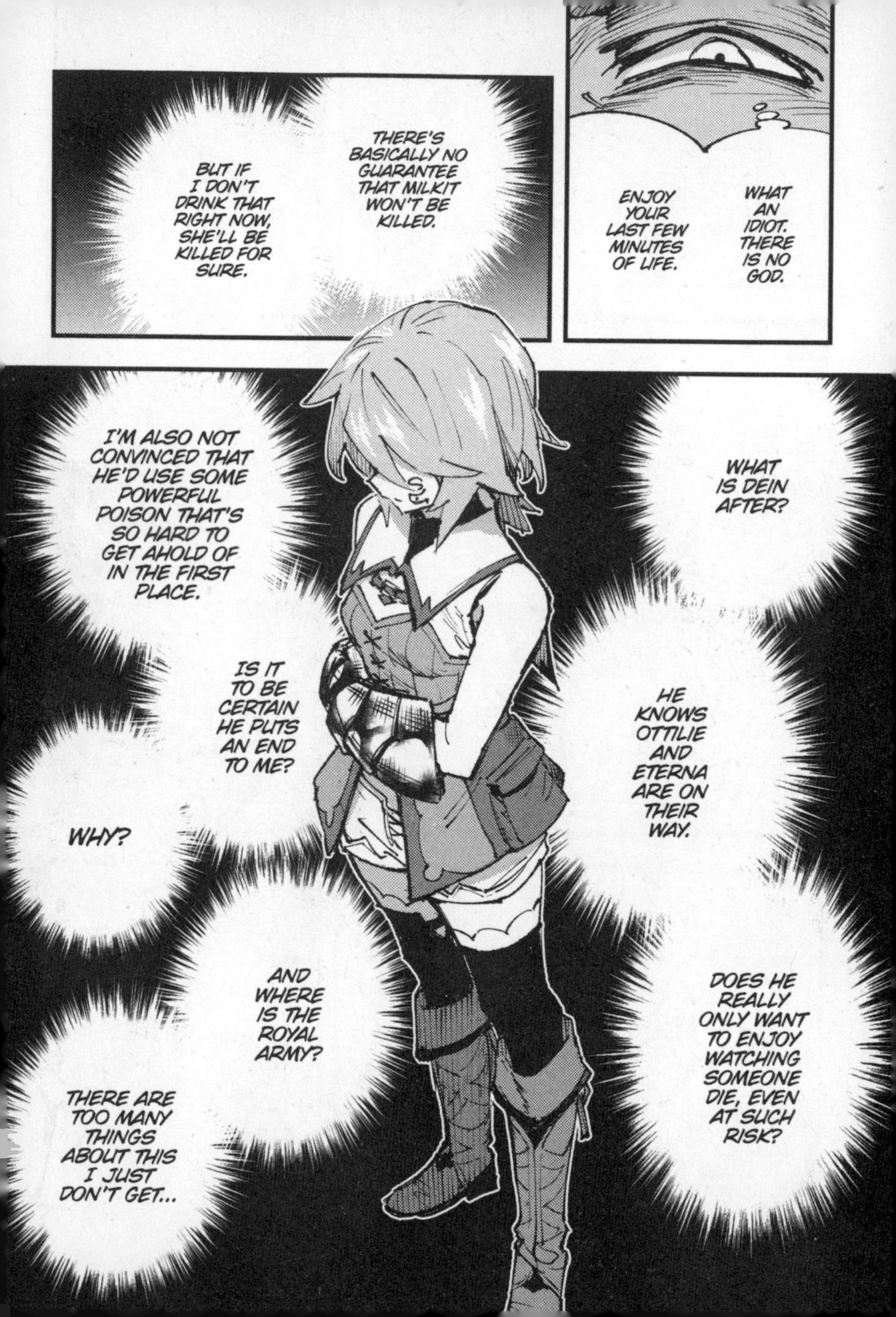
WHAT AN IDIOT. THERE IS NO GOD.
ENJOY YOUR LAST FEW MINUTES OF LIFE.
THERE'S BASICALLY NO GUARANTEE THAT MILKIT WON'T BE KILLED.
BUT IF I DON'T DRINK THAT RIGHT NOW, SHE'LL BE KILLED FOR SURE.
WHAT IS DEIN AFTER?
I'M ALSO NOT CONVINCED THAT HE'D USE SOME POWERFUL POISON THAT'S SO HARD TO GET AHOLD OF IN THE FIRST PLACE.
HE KNOWS OTTILIE AND ETERNA ARE ON THEIR WAY.
IS IT TO BE CERTAIN HE PUTS AN END TO ME?
WHY?
DOES HE REALLY ONLY WANT TO ENJOY WATCHING SOMEONE DIE, EVEN AT SUCH RISK?
AND WHERE IS THE ROYAL ARMY?
THERE ARE TOO MANY THINGS ABOUT THIS I JUST DON'T GET...

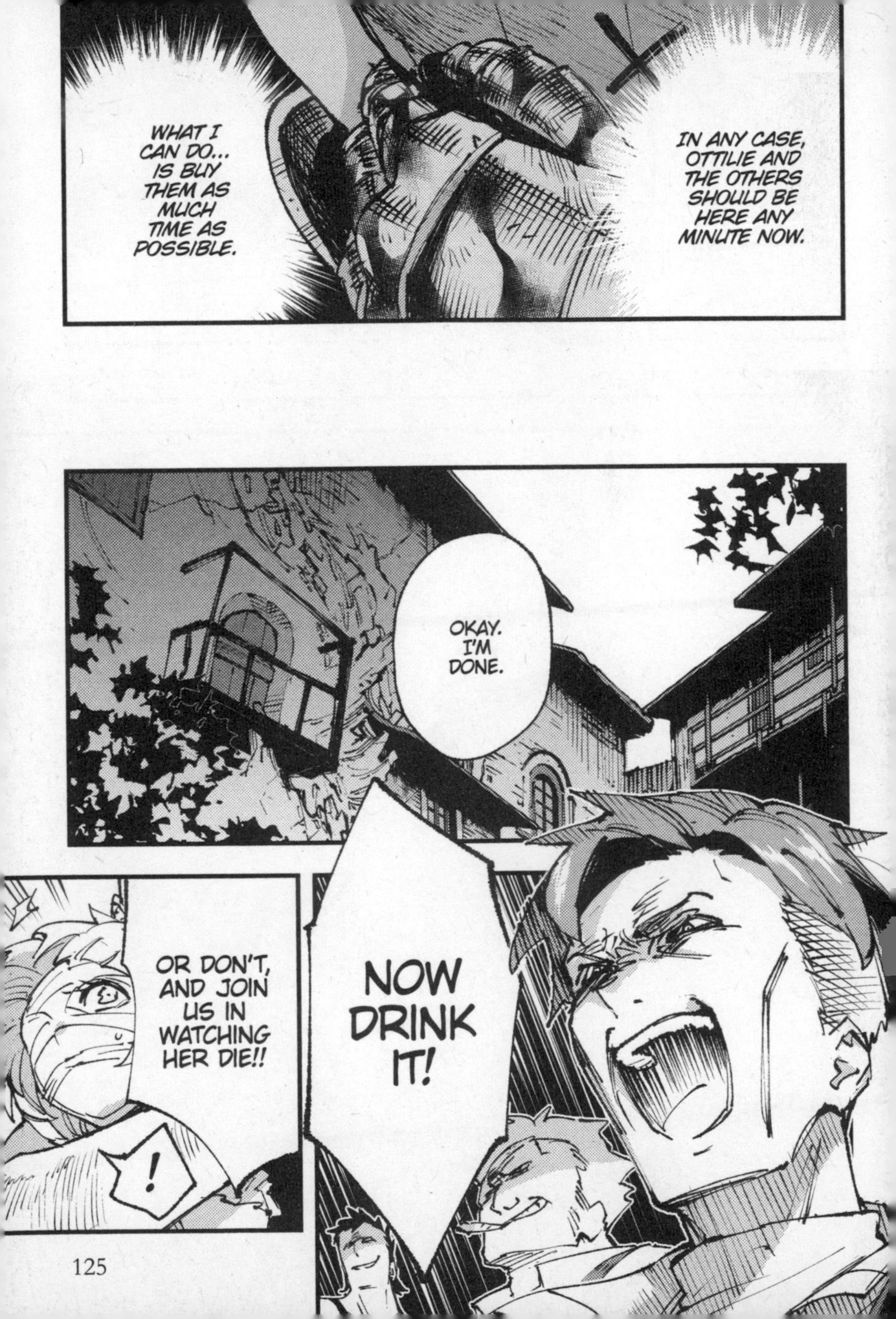
IN ANY CASE, OTTILIE AND THE OTHERS SHOULD BE HERE ANY MINUTE NOW.
WHAT I CAN DO... IS BUY THEM AS MUCH TIME AS POSSIBLE.
OKAY. I'M DONE.
NOW DRINK IT!
OR DON'T, AND JOIN US IN WATCHING HER DIE!!
!

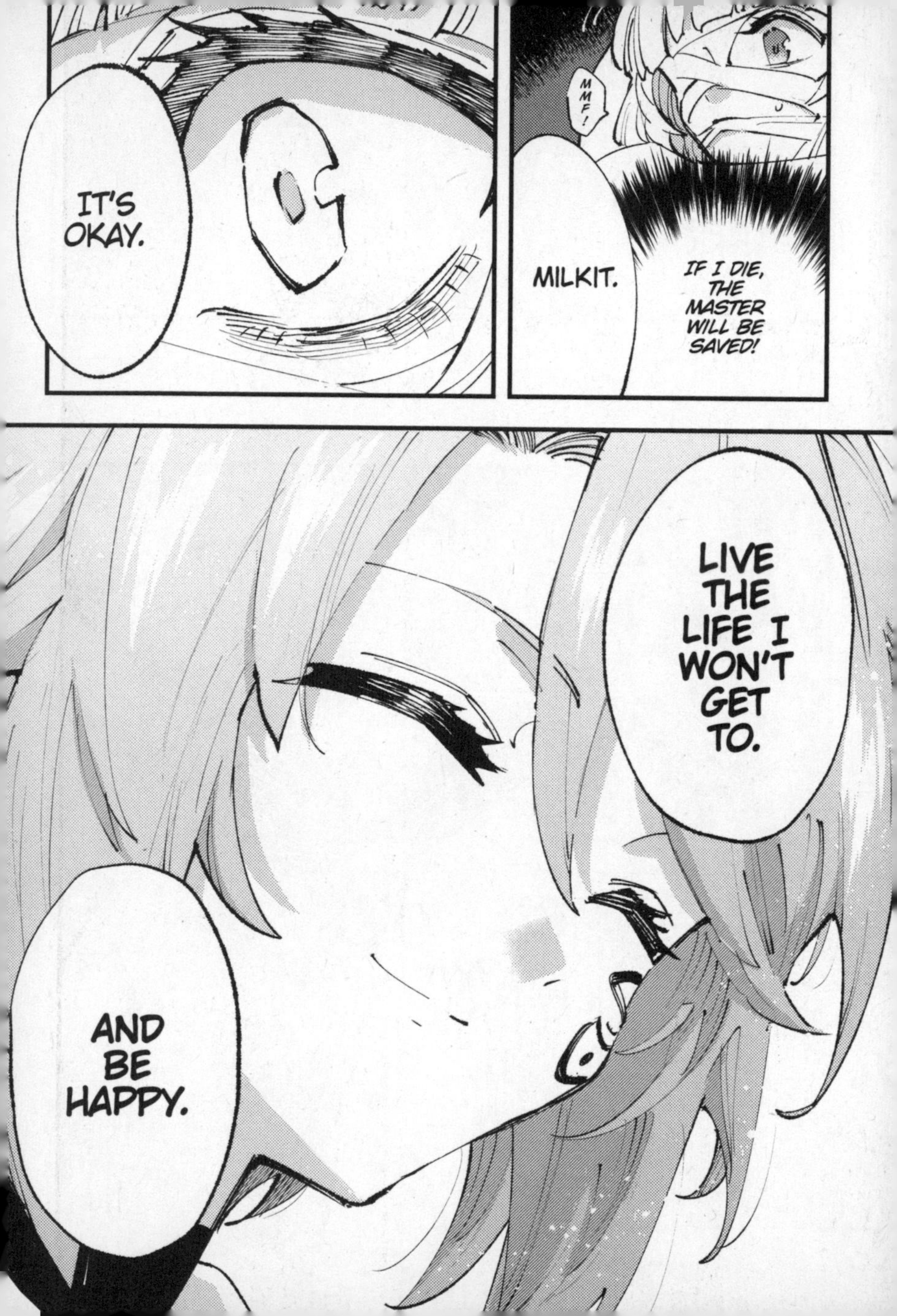
MMF!
IF I DIE, THE MASTER WILL BE SAVED!
MILKIT.
IT'S OKAY.
LIVE THE LIFE I WON'T GET TO.
AND BE HAPPY.

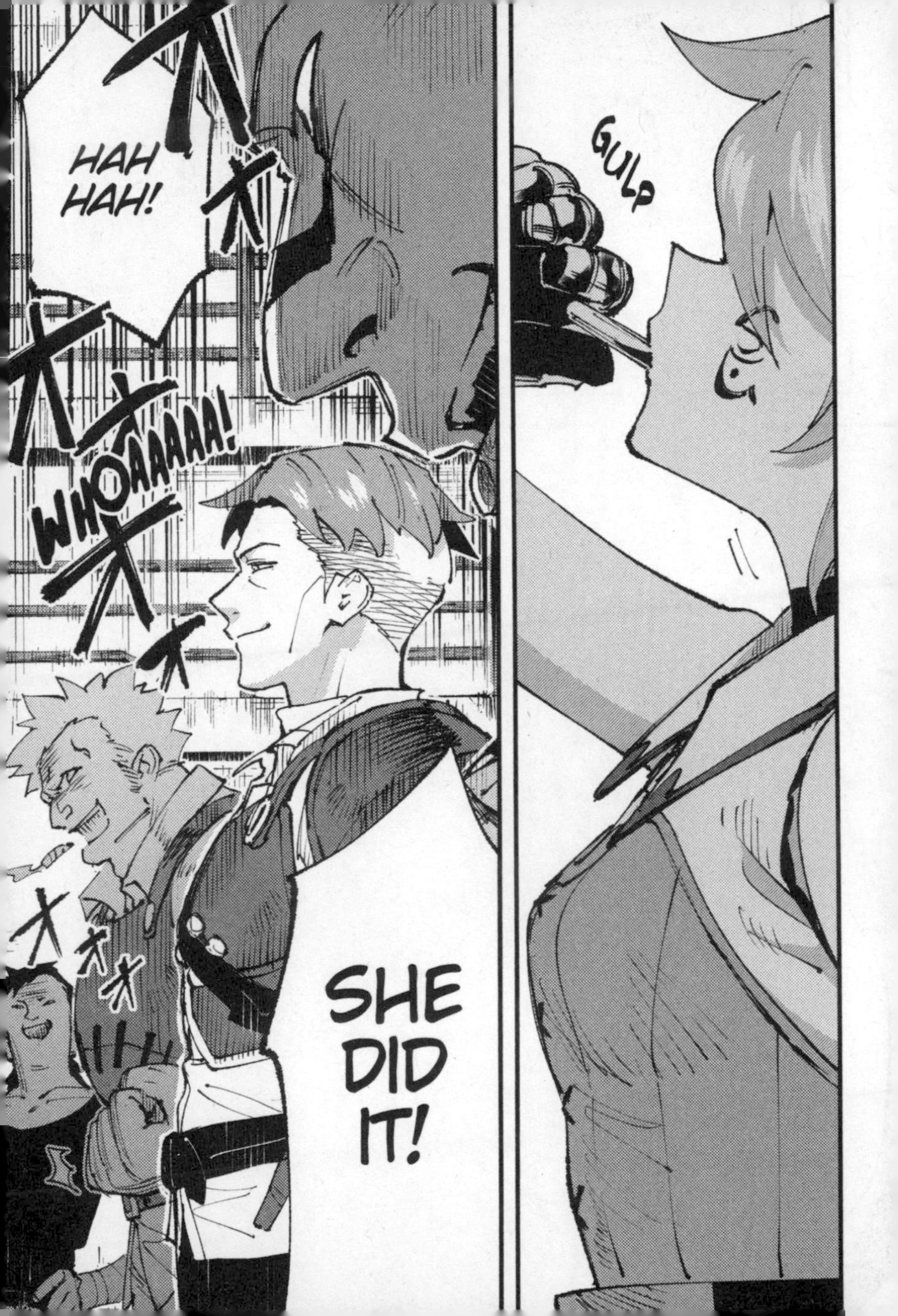
GULP
HAH HAH!
WHOAAAAAA!
SHE DID IT!

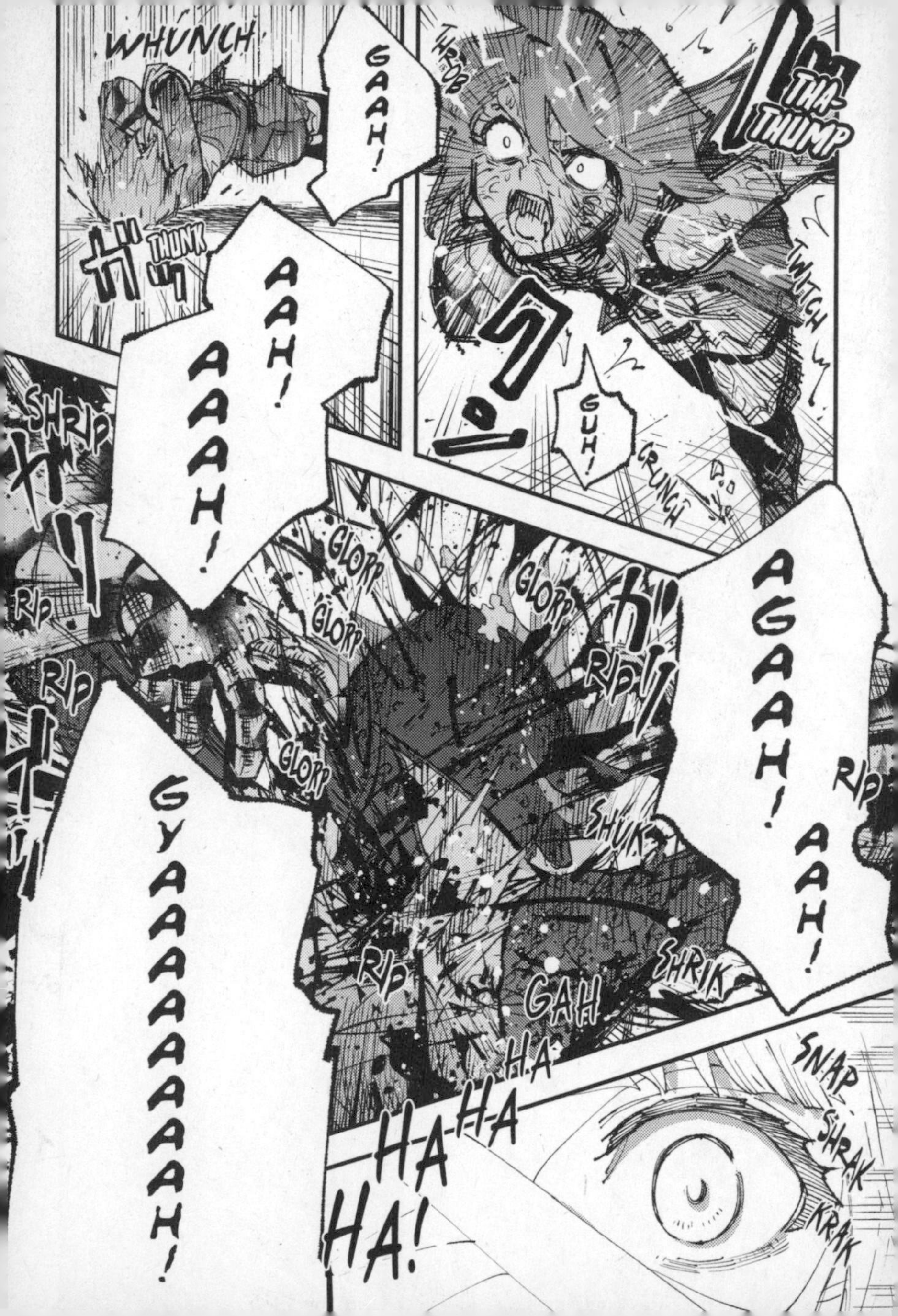
THROB
THA-THUMP
TWITCH
GUH!
CRUNCH
GAAH!
WHUNCH
THONK
AAH! AAAAH!
AGAAAH! AAH!
RIP
GLORP
GLORP
GLORP
RIP
SHRIP
RIP
RIP
GLORP
SHUK
SHRIK
GAH
RIP
GYAAAAAAAAAAAH!
SNAP
SHRAK
KRAK
HA
HA-HA
HA HA!

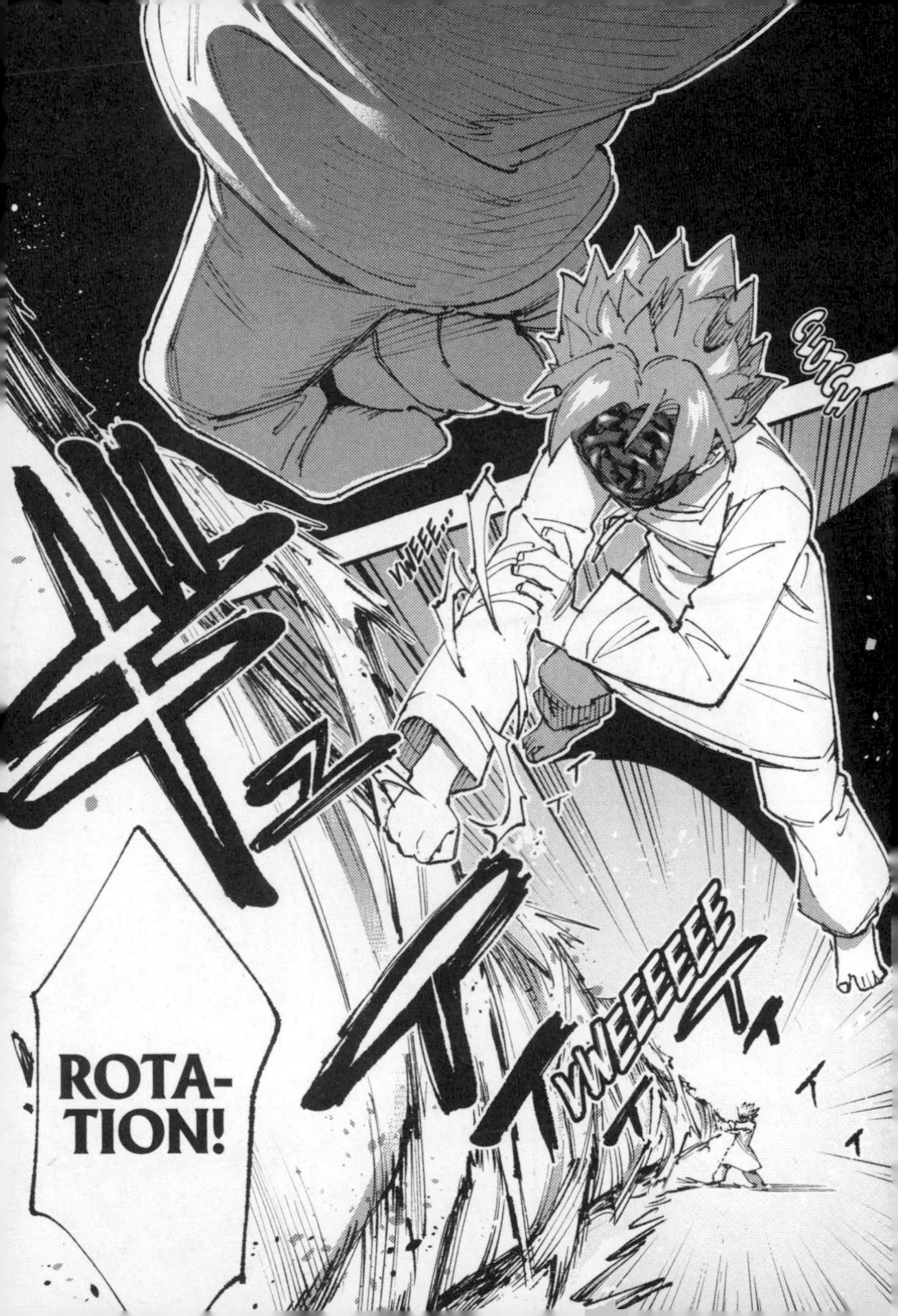
CLUTCH
VWEEE...
VWEEEEEE
ROTA-
TION!

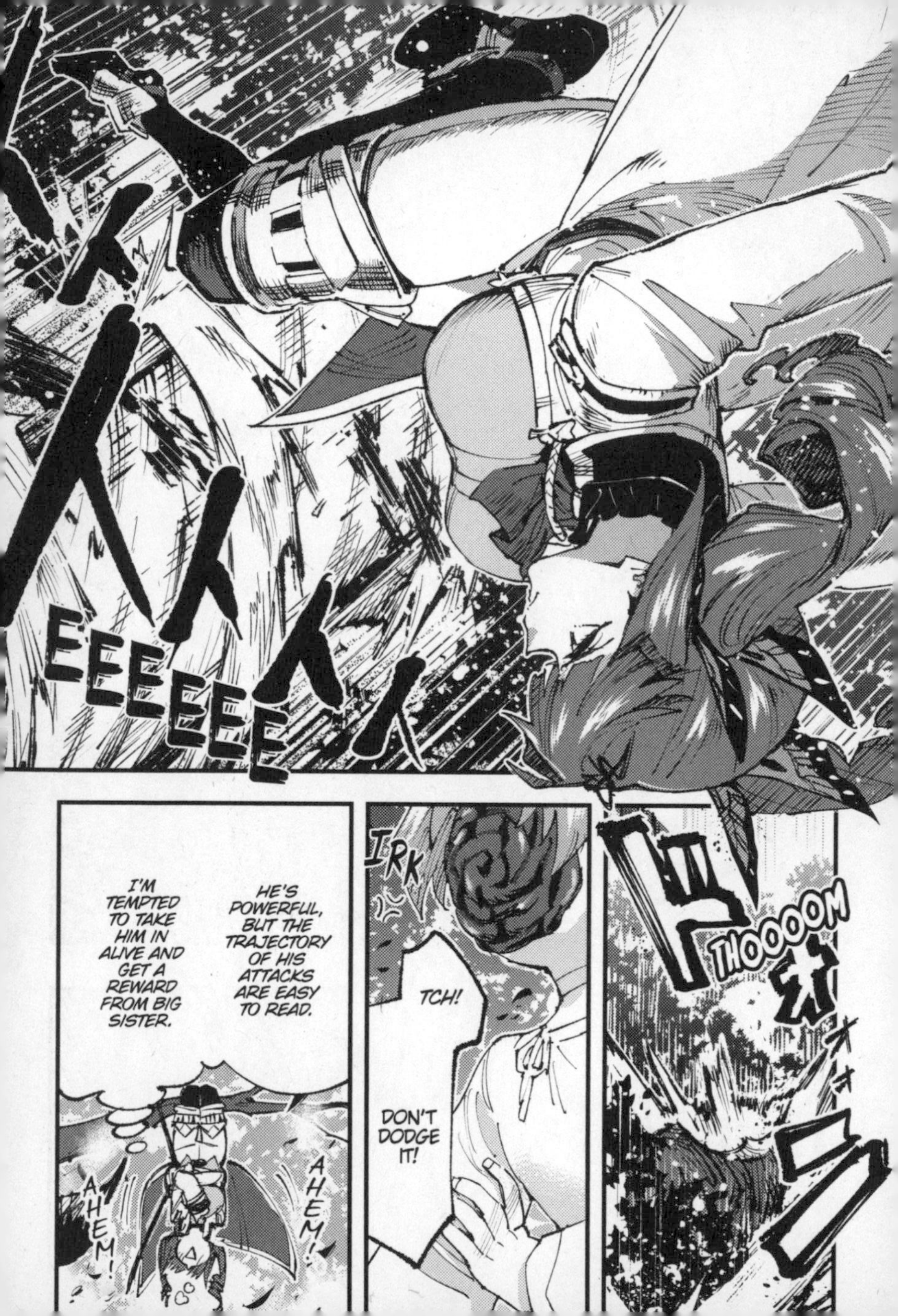
EEEEEEE
THOOOOM
IRK
TCH!
DON'T DODGE IT!
HE'S POWERFUL, BUT THE TRAJECTORY OF HIS ATTACKS ARE EASY TO READ.
I'M TEMPTED TO TAKE HIM IN ALIVE AND GET A REWARD FROM BIG SISTER.
AHEM!
AHEM!

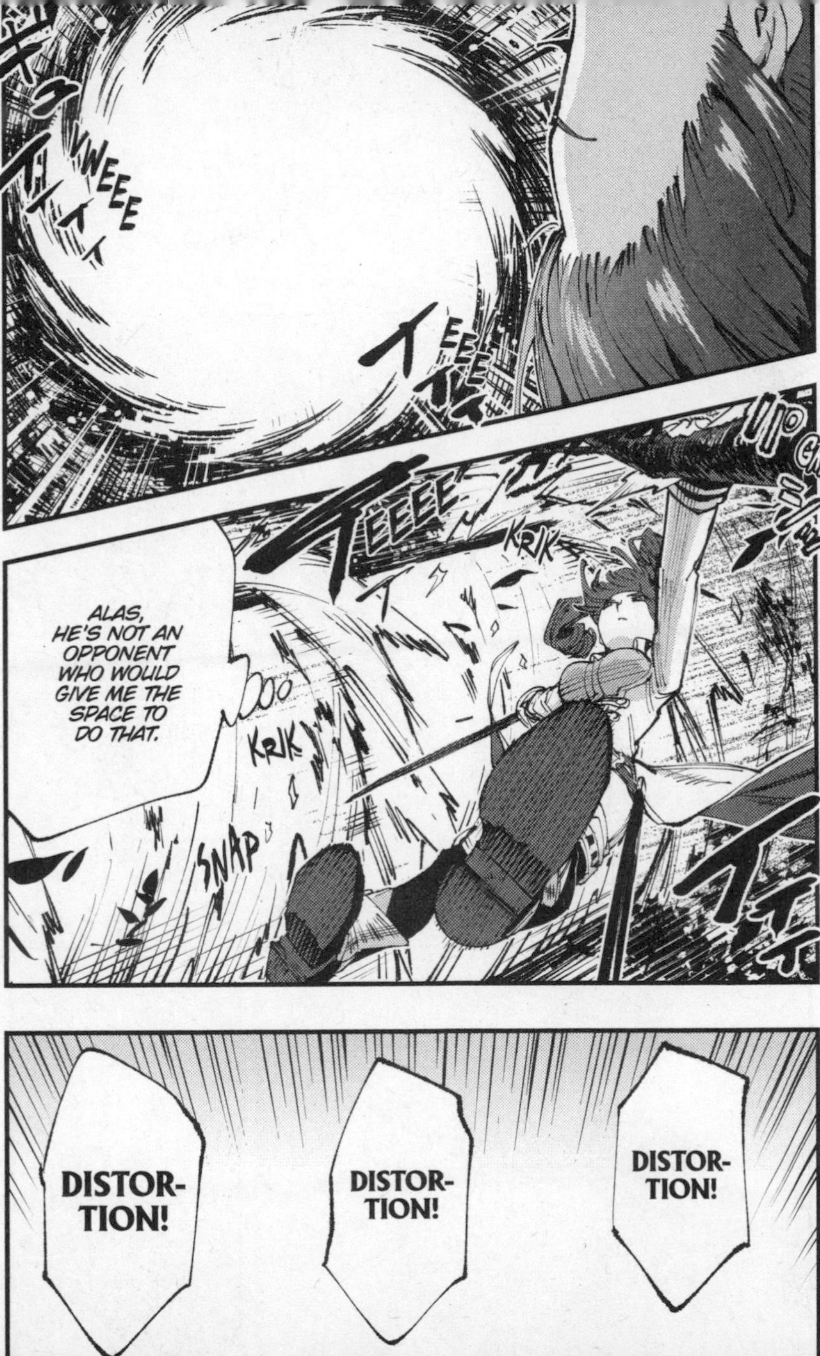
VWEEEE
EEEE
GRAB
TEEEE
KRIK
ALAS, HE'S NOT AN OPPONENT WHO WOULD GIVE ME THE SPACE TO DO THAT.
KRIK
SNAP
DISTOR-TION!
DISTOR-TION!
DISTOR-TION!

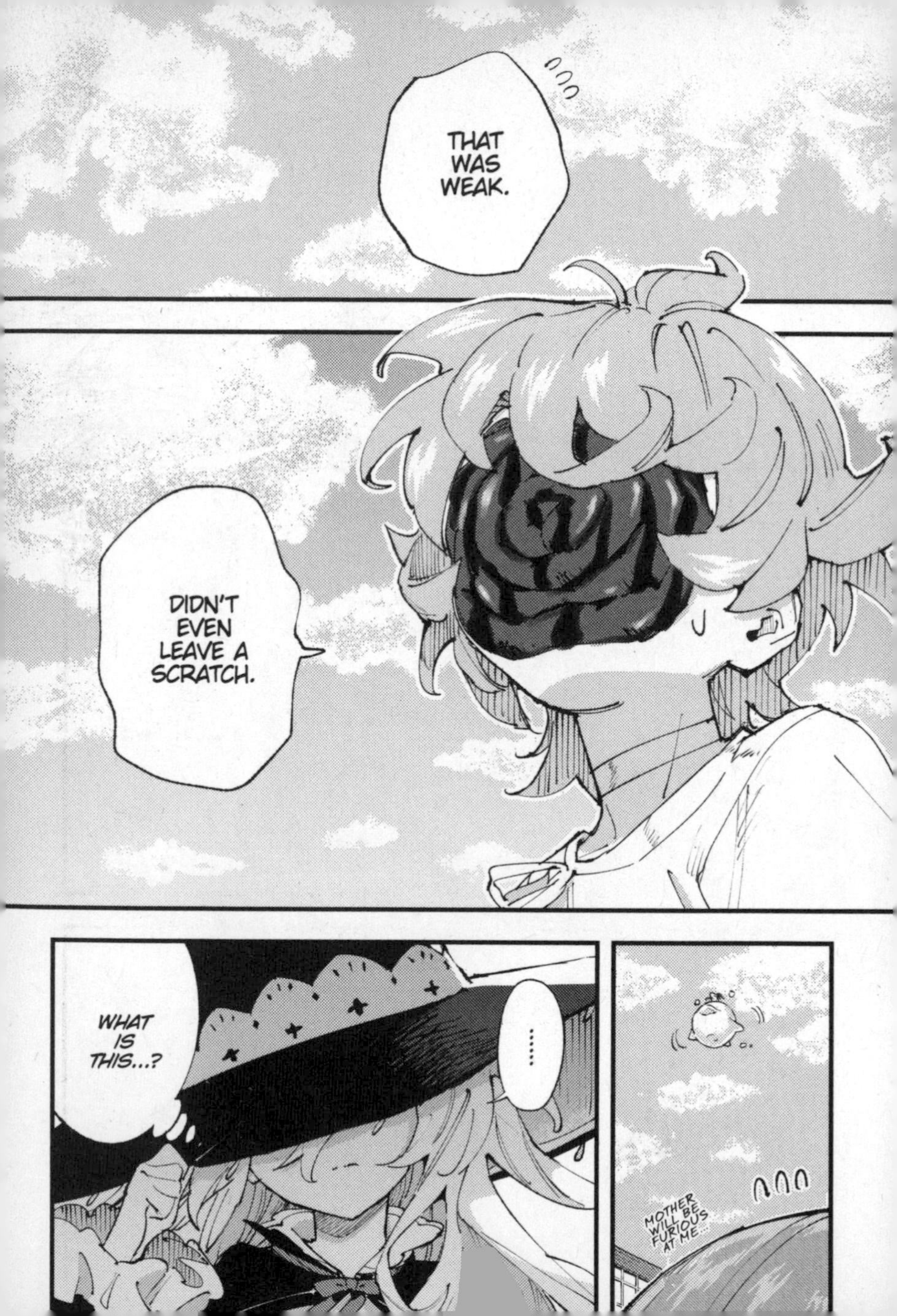
THAT WAS WEAK.
DIDN'T EVEN LEAVE A SCRATCH.
MOTHER WILL BE FURIOUS AT ME...
......
WHAT IS THIS...?

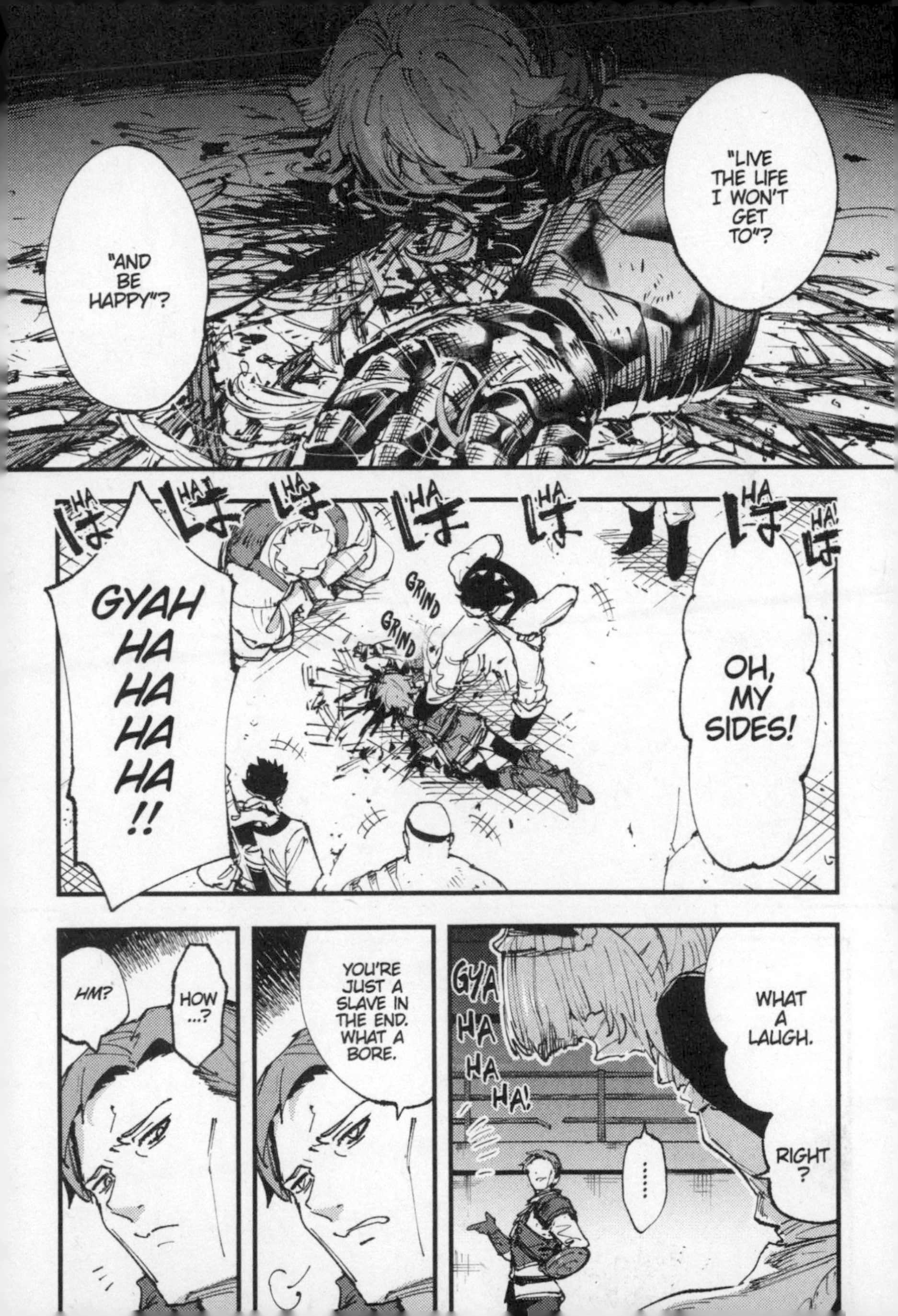
"LIVE THE LIFE I WON'T GET TO"?
"AND BE HAPPY"?
HA! HA HA HA HA HA HA!
OH, MY SIDES!
GRIND GRIND
GYAH HA HA HA HA HA!!
WHAT A LAUGH.
GYA HA HA HA!
RIGHT?
......
YOU'RE JUST A SLAVE IN THE END. WHAT A BORE.
HOW ...?
HM?

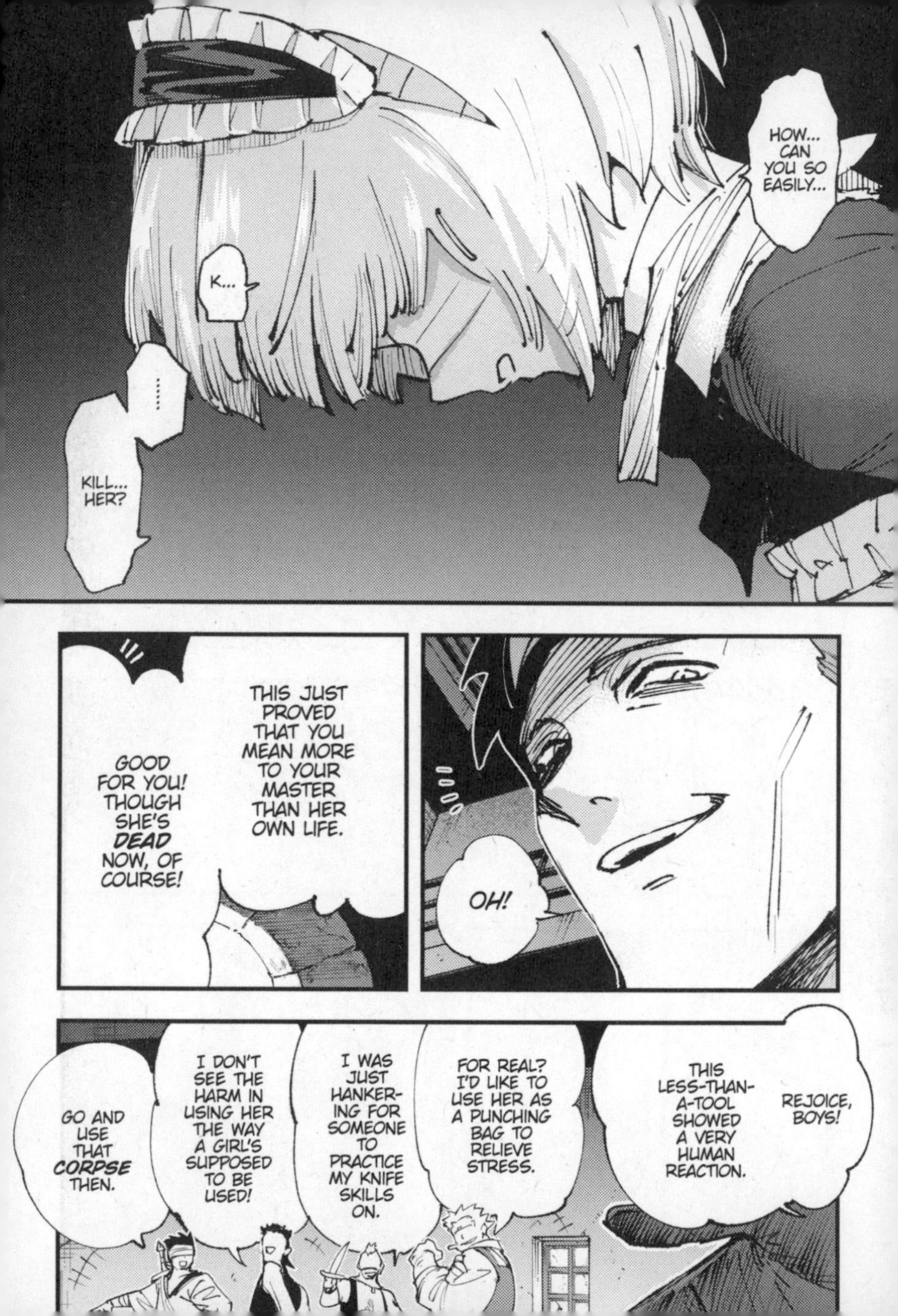
HOW... CAN YOU SO EASILY...
K...
......
KILL... HER?
OH!
THIS JUST PROVED THAT YOU MEAN MORE TO YOUR MASTER THAN HER OWN LIFE.
GOOD FOR YOU! THOUGH SHE'S DEAD NOW, OF COURSE!
REJOICE, BOYS!
THIS LESS-THAN-A-TOOL SHOWED A VERY HUMAN REACTION.
FOR REAL? I'D LIKE TO USE HER AS A PUNCHING BAG TO RELIEVE STRESS.
I WAS JUST HANKERING FOR SOMEONE TO PRACTICE MY KNIFE SKILLS ON.
I DON'T SEE THE HARM IN USING HER THE WAY A GIRL'S SUPPOSED TO BE USED!
GO AND USE THAT CORPSE THEN.

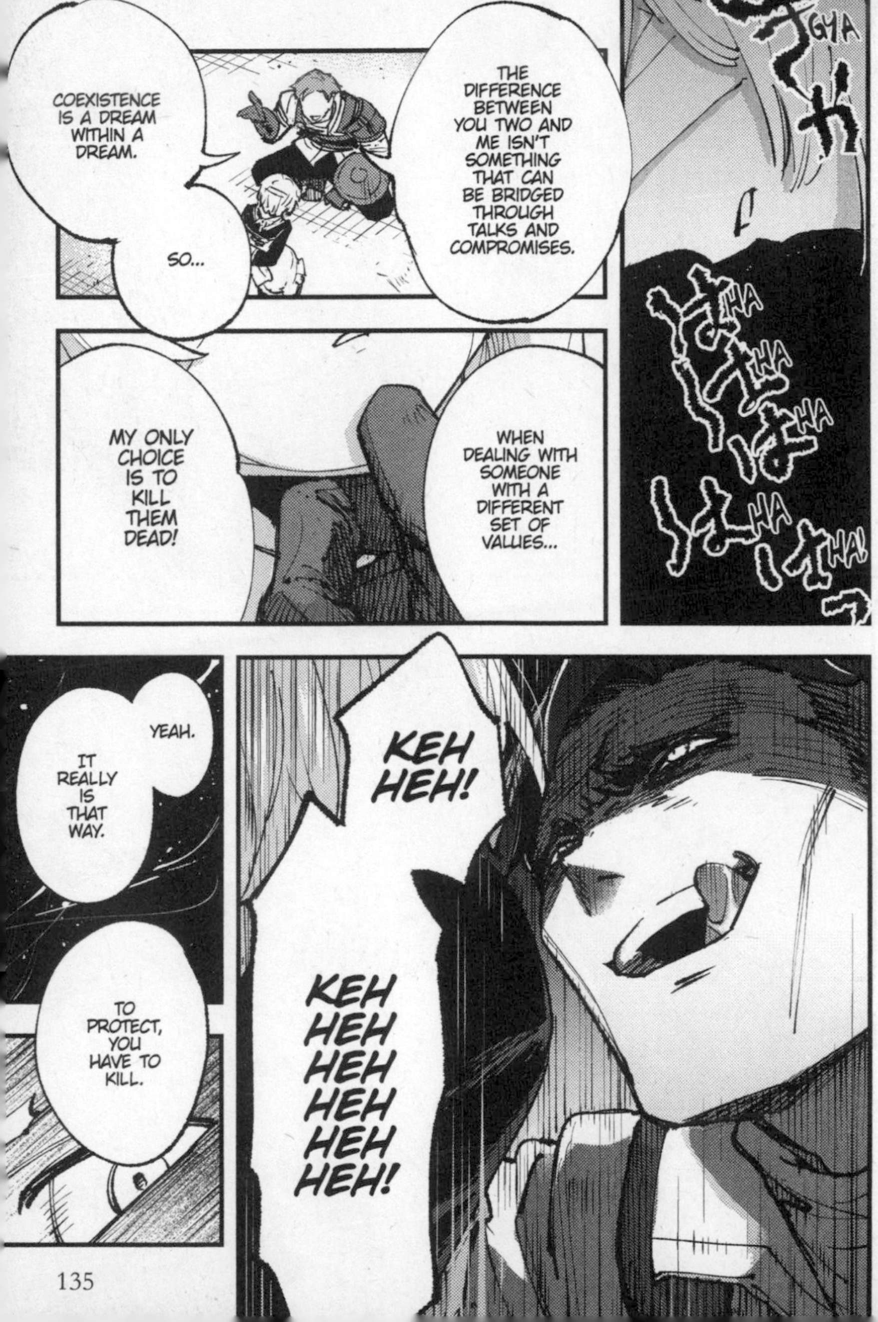
GYA
HA HA HA HA!
THE DIFFERENCE BETWEEN YOU TWO AND ME ISN'T SOMETHING THAT CAN BE BRIDGED THROUGH TALKS AND COMPROMISES.
COEXISTENCE IS A DREAM WITHIN A DREAM.
SO...
WHEN DEALING WITH SOMEONE WITH A DIFFERENT SET OF VALUES...
MY ONLY CHOICE IS TO KILL THEM DEAD!
KEH HEH!
KEH HEH HEH HEH HEH HEH!
YEAH.
IT REALLY IS THAT WAY.
TO PROTECT, YOU HAVE TO KILL.

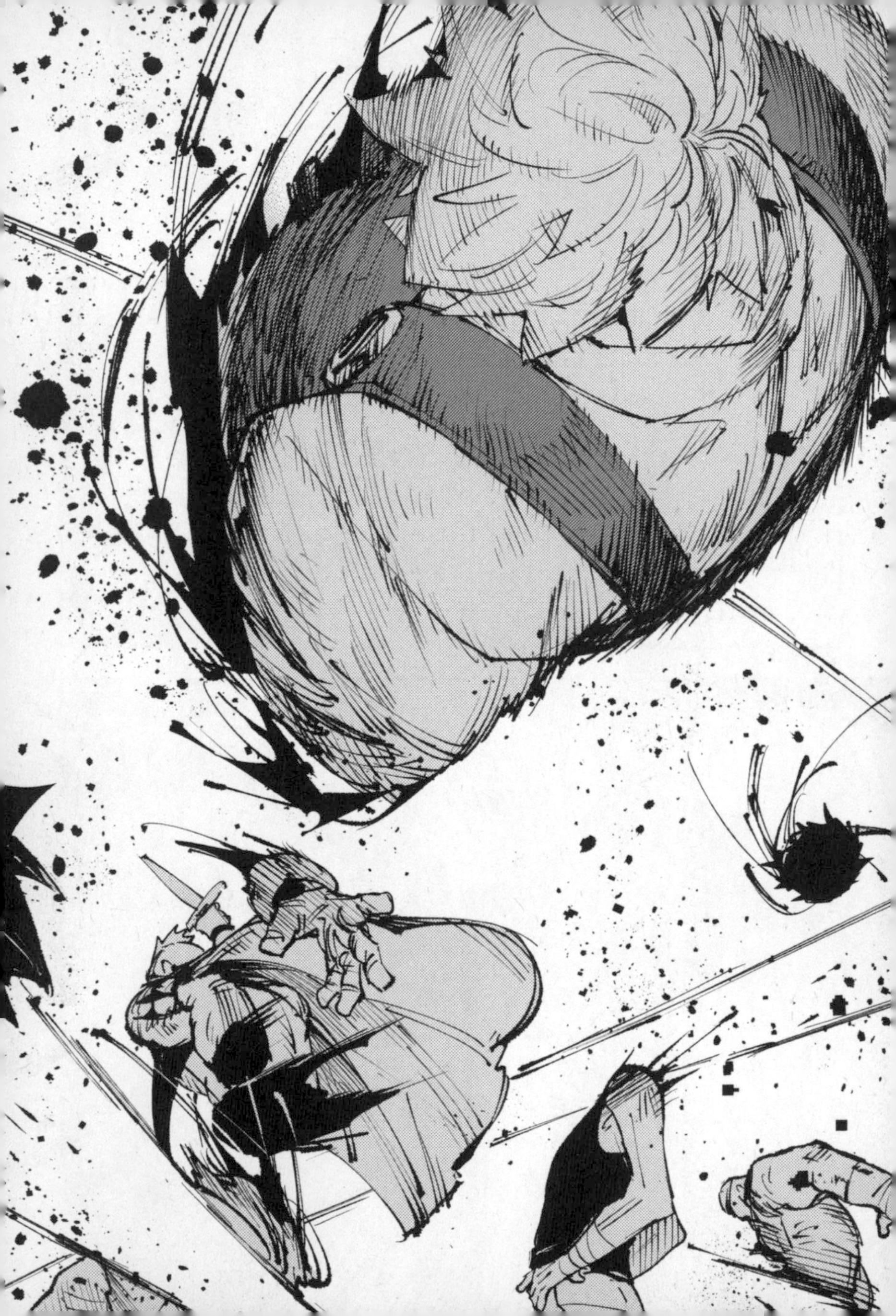

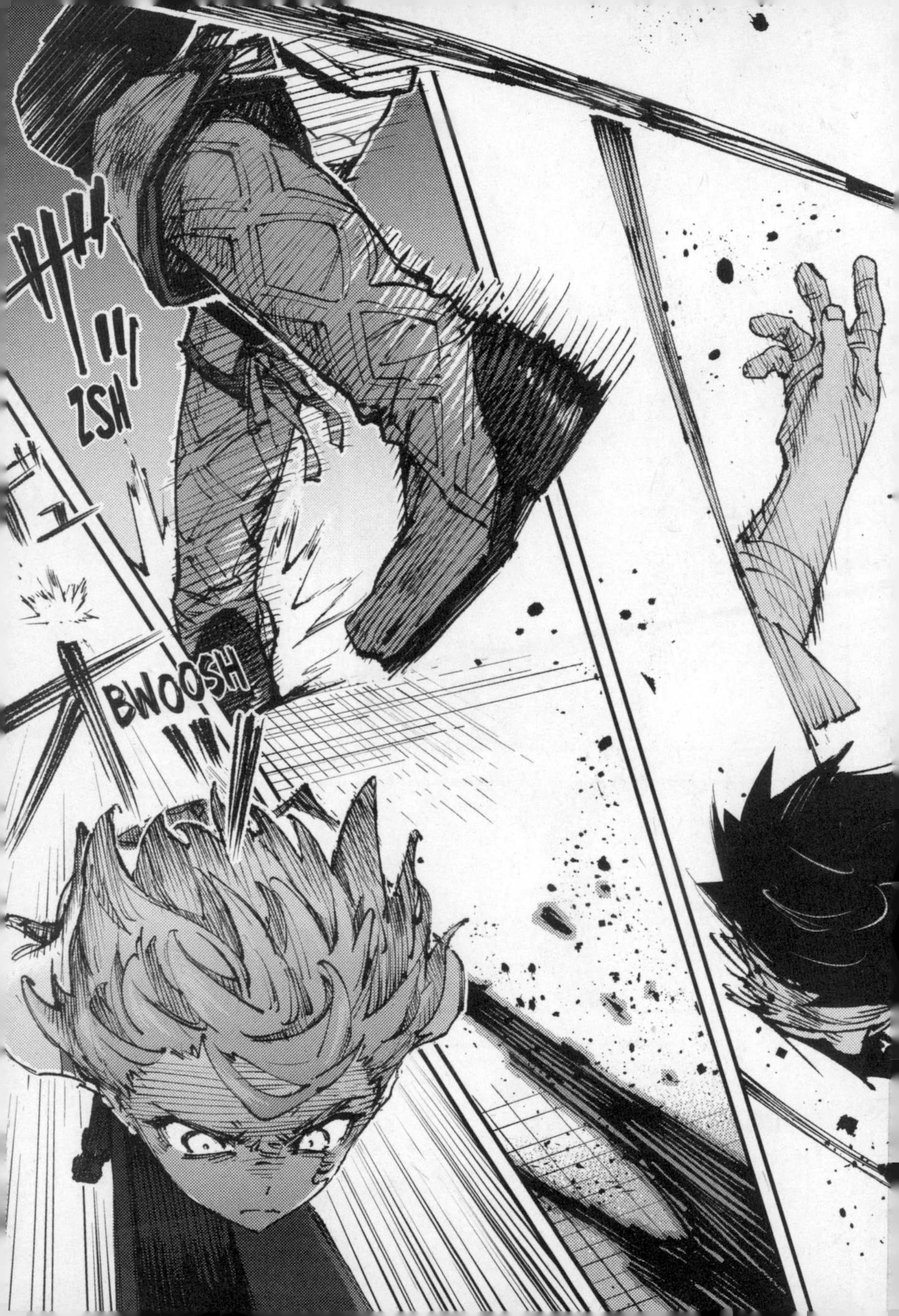
ZSH
BWOOSH

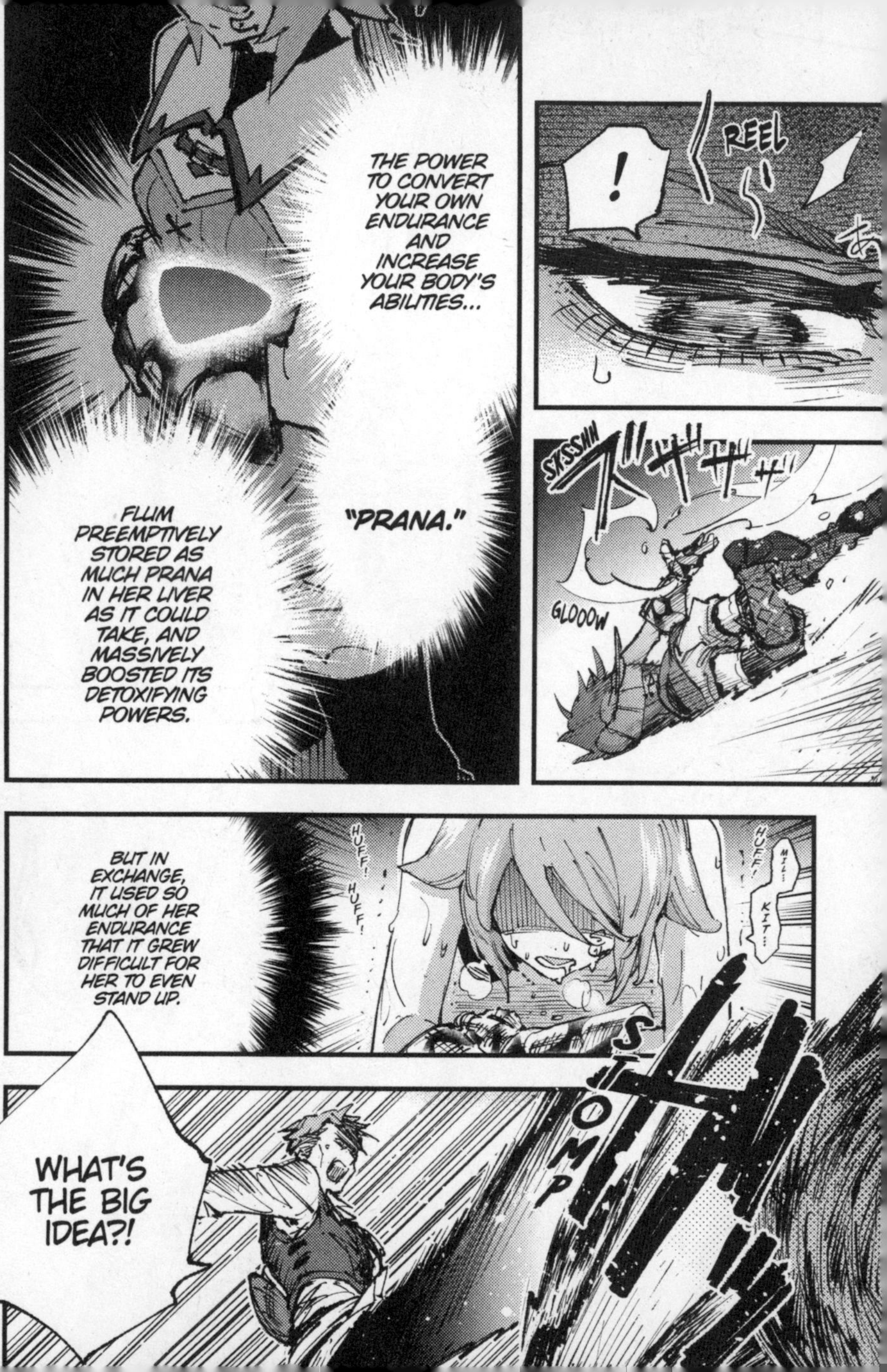
!
REEL
SX-S-SHHH
GLOOOW
THE POWER TO CONVERT YOUR OWN ENDURANCE AND INCREASE YOUR BODY'S ABILITIES...
"PRANA."
FLUM PREEMPTIVELY STORED AS MUCH PRANA IN HER LIVER AS IT COULD TAKE, AND MASSIVELY BOOSTED ITS DETOXIFYING POWERS.
HUFF!
MIL... KIT...
HUFF! HUFF!
BUT IN EXCHANGE, IT USED SO MUCH OF HER ENDURANCE THAT IT GREW DIFFICULT FOR HER TO EVEN STAND UP.
STOMP
WHAT'S THE BIG IDEA?!

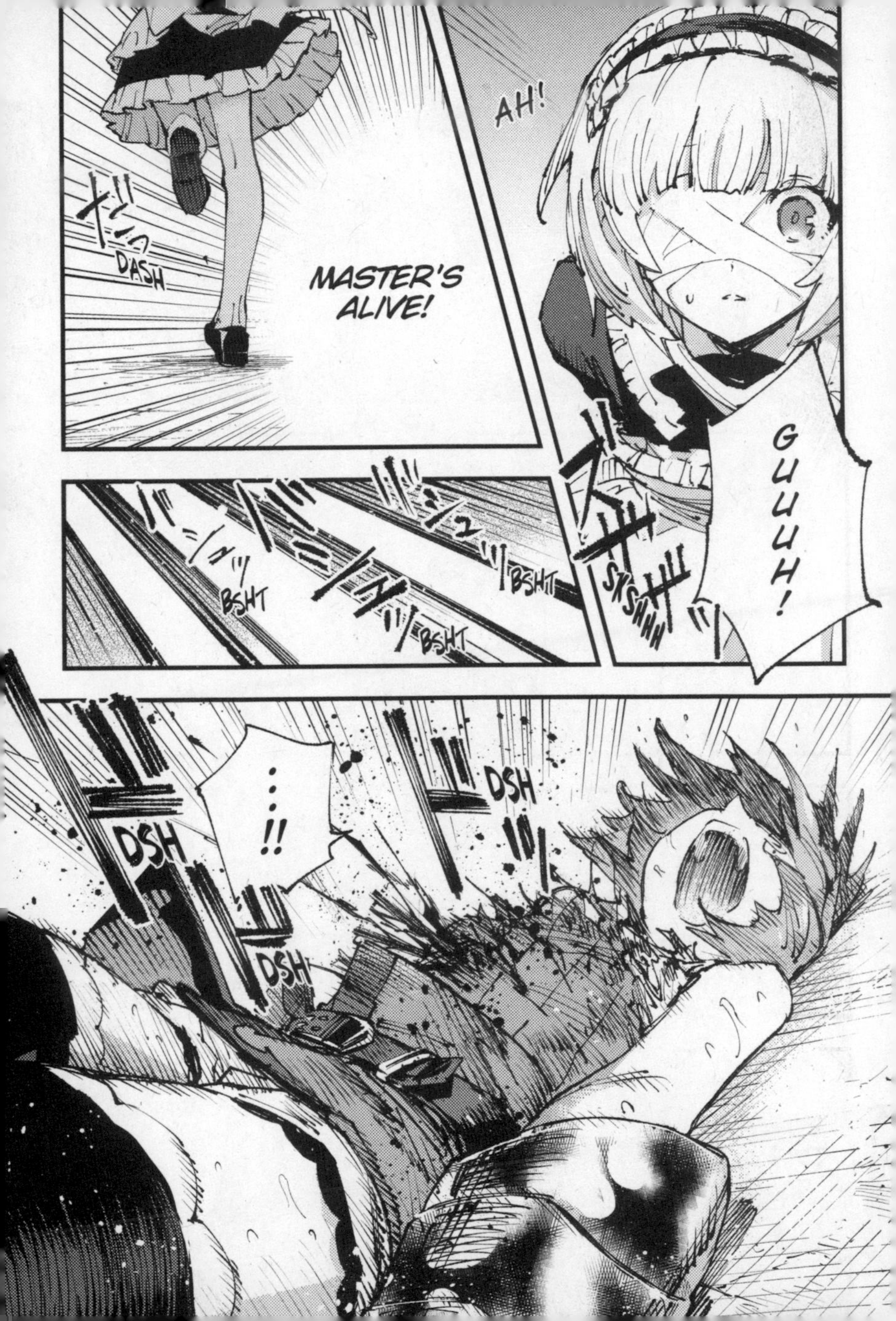
AH!
GUUUH!
SKSHHH
DASH
MASTER'S ALIVE!
BSHT
BSHT
BSHT
DSH
...!!
DSH
DSH

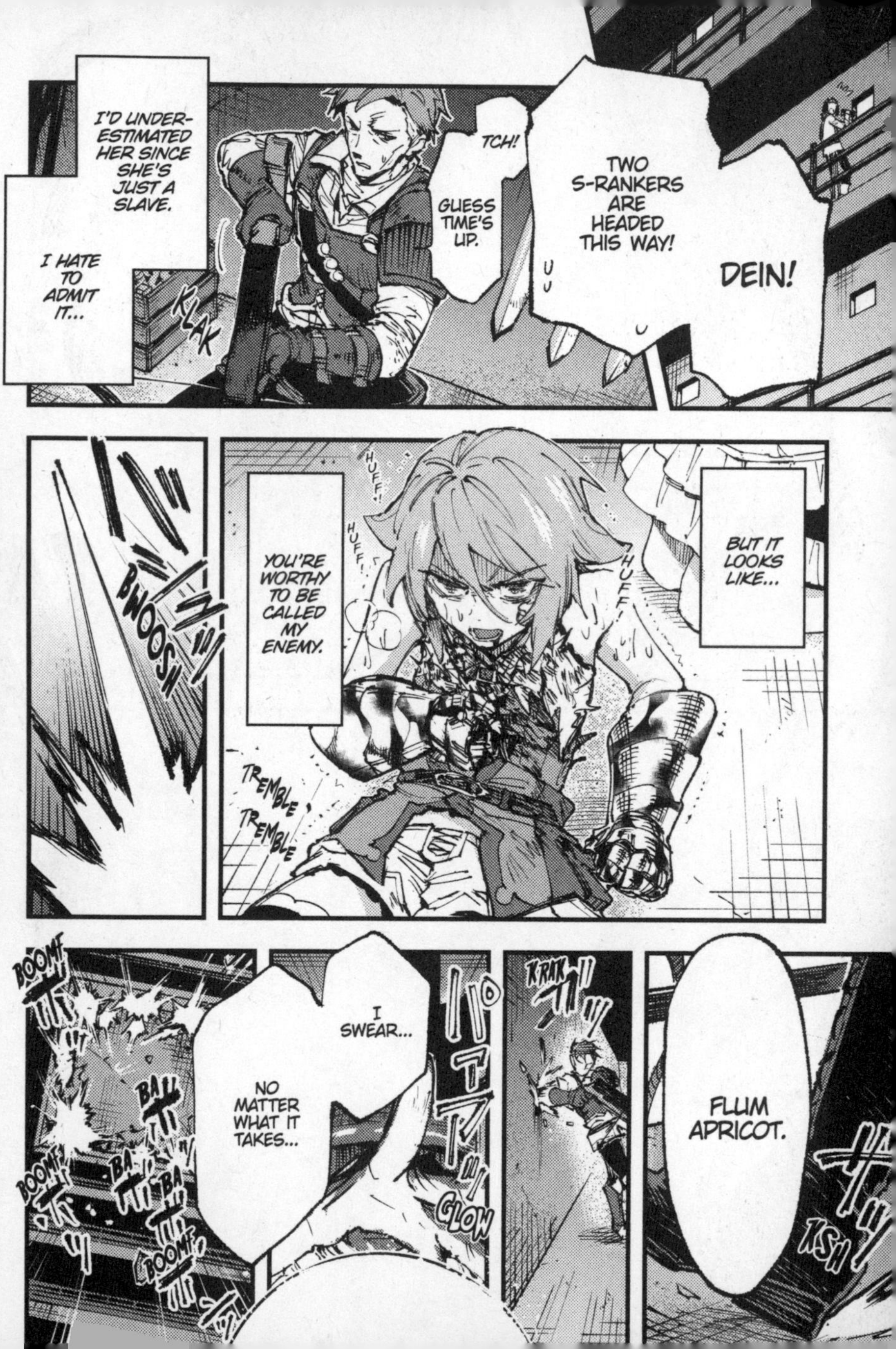
DEIN!
TWO S-RANKERS ARE HEADED THIS WAY!
TCH!
GUESS TIME'S UP.
I'D UNDER-ESTIMATED HER SINCE SHE'S JUST A SLAVE.
I HATE TO ADMIT IT...
KLAK
BUT IT LOOKS LIKE...
HUFF
HUFF
HUFF
YOU'RE WORTHY TO BE CALLED MY ENEMY.
TREMBLE TREMBLE
BWOOSH
FLUM APRICOT.
KSH
KRAK
I SWEAR...
NO MATTER WHAT IT TAKES...
GLOW
BOOMF
BA
BA
BA
BOOMF
BOOMF

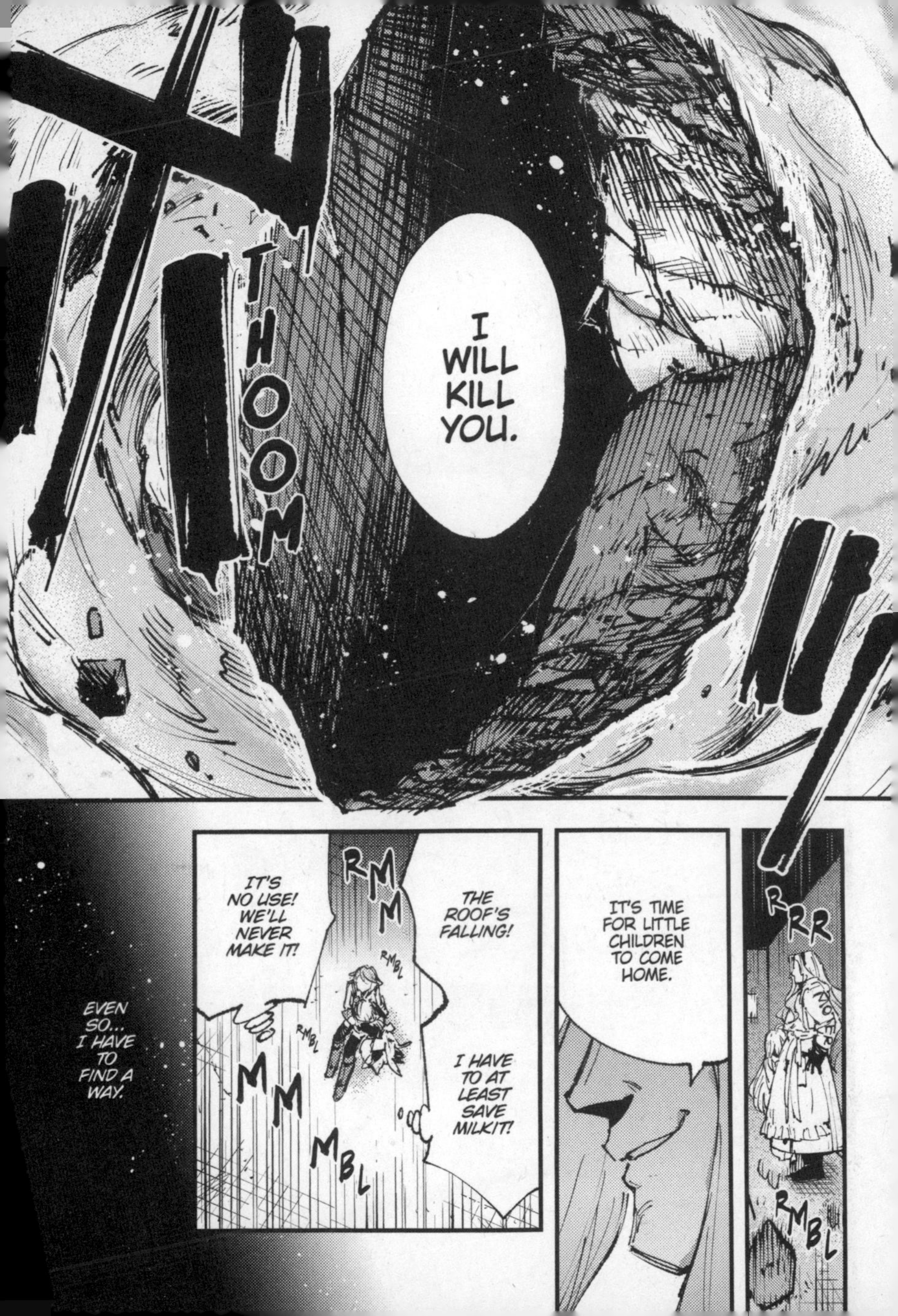
I WILL KILL YOU.
THOOM
RRR
RMBL
IT'S TIME FOR LITTLE CHILDREN TO COME HOME.
THE ROOF'S FALLING!
RMMM
IT'S NO USE! WE'LL NEVER MAKE IT!
RMBL
RMBL
I HAVE TO AT LEAST SAVE MILKIT!
MMMMBL
EVEN SO... I HAVE TO FIND A WAY.

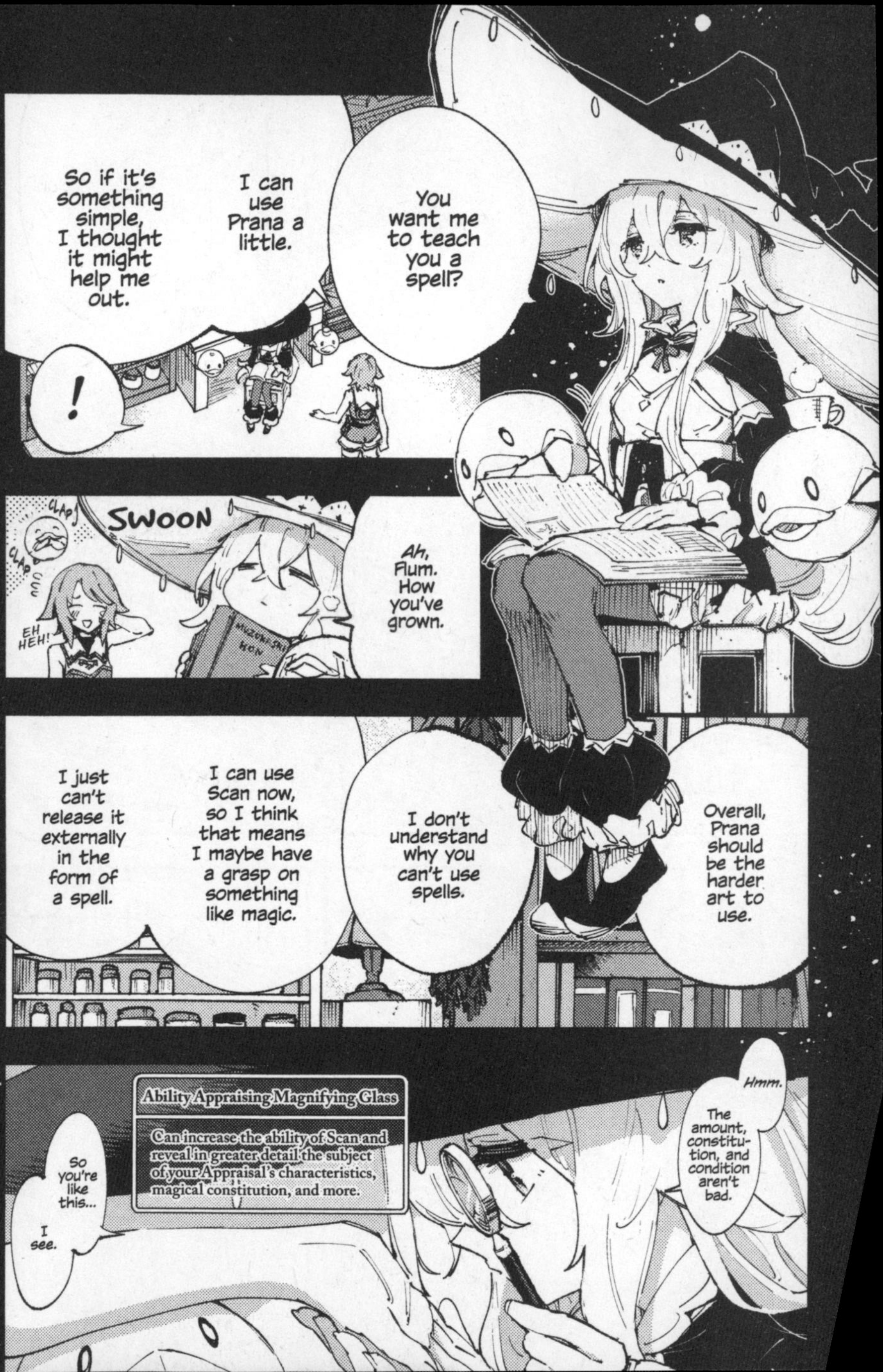
You want me to teach you a spell?
I can use Prana a little.
So if it's something simple, I thought it might help me out.
!
Ah, Flum. How you've grown.
SWOON
CLAP CLAP
EH HEH!
Overall, Prana should be the harder art to use.
I don't understand why you can't use spells.
I can use Scan now, so I think that means I maybe have a grasp on something like magic.
I just can't release it externally in the form of a spell.
Hmm.
The amount, constitution, and condition aren't bad.
Ability Appraising Magnifying Glass
Can increase the ability of Scan and reveal in greater detail the subject of your Appraisal's characteristics, magical constitution, and more.
So you're like this...
I see.

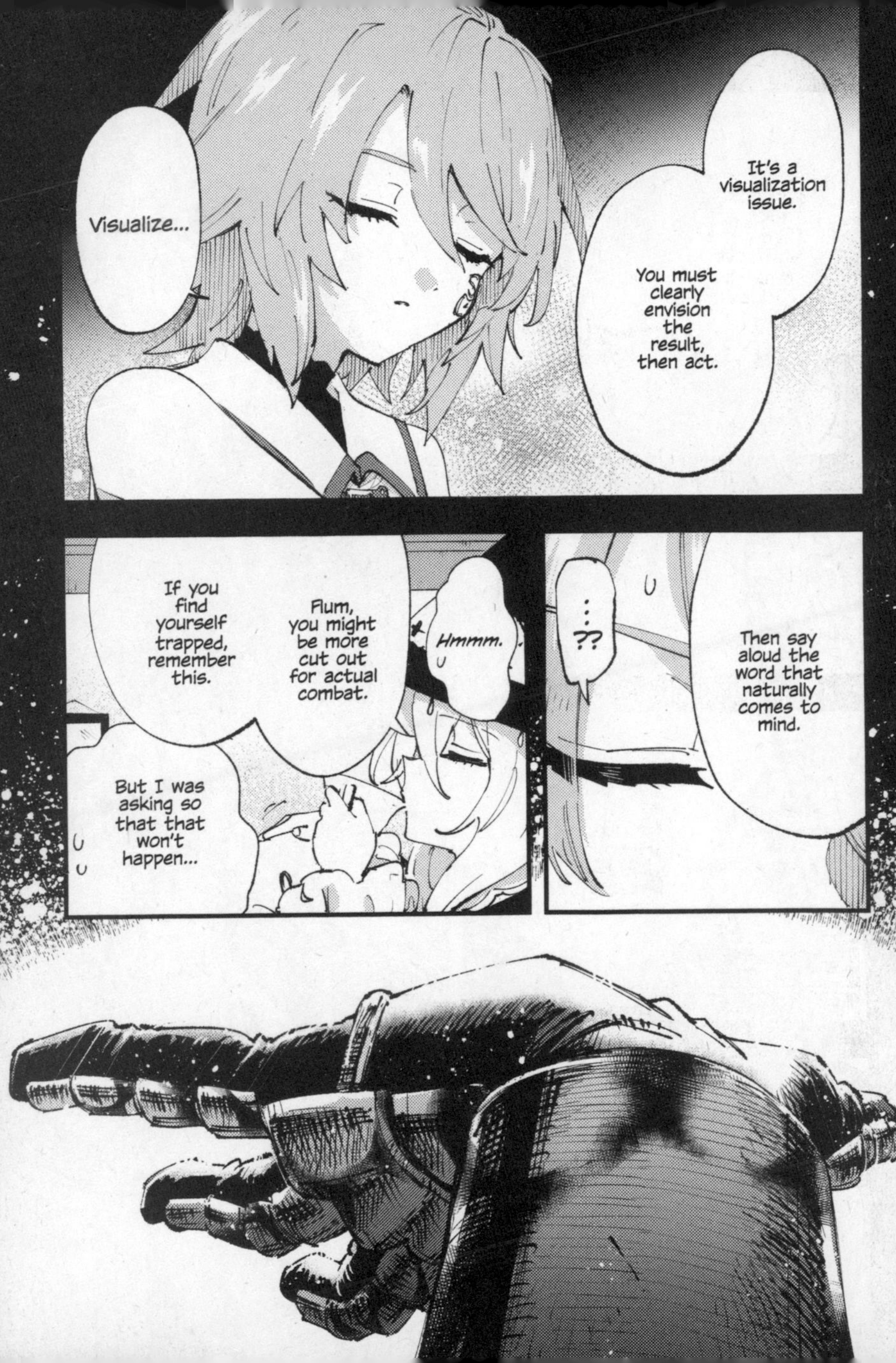
It's a visualization issue.
You must clearly envision the result, then act.
Visualize...
Then say aloud the word that naturally comes to mind.
...??
Hmmm.
Flum, you might be more cut out for actual combat.
If you find yourself trapped, remember this.
But I was asking so that that won't happen...

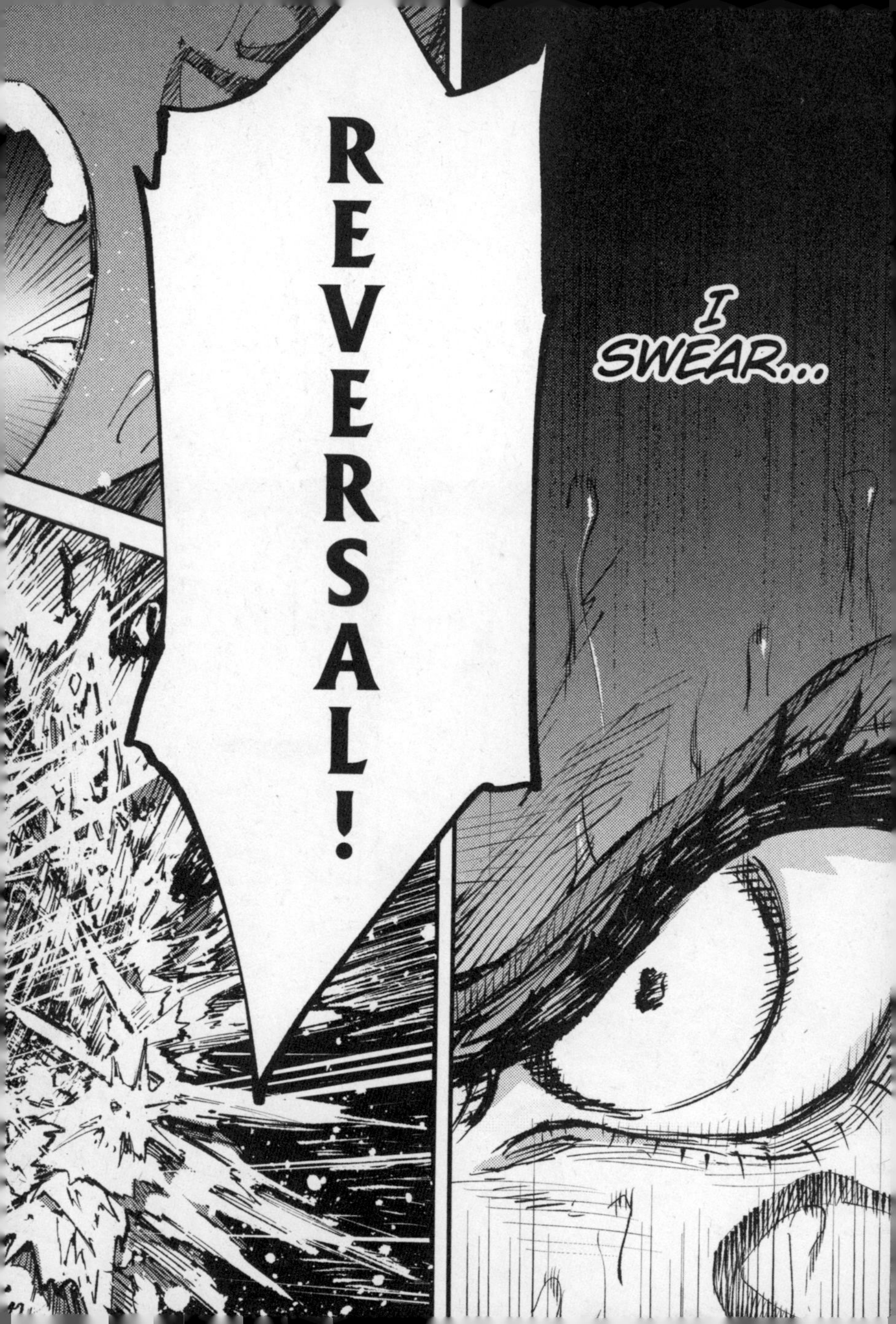
I SWEAR...
REVERSAL!

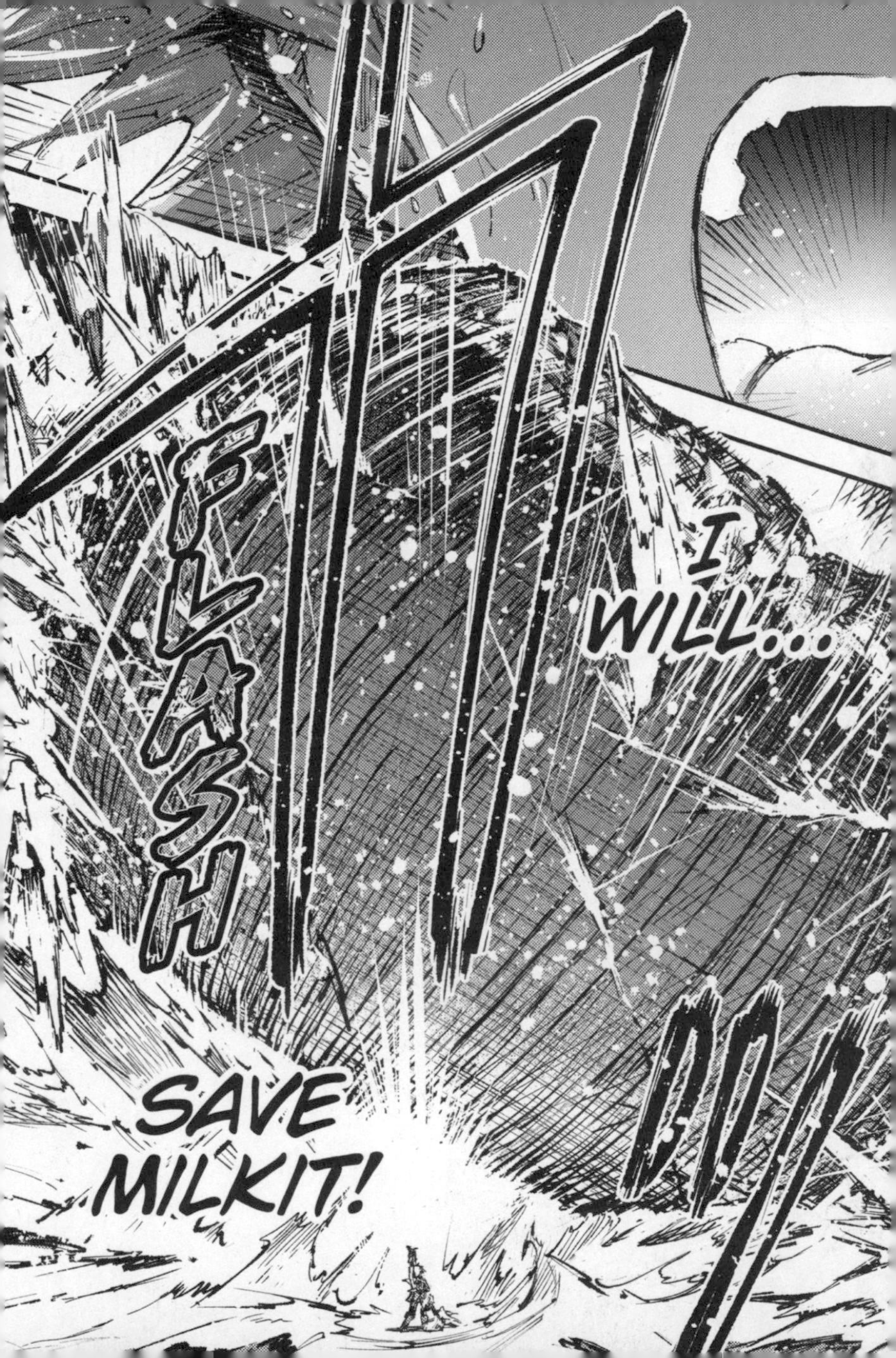
I WILL...
FLASH
SAVE MILKIT!

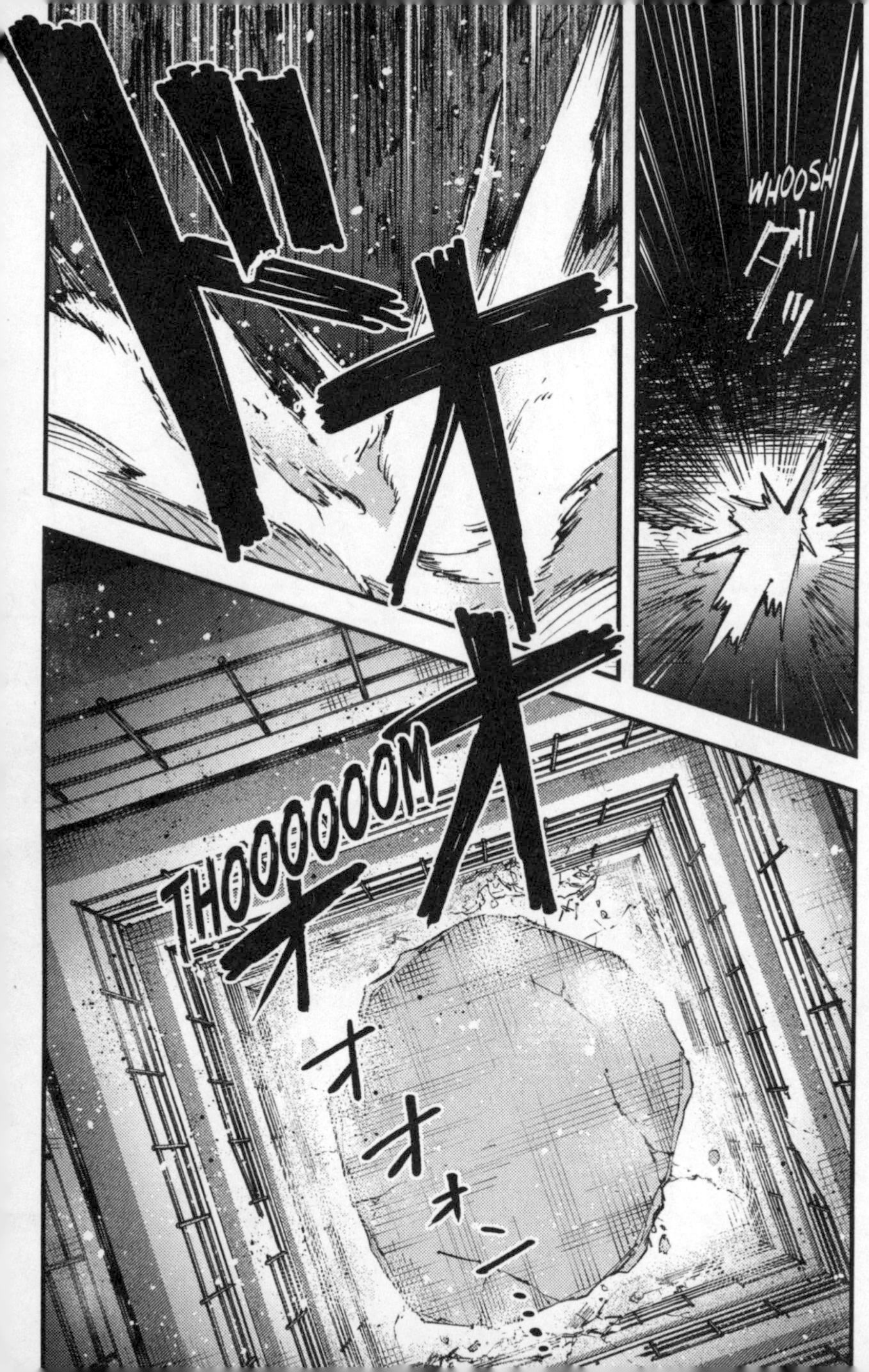
WHOOSH
THOOOOOM

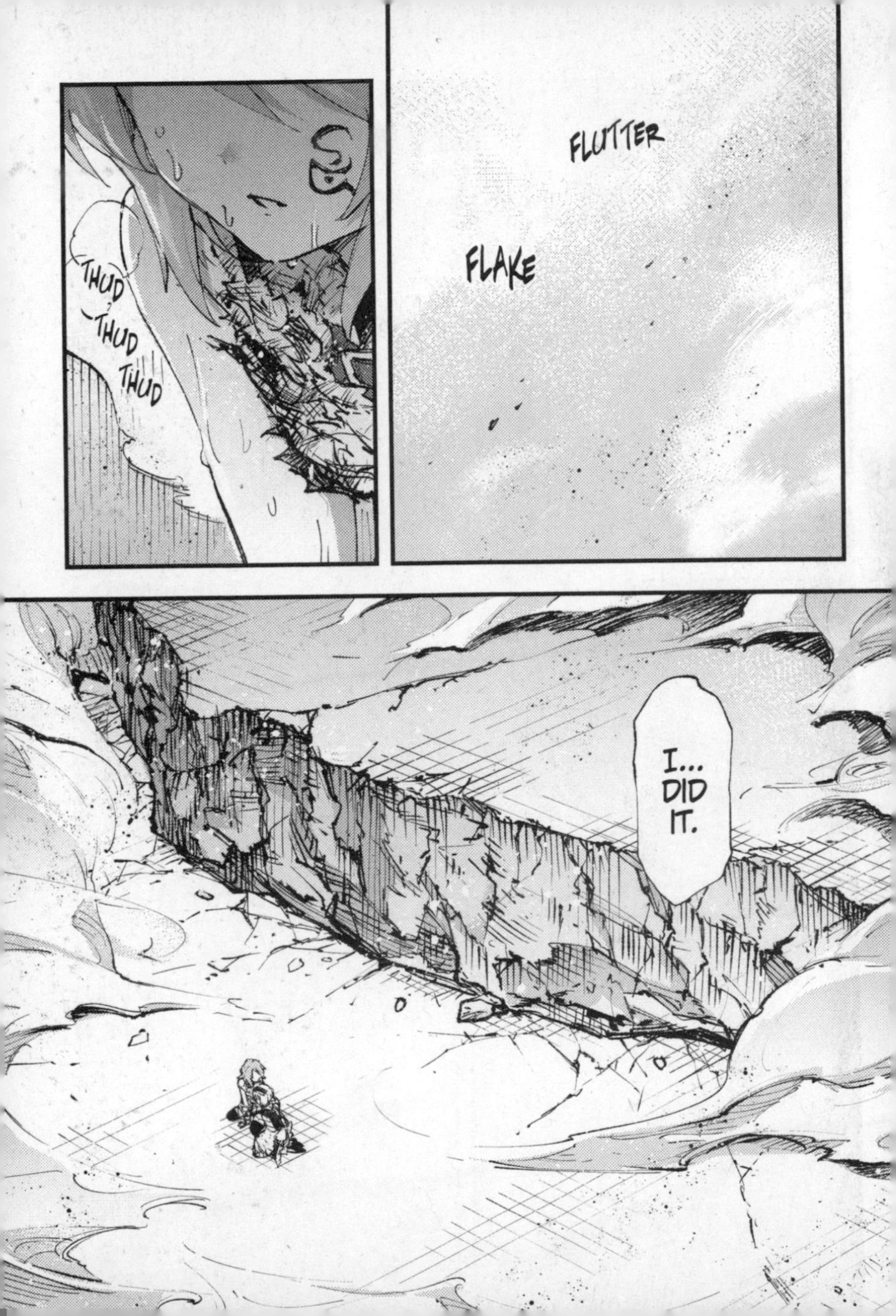
FLUTTER
FLAKE
THUD THUD THUD
I... DID IT.

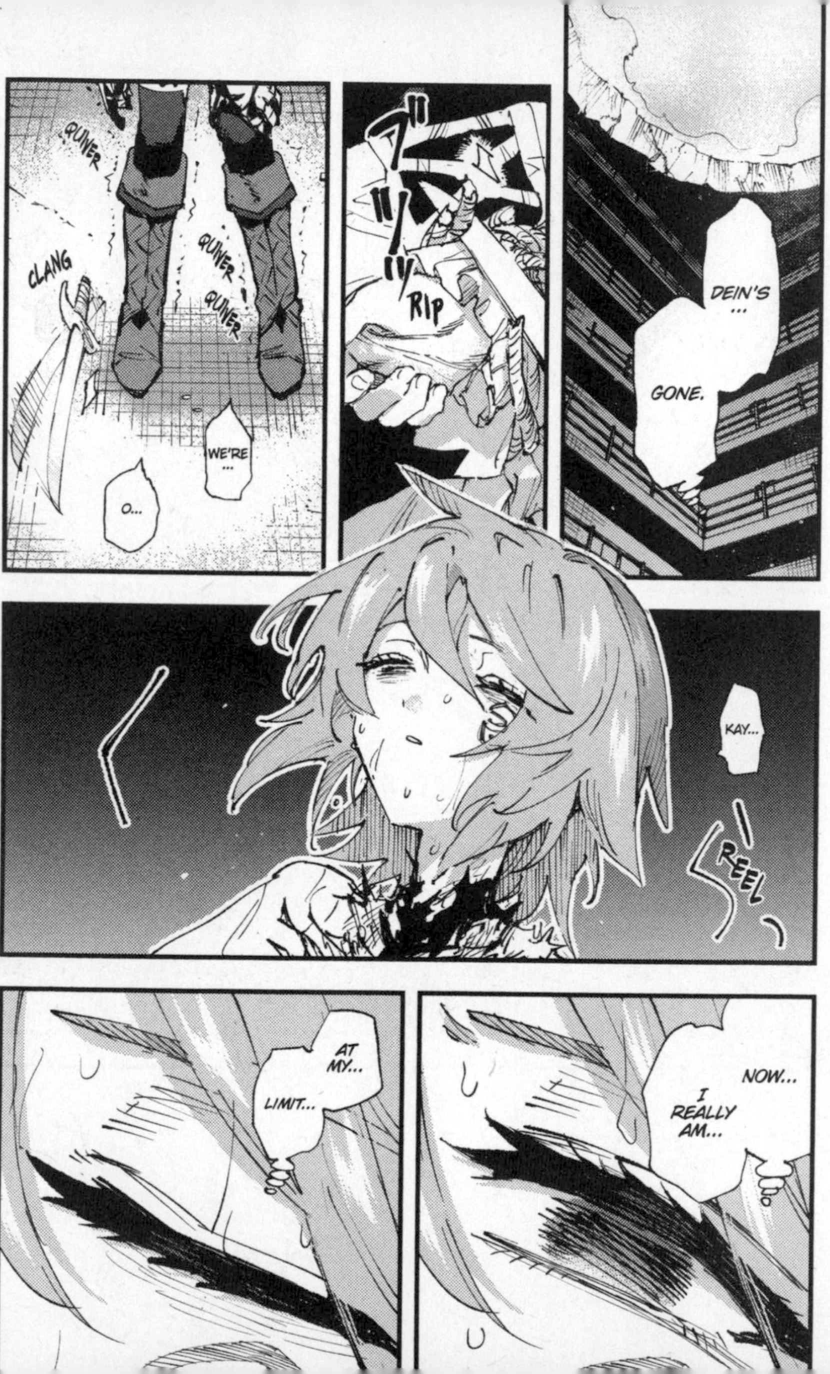
DEIN'S...
GONE.
RIP
QUIVER
QUIVER
QUIVER
CLANG
WE'RE...
O...
KAY...
REEL
NOW... I REALLY AM...
AT MY... LIMIT...

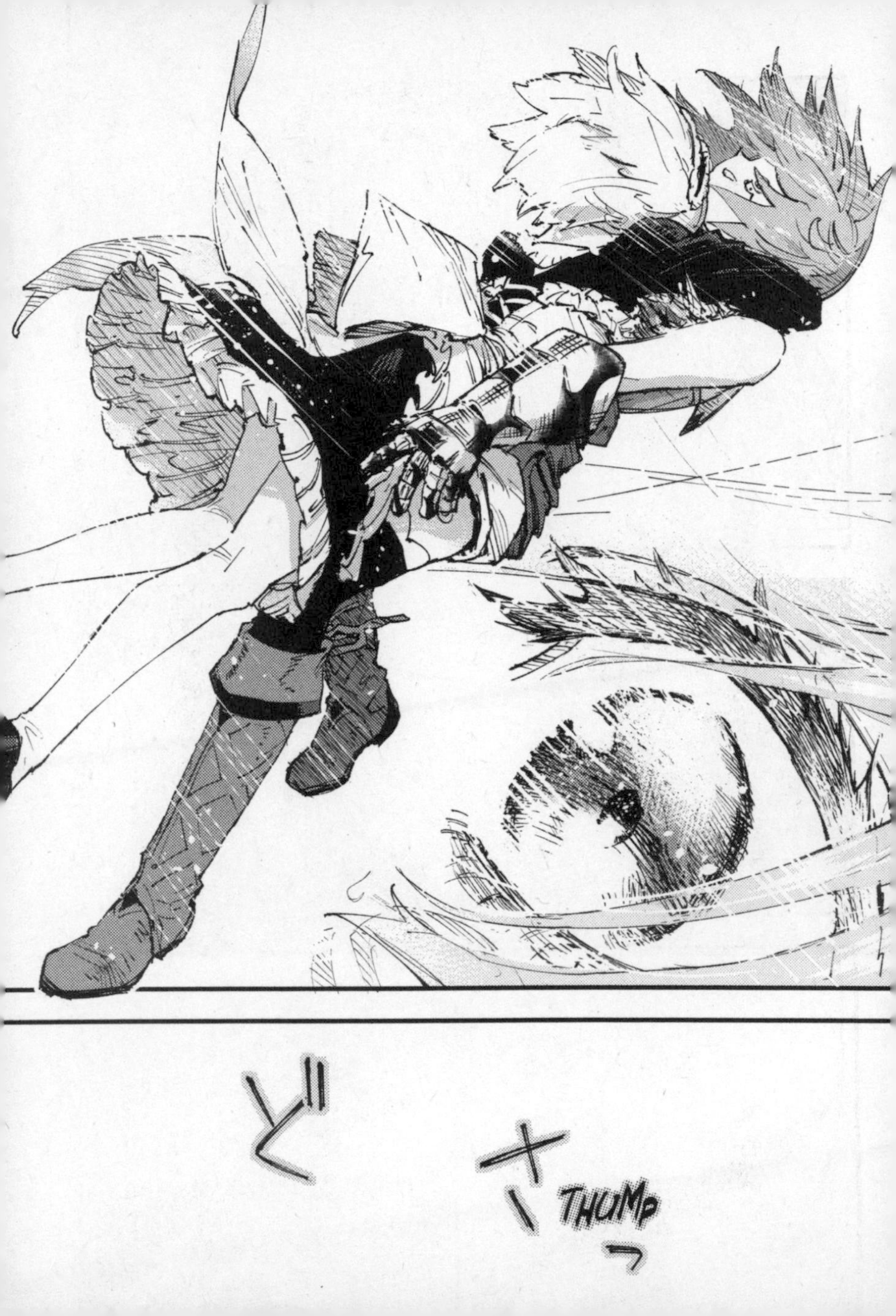
どさッ
THUMP

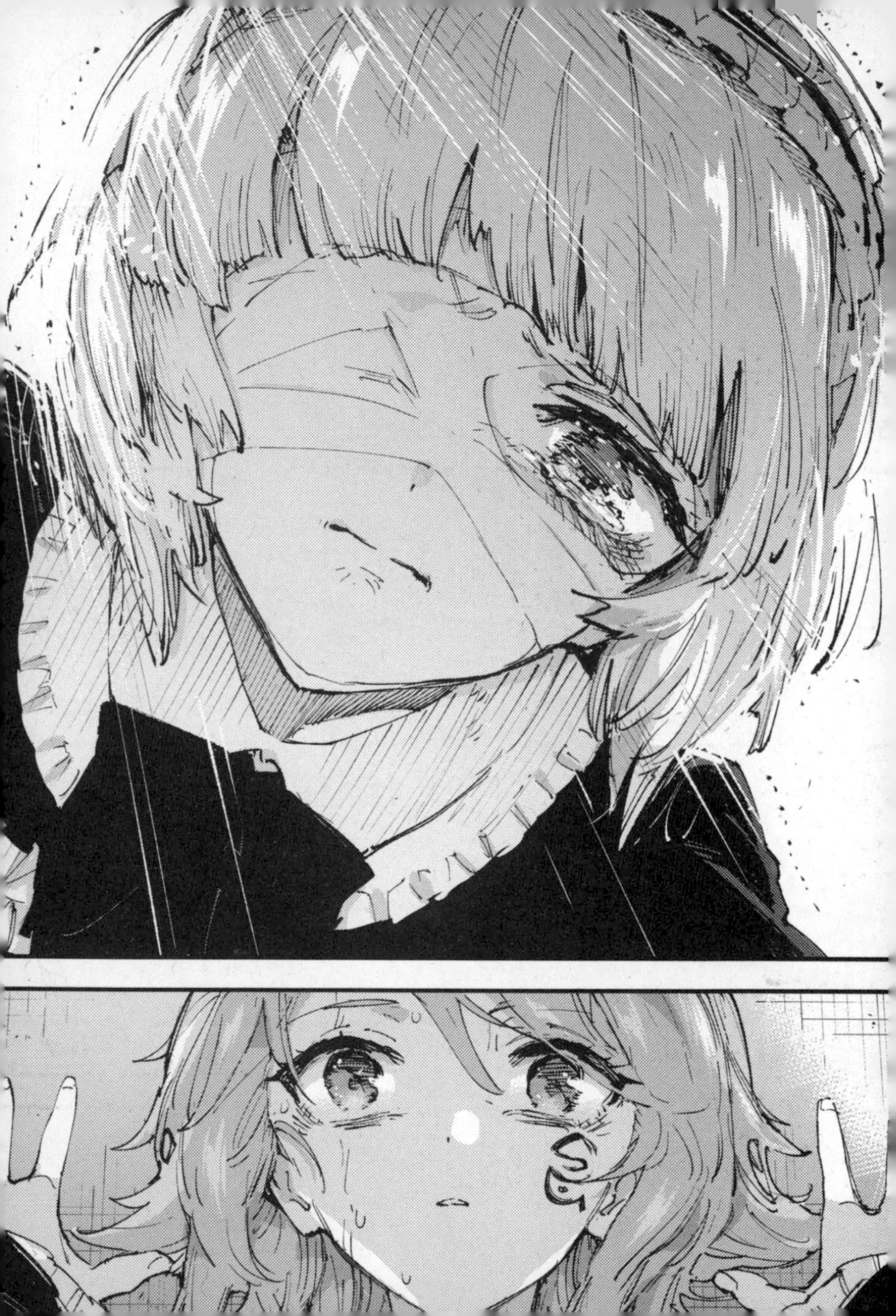

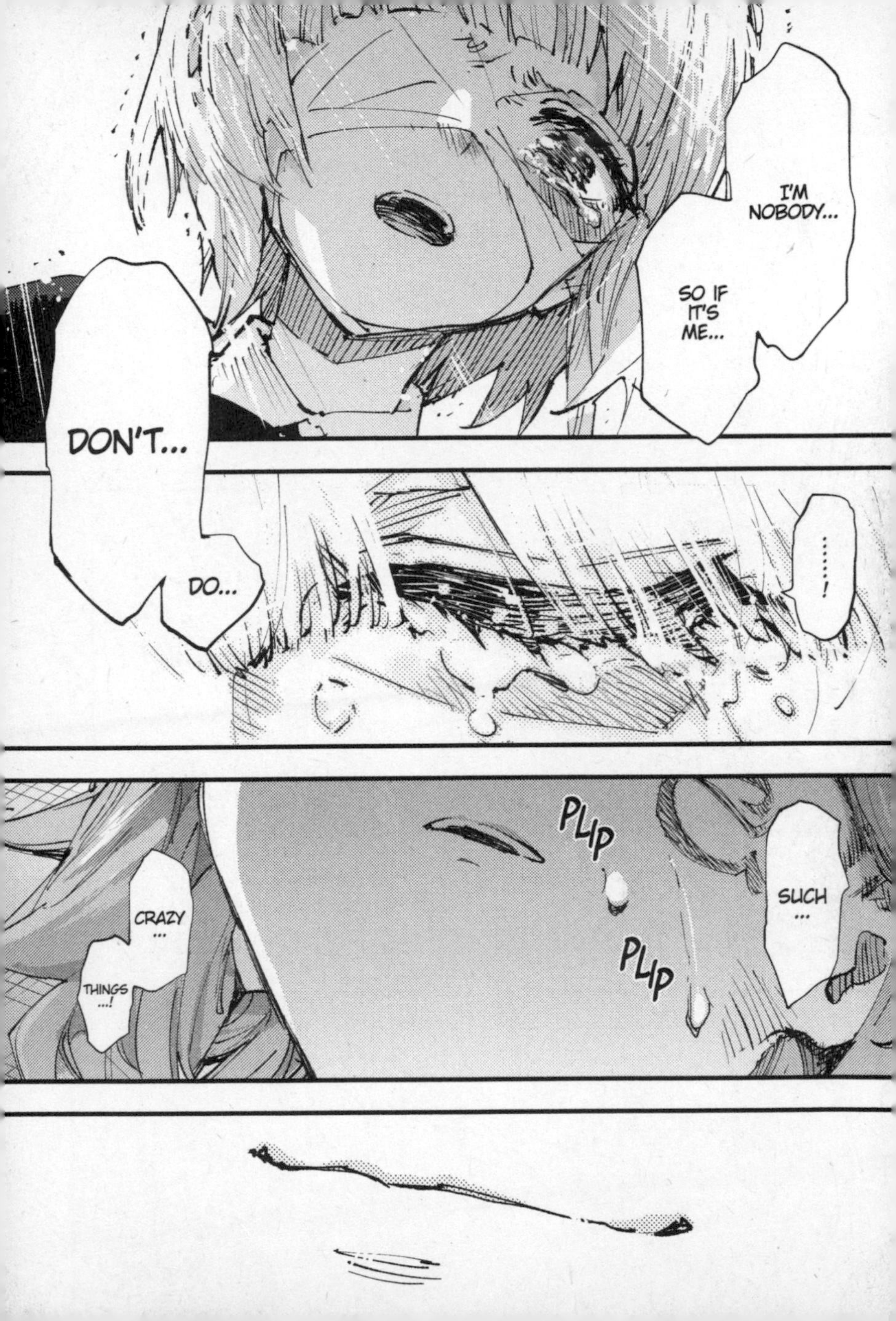
I'M NOBODY...
SO IF IT'S ME...
DON'T...
DO...
......!
SUCH...
PLIP
PLIP
CRAZY...
THINGS...!

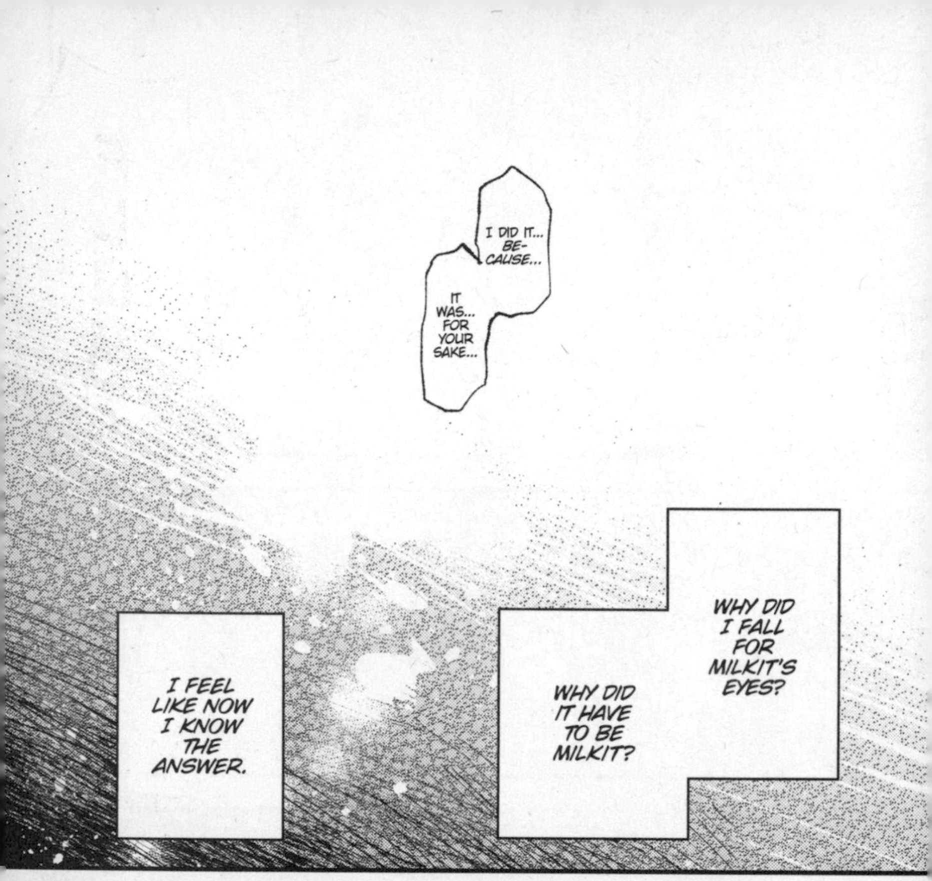
I DID IT... BE-CAUSE...
IT WAS... FOR YOUR SAKE...
WHY DID I FALL FOR MILKIT'S EYES?
WHY DID IT HAVE TO BE MILKIT?
I FEEL LIKE NOW I KNOW THE ANSWER.
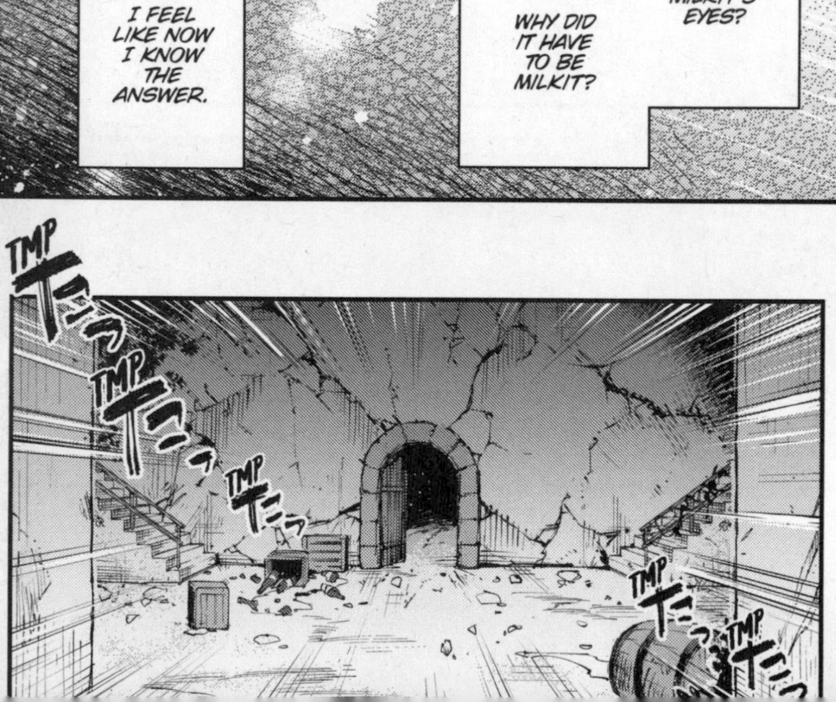
TMP
TMP
TMP
TMP
TMP

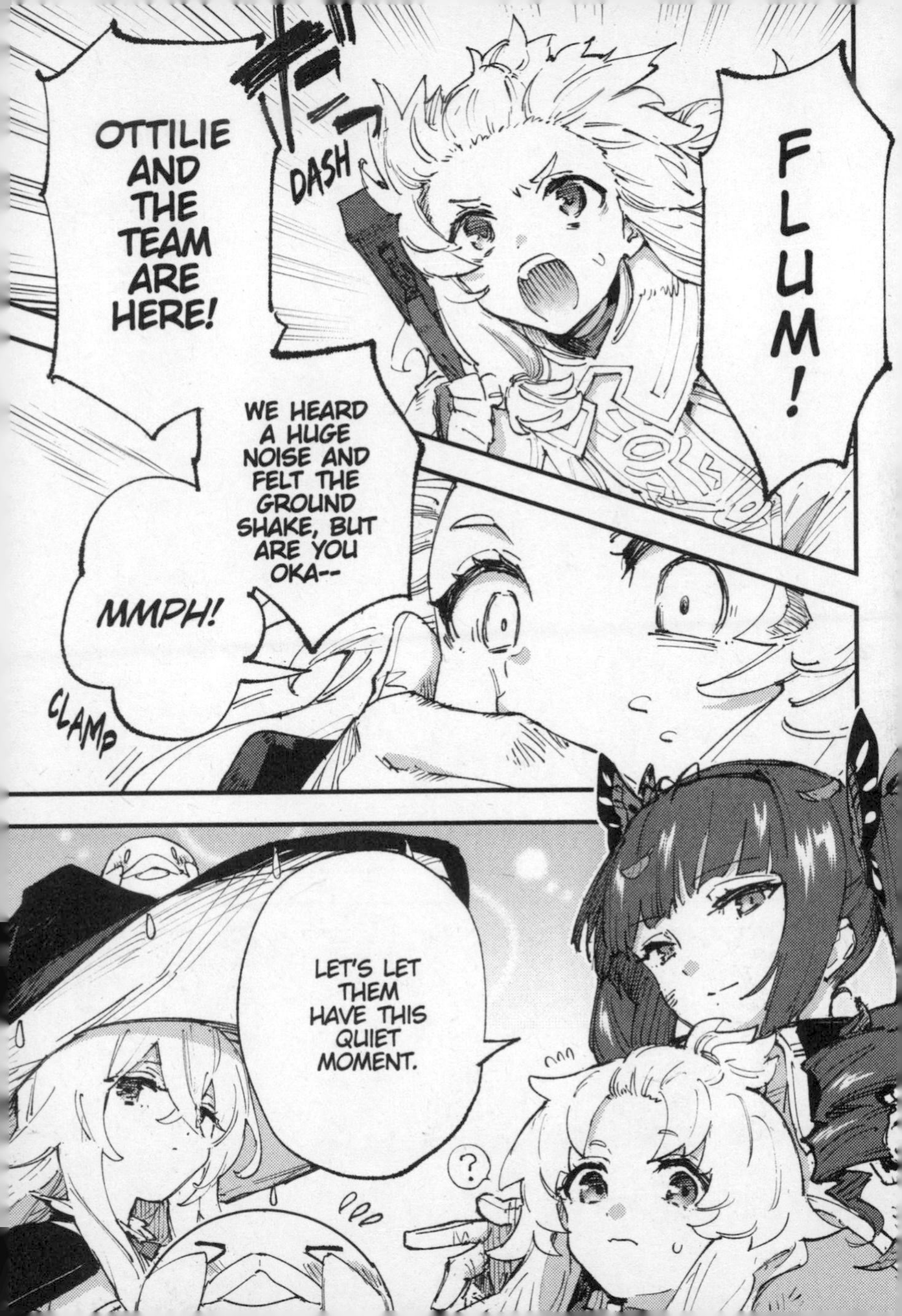
FLUM!
DASH
OTTILIE AND THE TEAM ARE HERE!
WE HEARD A HUGE NOISE AND FELT THE GROUND SHAKE, BUT ARE YOU OKA--
MMPH!
CLAMP
LET'S LET THEM HAVE THIS QUIET MOMENT.
?

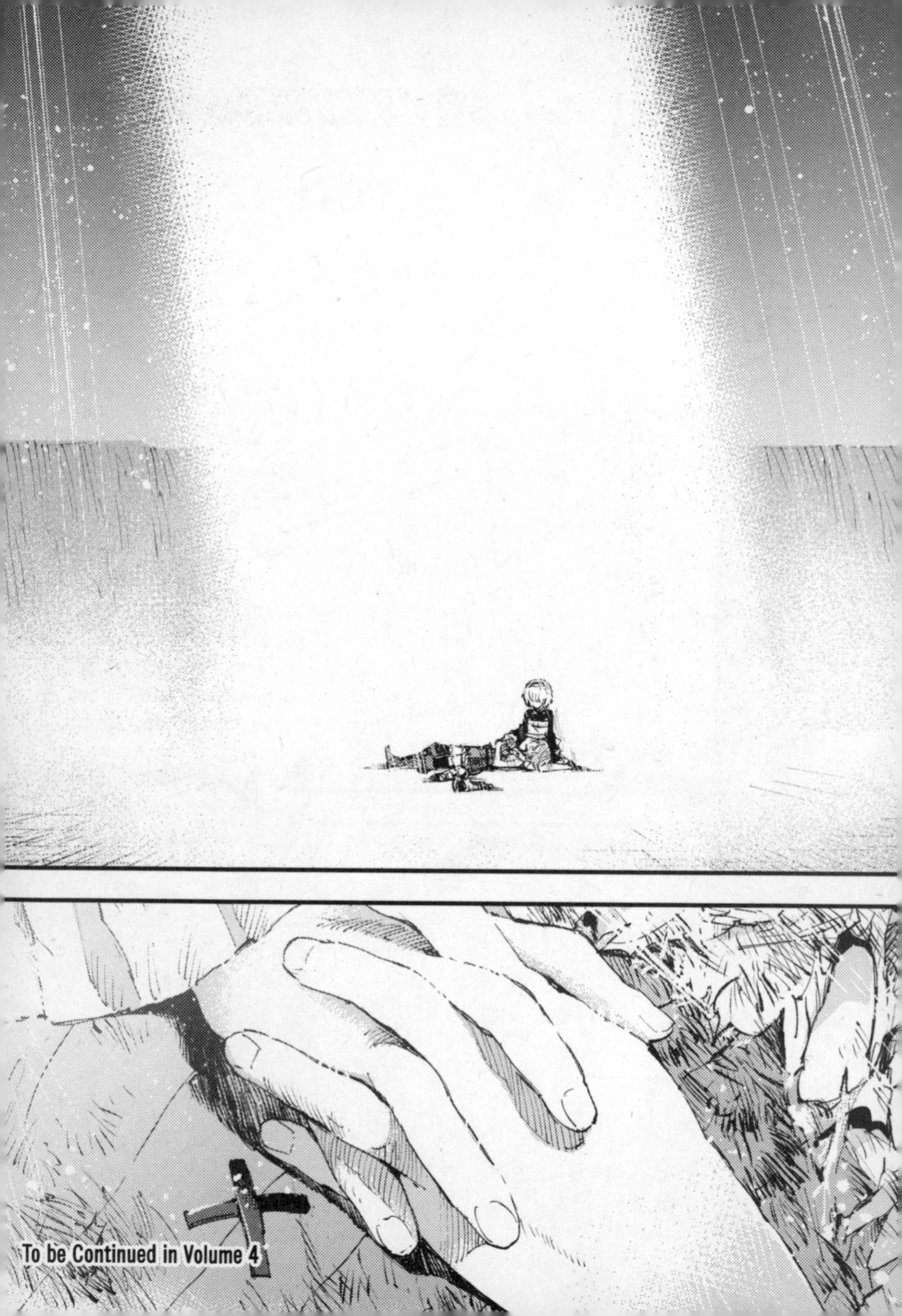
To be Continued in Volume 4

AFTERWORD

A Message from the Author

Thank you for purchasing this volume. It's the author, Kiki. I hope you all enjoyed volume 3 of *Roll Over & Die.* I enjoyed it like crazy!

In volume 3, the story starts focusing on the capital. It's the same as having ninety percent of the title fulfilled. As for the remaining ten percent "I Just Want to Live an Ordinary Life," who knows when that part will be fulfilled. Not even I can tell you.

Now then, Dein played a kind of pretty big role in this volume, but he is a higher-ranking Adventurer than Flum. Of course, he's inferior compared to Eterna and Ottilie, but his brute strength and experience top Flum's. He's not wholly wrong when he says he's the "King of the West District," and he has backing from all the shops and establishments, meaning that he has the trust and support of the residents of the slums. He gave such ample compensation for the bombing of the church that the residents are in fact grateful to him. He and his plans have been ripped asunder, and he was driven into a corner by Flum and the gang, but their paths will inevitably cross again.

New "vortexes" have shown up, and Flum's battles are intensifying. Of course, her relationship with Milkit is sure to continue to deepen, too. Best regards going forward for *Roll Over & Die* and its many promising highlights!

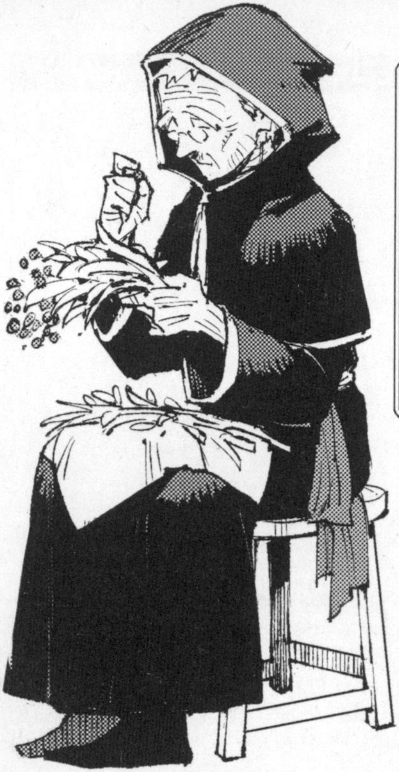

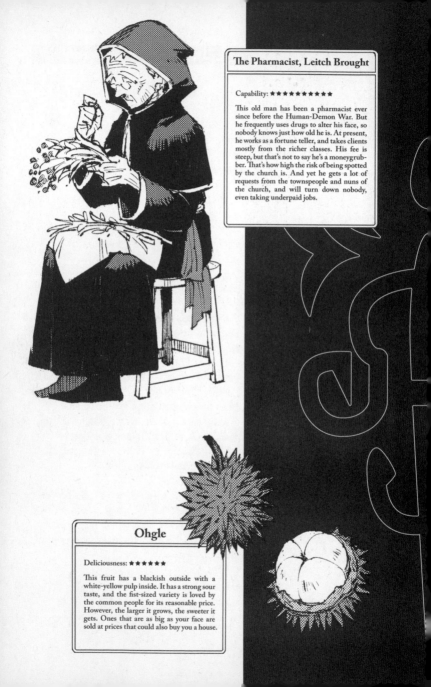

The Pharmacist, Leitch Brought

Capability: ★★★★★★★★★★★

This old man has been a pharmacist ever since before the Human-Demon War. But he frequently uses drugs to alter his face, so nobody knows just how old he is. At present, he works as a fortune teller, and takes clients mostly from the richer classes. His fee is steep, but that's not to say he's a moneygrubber. That's how high the risk of being spotted by the church is. And yet he gets a lot of requests from the townspeople and nuns of the church, and will turn down nobody, even taking underpaid jobs.

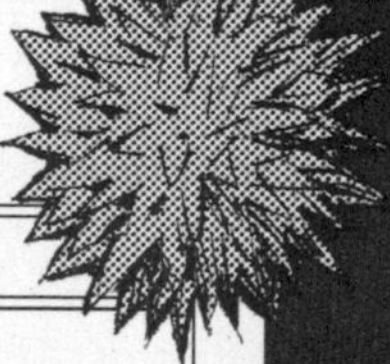

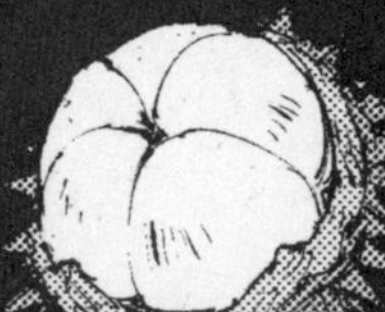

Ohgle

Deliciousness: ★★★★★★

This fruit has a blackish outside with a white-yellow pulp inside. It has a strong sour taste, and the fist-sized variety is loved by the common people for its reasonable price. However, the larger it grows, the sweeter it gets. Ones that are as big as your face are sold at prices that could also buy you a house.

Eterna's Ride

Comfort: ★★★★★★★

It's like a balloon with a film of water on it, full of lighter-than-air gas. It takes a high-level spell technique to create this gas from water. It can increase its speed by rigorously flapping its wings up and down and rotating its tail like a propeller, but it's fundamentally not fast. It will explode when in close proximity to an open flame.

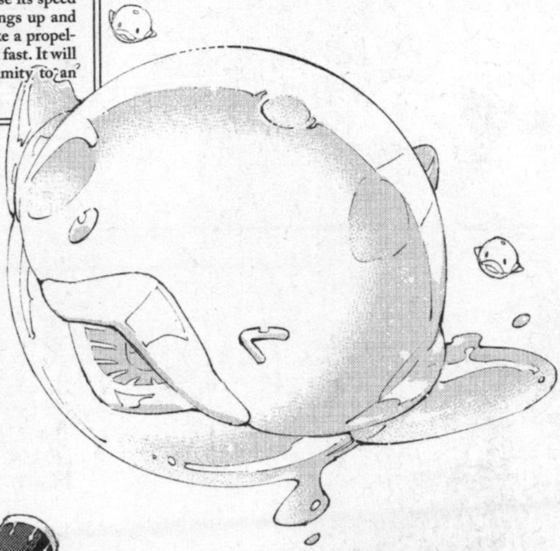

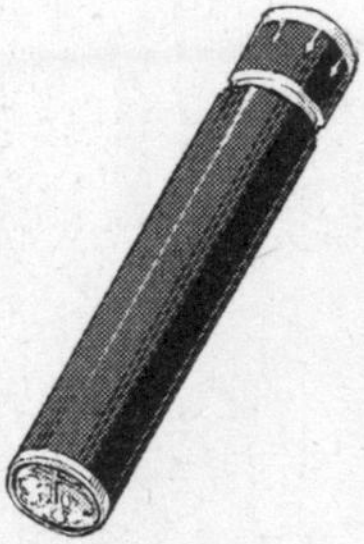

Magic-Powered Flare

Price: ★★

A cylinder filled with gunpowder; a minute amount of magic will activate an ignition technique to generate smoke. There are also easier-to-use models that are purely magic instead of using gunpowder to produce smoke. Lightweight, resistant to moisture, and capable of creating a lot of smoke, they can be used for smokescreens too. However, from a cost perspective, the royal army prefers the gunpowder variety. General Henriette's been known to mourn the fact that their budget is not equal to that of the church knights.

Dein's Lethal Poison

Danger Level: ★★★★★★★★★★

With a catchphrase that claims it can kill even a dragon, this lethal poison is circulated by shady merchants. It's a mystery as to whether it could really kill a dragon or not, but at the very least, when used on a human, even an A-Rank Adventurer cannot escape immediate death. Its scarcity means a high value, and the fact that Dein used it on the low-ranking Flum goes to show how cautious he is.

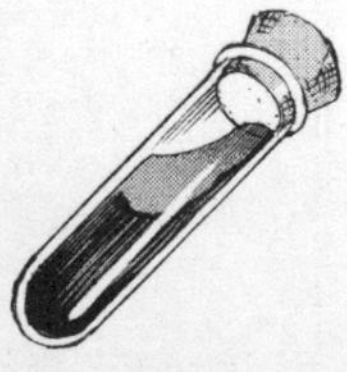

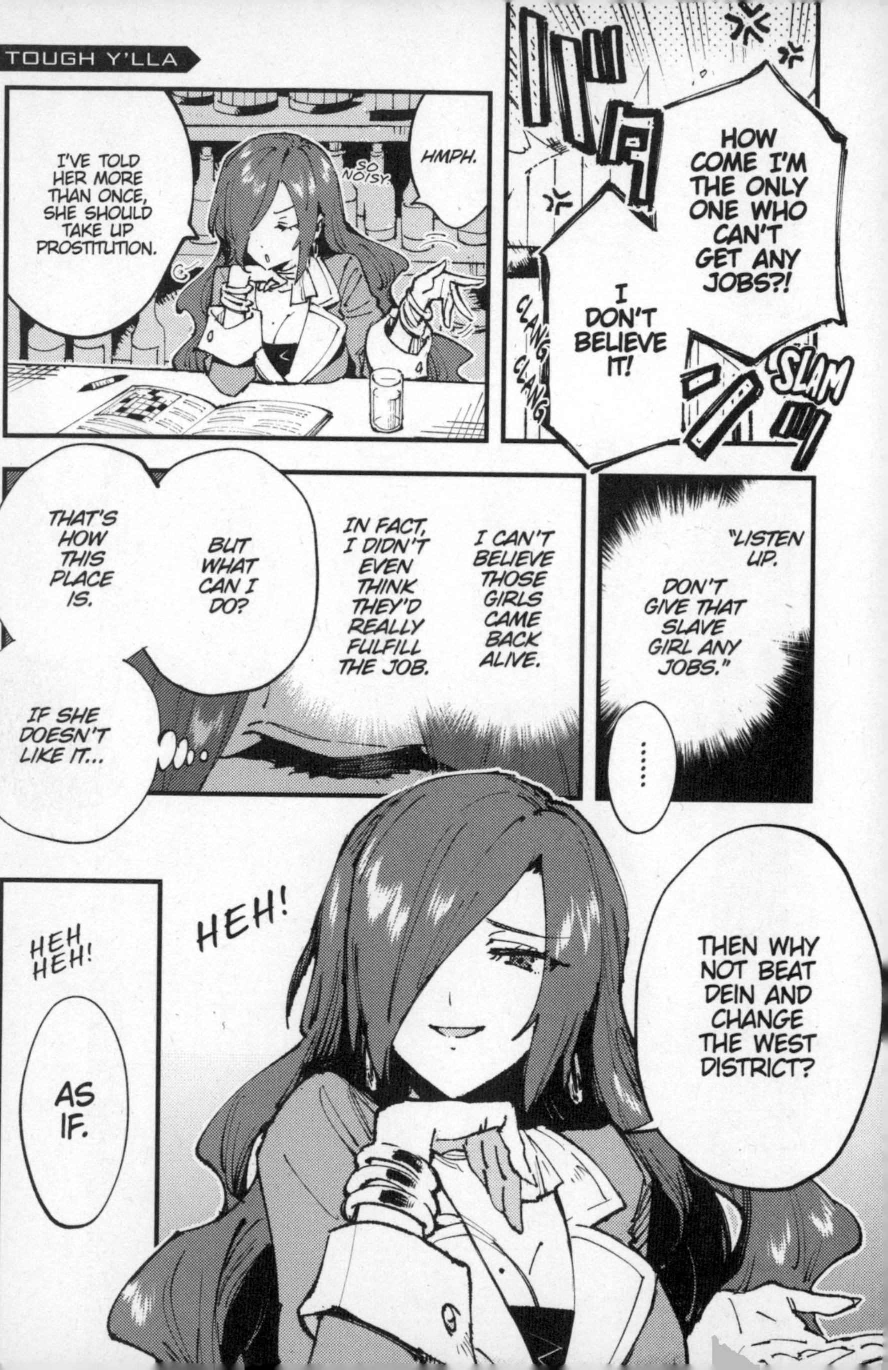
HOW COME I'M THE ONLY ONE WHO CAN'T GET ANY JOBS?!
I DON'T BELIEVE IT!
CLANG CLANG
SLAM
HMPH.
SO NOISY.
I'VE TOLD HER MORE THAN ONCE, SHE SHOULD TAKE UP PROSTITUTION.
"LISTEN UP.
DON'T GIVE THAT SLAVE GIRL ANY JOBS."
......
I CAN'T BELIEVE THOSE GIRLS CAME BACK ALIVE.
IN FACT, I DIDN'T EVEN THINK THEY'D REALLY FULFILL THE JOB.
BUT WHAT CAN I DO?
THAT'S HOW THIS PLACE IS.
IF SHE DOESN'T LIKE IT...
THEN WHY NOT BEAT DEIN AND CHANGE THE WEST DISTRICT?
HEH!
HEH HEH!
AS IF.